Racism and antiracism
in real schools

theory • policy • practice

David Gillborn

Open University Press
Buckingham • Philadelphia

For Dom,
Rebecca and Sarah
– without whom
there's no point

Open University Press
Celtic Court
22 Ballmoor
Buckingham
MK18 1XW

email: enquiries@openup.co.uk
world wide web: http://www.openup.co.uk

and 325 Chestnut Street
Philadelphia, PA 19106, USA

First Published 1995
Reprinted 2000

A catalogue record of this book is available from the British Library

ISBN 0 335 19092 8 (pb) 0 335 19093 6 (hb)

Library of Congress Cataloging-in-Publication Data
Gillborn, David.
    Racism & antiracism in real schools / David Gillborn.
        p. cm.
    Includes bibliographical references and index.
    ISBN 0–335–19093–6 (hb). — ISBN 0–335–19092–8 (pb)
    1. Discrimination in education—Great Britain. 2. Racism—Great Britain. 3. Racial discrimination—Great Britain. 4. Educational sociology—Great Britain. I. Title. II. Title: Racism and antiracism in real schools.
LC212.3.G7G45   1995
371.19′342—dc20   94–25726
                                                        CIP

Typeset by Graphicraft Ltd, Hong Kong
Printed and bound in Great Britain by Biddles Limited, www.biddles.co.uk

Contents

Acknowledgements _____

Most authors seem to get the acknowledgements over with quite quickly – a paragraph or two and they're done. The length of this section, therefore, may perhaps give a clue as to my dependence on others. A mention here does not begin to repay some people, but it does, at least, acknowledge the debt.

My first debt is to the teachers and students of the schools I visited during the research: without their insight, courage and determination the future would look especially bleak. Special thanks also must go to BP (British Petroleum) who funded the research; in particular, to Chris Marsden (who saw the need for such a project) and to Brian Palmer.

I started work on the project while lecturing in the Division of Education at Sheffield University. I am grateful to all those at Sheffield who helped me, particularly John Gray and Jean Rudduck. Special thanks to Len Barton (who kept me sociological), Tina Cartwright (who transcribed all the tapes and kept me cheerful), Sue Cramp (for saving me at short notice), Dave Drew (for the help with numbers), Suzy Harris (who will never learn about Celtic), Don Howes (*still* helping me cope with computers), Pam Poppleton (for putting up with the interruptions), George Riseborough (for believing in what we do), Nick Sime (for the football and humour), Mark Tranmer (be seeing you) and Shafeeq Ulhaq (for help with the graphics).

I wrote this book in London, where several colleagues helped by sharing ideas and problems with me. Tony Green and Geoff Whitty have been stimulating, challenging and, above all, supportive: the book would not have been written without them and it is better for their help. Many other friends and colleagues also took time to read chapters and/or comment on work in progress: I hope the final version repays their investment. They are Paul Atkinson, Stephen Ball, Bob Burgess, Maud Blair, Nazir Carrim, Amanda Coffey, Sara Delamont, Eva Gamarnikow, Greta Gibson, Anne Gold, Harvey Goldstein, Jagdish Gundara, Crispin Jones, Danny Lawrence, Tariq Modood, Gemma Moss, Jon Nixon, Desmond Nuttall, Euan Reid, Gabrielle Rowe, Barry Troyna, Jef Verhoeven, Carol Vincent and Cecile Wright. Máirtín Mac an Ghaill gets a special round of applause for grappling with more than half the manuscript, even though he had a book of his own to complete. Any remaining deficiencies are, I'm afraid, entirely my fault.

Finally, place of honour is reserved for my family. They know that I couldn't do anything without them. To Joyce, Jim and Dorn – thank you with all my heart.

Key to transcripts _____

italic text	Denotes emphasized speech or raised voice
. . .	Pause
(. . .)	Material has been edited out
[square brackets]	Paraphrased for sake of clarity
<angled brackets>	Stage direction: non-verbal action or tone of voice

one _____

Racism and schooling _____

WHO SAYS BRITAIN IS RACIST?

67% of whites
79% of blacks
56% of Asians

(Runnymede Trust 1992: 2[1])

'Race' is a word that we all recognize. Part of the English language for hundreds of years, the term has been the subject of heated political and academic debate for more than a century. And yet, for all the controversy, it is still the case that people routinely (often unthinkingly) categorize themselves and others according to 'racial' criteria. Although the word remains unchanged, the meaning and significance of 'race' have not. It is the complex and dynamic character of 'race' thinking, shielded by a veneer of apparent simplicity and *obviousness*, that makes 'race' such a powerful and dangerous aspect of contemporary society. This book focuses on 'race' at work within the education system. The concern with education is especially pertinent because education has come to occupy a pivotal role in contemporary 'race' politics.

Attempts to challenge racism in education have a long (and troubled) history. Indeed, educationists have been among the most active professional groups in the struggle against racism. Additionally, in the late 1980s and early 1990s, education has emerged as a major ideological battleground in British politics. Arguments about the 'national character', morality and economic decline have coalesced into policy reforms that picture an imaginary, homogeneous (white) Britain; a Britain where ethnic minorities pose an 'alien' threat to Britishness itself:

> crime has been displaced recently at the centre of race politics by another issue . . . now it is the classrooms and staffrooms of the inner city school which frame the same conflict and provide the most potent terms with which to make sense of racial difference.

(Gilroy 1990: 76)

Like other institutions in contemporary Britain (e.g. the legal system and the economy) the education system operates in racialized ways, reproducing an inequitable distribution of rewards and punishment, success and failure.[2] In the classroom, the corridor and the playground, minority students experience school differently to their white peers, often in ways that disadvantage them and reinforce the message that 'Britain' and 'the British' are categories that can never truly include them (Gillborn 1992a).[3] In isolation, of course, no field of social policy can eradicate racism from society: racism gains strength from too many quarters simply to be 'taught' out of existence. Nevertheless, the education system does have the potential to challenge racism in ways that may have a lasting impact on school students (of all ages and ethnic backgrounds) and the communities of which they are part.

This study blends original school-based research with a critical reading of policy and theory. I argue that 'race' is a vital part of any attempt to understand education. 'Race' and ethnic identity are complex and changing factors that we must constantly review against the real world experiences of teachers and students. Despite the size, complexity and political nature of the task, schools *can* take action to challenge the racism at work within and beyond the school walls. This is not a matter of polemic, but of research: my analysis is grounded in the experiences of teachers and students in real schools. Throughout the account, priority is given to understanding the social and political processes at work within educational contexts. Before explaining the nature of the research, however, it is useful briefly to reflect on the concepts that lie at the heart of the study.

'Race', racism and antiracism

It is customary to define key terms before getting to grips with the bulk of an original analysis. In this case, however, the ways in which central ideas have been sustained and reworked (in policy, in research, in theory and in practice) form the focus of the book. 'Race', racism and antiracism are central to this study and, as the book progresses, I explore increasingly sophisticated and critical understandings of each term. At this stage, therefore, a *brief* introduction is appropriate, to set the scene.

'Race'

The idea of 'race' has a long and bitterly contested history. In the nineteenth century the main disputes concerned where to draw the boundaries between the genetically fixed and biologically discrete 'races' that were supposed to make up *mankind* (see Banton 1988; van den Berghe 1988;

Williams 1983: 248–50).[4] Ideas about the genetic heritability of educability and intelligence are far from dead, as signalled in attempts to rehabilitate the reputation of Cyril Burt (Burstall 1991; Joynson 1989).[5] Nevertheless, it is the case that arguments about fixed genetic differences and the innate superiority of certain human 'races' have now been widely discredited, not least by scientific advances that reveal the massive commonality of human DNA. Such developments establish beyond doubt the futility of seeking meaningful and consistent biological differences that would offer a 'scientific' basis for the groups usually treated as 'races' (see Demaine 1989). 'Race' is, therefore, exposed as a *social* construct.

Far from being a fixed, natural system of genetic difference, *'race' operates as a system of socially constructed and enforced categories, constantly recreated and modified through human interaction.* This understanding (sometimes known as 'social race') underlies most use of the term in contemporary social science.[6] In view of this, it has been suggested that the term may no longer be useful in social scientific research:

> when such concepts, like 'race', 'racial', 'race relations', do not survive critical scrutiny they should be abandoned. Given that there are no 'races' or 'race relations', to do sociology as if there were is irresponsible.
>
> (Carter and Green 1993: 8)

Bob Carter and Marci Green fear that sociologists' repeated use of certain terms may lend a spurious authenticity to the idea of separate and fixed human 'races':

> This is not to deny that many, if not most sociologists, now challenge hierarchical notions of 'race' and, especially since the Holocaust, the political ends these have served. Our point though is that we have continued to accept the analytical constituents of the discourse, using them to produce and reproduce accounts of 'race relations' in matters of housing, employment, health, education and identity formation. In our research we continue to draw on census data . . . we classify human subjects in similar census terms – by sex, age, class and 'race/ethnicity' and ask our subjects to do the same. These politically generated categories parade as neutral, demographic variables and serve as the working tools rather than the subjects of sociological analysis.
>
> (Carter and Green 1993: 6)

Carter and Green want to emphasize the complex and changing character of 'race' thinking. They assert that labels such as 'race' act to 'prevent people from recognising what they have in common by representing the contingent, signified differences between them as transhistorical and fixed' (Carter et al. 1992: 87). This view of 'race' and identity echoes much recent theoretical work, especially in postmodern and post-structuralist analyses, which stresses the contingent, dynamic nature of categories that are often taken for granted.[7] According to such theorists, society can no longer be seen as the working out of wider tensions and conflicts between large, relatively fixed social groups. Rather, there is emphasis on 'diversity, multiplicity, and heterogeneity' in a perspective that celebrates a version of society as 'provisional, variable, tentative, shifting, and changing' (West 1990: 203–4). I address these arguments in detail later (Chapter 4). For the moment, it is sufficient to note that such approaches add a new and important dimension to our understanding of 'race', racism and antiracism. To go a step further, by abandoning such categories, however, would be to misrepresent reality and frustrate sociological analysis.

First, all sociologists are not uniformly guilty of falling into the trap identified by Carter and Green. Indeed, they accept that 'many, if not most' now adopt an openly critical position when defining 'race' or discussing ethnic identities. True, our use of such terms can reflect the confusion and multiplicity of meanings that are attached in everyday use. A distinction is sometimes made, for example, between 'racial' and ethnic groups: where *'race'* is usually associated with physical differences (phenotype), such as skin colour, while *'ethnic'* refers to groups set apart by a shared cultural identity (e.g. on the basis of language, religion or history). In practice, however, the terms are often used interchangeably; despite the fact that many ethnic groups are in no way physically distinct.

There is a second and more important reason to retain categories such as 'race' in sociological work. Simply put, people use 'race' as a way of making sense of the world; if sociologists wish to engage with that world (possibly even help to change it), they must find means of connecting with people's perspectives. This may be easier if, by using recognizable terms, we can at least address ourselves to questions that people recognize. Simply rejecting the idea of 'race' will not help non-sociologists (teachers and minority students included) who have to deal with 'racial' issues every day of their lives.

Finally, Carter and Green claim that 'we classify human subjects in similar census terms . . . and ask our subjects to do the same' (Carter and Green 1993: 6). This presents sociologists as not merely recording people's views, but actively *encouraging* them to assign importance to 'race' and other 'census' categories, such as class and gender. It is doubtful that sociological research has a wide enough audience to contribute significantly to general understandings of 'race' among the population at large. However, in relation to the human subjects of sociological research – the people we question, observe and count as the material of empirical research – Carter and his colleagues raise an important issue. There is a danger that the research act might encourage, or even impose, 'race' thinking among the participants, for example, through the construction of question-naire items or the framing of interview questions (see Troyna and Carrington 1989). This is a difficult area, but the problems are not insurmountable. Qualitative research, in particular, offers the possibility of allowing respondents to describe the world in their own terms. For example, by avoiding loaded questions, which highlight 'racial' issues, researchers can have increased confidence in the validity of their data.[8]

Bob Carter and Marci Green are right, therefore, to warn sociologists against the dangers of replicating the very fictions they seek to expose. Their concern to identify the roots of 'race' thinking is an important task for further sociological analysis. The question arises, however, is it the *only* relevant task? Abandoning the term and championing a new vocabulary may not be the only (or even the best) means of addressing the complex ways in which people routinely adopt 'race' thinking. An urgent task is to understand the ways 'race' figures in educational policy, theory and school practices.

Racism

> The question of how to conceptualise racism is not purely an academic matter, it is connected with a wider political culture in any given historical conjuncture.
>
> (Solomos and Back 1994: 156)

Like 'race', the related concept of racism has been the centre of considerable debate. In common usage racism is often equated with *prejudice*, implying a position of ignorance, an irrational hatred or fear of another racial group. In the 1960s and 1970s a rather different conception emerged, linked with growing support for civil rights and anti-discrimination legislation (on both sides of the Atlantic). A 'radical' conception of equality of opportunity came to prominence; one that judged substantive *opportunity* in relation to differences in average group *achievement*.

This approach removes *intent* from the equation; actions and/or rules that disproportionately disadvantage people of minority ethnic background may be judged racist in their consequences, whatever the conscious intent behind them. This perspective has been widely adopted in research on 'race' and education in Britain, including work commissioned by central Government (see Rampton 1981; Swann 1985). Nevertheless, disputes about the proper definition of racism continue and must be treated with caution. These definitional issues are not arcane technical matters, but politically significant decisions:

> to marginalise the matter of definition is to grant to the racists an autonomy to deny their avowal of racism. For if we 'retreat' to the

position that racism is whatever we define it to be at any time, we concede to the racists the opportunity to argue (with justification) that the notion is no more than an item in the arsenal of 'left-wing' rhetoric.

(Miles 1993: 9)

In this way, apparently 'technical', academic concerns are directly implicated in the politics of 'race' and racism. These issues are examined at length in Chapter 3.

Antiracism

At its most basic, the term 'antiracist' can be understood to denote opposition to racism. In Britain, however, the term has such a long and politically explosive history that no simple definition is possible. Antiracist approaches are commonly contrasted with multicultural strategies, where the latter are criticized for a narrow focus on curriculum content and 'positive images' which do not engage with questions of power and racism in interpersonal and institutional contexts (see Brandt 1986; Troyna and Carrington 1990).

A bewildering variety of initiatives and perspectives have claimed and/or been described using the term 'antiracist'. Some of these have achieved great notoriety, but do not adequately cover the range of practice and possibility in this area. Again, as the book progresses so I outline a *critical* understanding of antiracism; one that builds on the achievements and problems of the past, and suggests concrete strategies for future work at the school and classroom level.

The research

This book grew out of a research project sponsored by BP (British Petroleum). The original study formed part of a wider initiative (based at Sheffield University) that focused on a series of issues (such as discipline, gender, 'race', expectations) which have generated much debate, but where clear data on new school-based approaches are comparatively rare. The initiative aimed to apply critical qualitative approaches to the study of schools that are making genuine progress in relation to the chosen topics.

Finding the case study schools

The first project to be undertaken within the initiative focused on discipline in urban comprehensives (Gillborn et al. 1993). Suitable schools were identified by the research team (Jon Nixon, Jean Rudduck and myself) using a range of personal and professional contacts, including local inspectors and advisers, members of Her Majesty's Inspectorate (HMI) and colleagues in higher education institutions. School discipline was an especially high profile issue when the project began, with frequent attacks (by politicians and the media) on the standards of urban schools. Colleagues in many parts of the country nevertheless felt confident that they could recommend schools where new and valuable approaches were being developed; approaches that moved away from narrow concepts of discipline as control, and sought to make it a positive – enabling – aspect of interpersonal relations within school. Unfortunately, the same network proved much less fruitful when considering issues of 'race' and racism.

My work in this field has helped me build a network of contacts among groups and individuals specifically working on 'race' and antiracism. Despite these additional 'informants', however, recommendations were still difficult to come by. In the eyes of many observers, and practitioners, school-based progress on these issues is rare and always piecemeal. Some simply see schools as part of the problem rather than the solution. Consequently I found few people confident enough to recommend a school as genuinely addressing racism and antiracism as whole-school issues. Several people pointed to interesting work by individuals, but most recognized that the progress was limited to a small part of the students' experience, leaving the rest of the school untouched. The difficulty I experienced at this stage of the project suggested a massive gap between reality and the rhetoric of multicultural and antiracist policy statements, now common to many Local Education Authorities (LEAs) (Troyna 1992).

Eventually a small number of potential research sites were identified. In each case I contacted the school (usually through the headteacher) to arrange a visit, so that I could discuss the project with teachers and look at some of the school's work.[9] I gathered preliminary interview material in several schools and, finally, settled on two that would provide the major focus for the study.[10] Both had been recommended by members of the HMI national team on 'ethnic diversity'. In both schools I had spoken with teachers who were honest about the difficulties they had encountered and the fact that more work was necessary. Nevertheless, it was clear that 'race' and racism were taken seriously as whole-school issues that affected all teachers and students; indeed, an HMI report described one of the schools as 'in the forefront of good practice in relation to equal opportunities (race, sex, disability)'.

The fieldwork

My principal aim during the empirical stage of the project was to build a relatively detailed and vivid picture of how the schools had changed to address the issues of 'race' and racism. In particular, I wanted to explore how teachers and students experienced the changes: How had such sensitive and personally challenging issues been raised within the school? How did different sections of the school population receive the changes? What work was in progress to ensure that the changes affected the whole school and would not collapse if one or two key individuals left?

I aspired to the kind of detail and insight that are possible through *ethnographic* research; that is, a form of qualitative fieldwork that blends multiple sources of data, collected over an extended period, to generate new insights concerning the intricacies of organizational life (cf. Hammersley and Atkinson 1983).[11] Unfortunately, long periods 'in the field' were not possible because of the practicalities of travel around the country and the limits of available time and funding. As a compromise, the project relied on short but intensive periods of data collection.

By working with an appointed 'liaison teacher' in each school, I was able to organize a series of day visits and/or short blocks of fieldwork. The liaison teachers (senior members of staff who had been involved in the antiracist developments) took responsibility for organizing a detailed timetable of interviews and observations, based on specific requests that I outlined in advance. In this way I could ensure that, despite limited time in each school, I saw a representative sample of students (covering the range of abilities and ethnic backgrounds) and teachers (including different areas of responsibility, a variety of subject specialisms and lengths of experience). The timetable was drawn up in advance of each visit, allowing me to compare the schedule with my knowledge of the school's composition and giving me the chance to request additions or other alterations.

In both schools my timetable of interviewees and activities was made available to all staff. Additionally, I had free access to the staffroom and was allocated a room of my own for the duration of the fieldwork (where interviews were conducted in private and where teachers and students knew they could find me or leave messages). Although it is conceivable that interviewees presented a biased or unrealistically 'rosy' picture of their schools, all reasonable steps were taken to ensure that all staff knew of my work, could form a judgement about the representativeness of my sources and had opportunities (both formal and informal) to make known any objections or additional points they felt relevant. What is more important, by talking with students as I walked around the schools, I felt safe that teachers could not substantially misrepresent the reality of their work on 'race' and racism.

The data

Interviews form the bulk of my data but I also organized some observational work and collected a good deal of documentation (including school policy statements; local authority guidelines; and the minutes of staff meetings and working parties). Although I could not hope to collect the depth of material generated by extended ethnographic research (conducted over months – even years – in the field) I was able to retain the degree of flexibility necessary to adjust fieldwork to new issues and concerns as they emerged (see Burgess 1985: 9–10). Besides requesting more documentation and arranging further interviews after the initial fieldwork, I also kept some time 'free' when I visited the schools. This meant that I could arrange new interviews or observations at very short notice. This was invaluable where unexpected issues arose during interviews, suggesting new people I needed to speak with. It also enabled me to respond to requests from people (teachers *and* students) who wanted to talk to me but were not part of the original fieldwork schedules.

Preliminary interviews and data gathering began in 1991, with the main periods of intensive fieldwork conducted in the spring and summer of 1992. This was a time when many teachers' morale was particularly low. Several major reforms of education were being felt across the entire system, including massive changes in curriculum management (caused by the imposition of the National Curriculum) and cuts in funding available for local projects and Section 11 schemes (which had played a key role in early 'race' work in most of the schools I contacted).[12] I was visiting the schools, therefore, at a time when past successes were having to be defended against other priorities; emphasizing that none of the changes were complete and that the struggle to maintain/improve the schools' work is continual.

An outline of the book: perspective and content

The book is split into two parts. The first deals with wide ranging issues of a relatively theoretical and abstracted nature; the second focuses on practical issues of 'race', racism and antiracism in school settings. Teachers, headteachers and governors might wish to start with Part Two; researchers and other academics will gain most by reading the chapters in their original order. The division between theory and practice is a useful heuristic, but nothing more. As the book progresses it becomes clear that theoretical insight can best be generated through a critical analysis of practice. By looking at change and antiracism in real situations, new questions are generated and new ideas tested. In this way the book embodies an attempt to develop a 'language of possibility' about 'race' and racism in schools. That is, using research to explore possibilities for change and progress, rather than being locked endlessly into a purely negative 'language of critique' (McCarthy and Apple (1988: 31) after Aronowitz and Giroux). This raises a wider point, about the way that sociologists theorize school-based work.

Because of their position in the social structure, schools and teachers must contend with a variety of factors that are likely to render partial and incomplete all attempts at radical reconstruction. The legal framework for education in England and Wales, for example, now allows for much of the curriculum in state schools to be dictated centrally. Such constraints cannot be ignored. However, these factors do not, by definition, render all school-based work necessarily worthless or inevitably doomed to reproduce existing inequalities. This is a recurring issue for those sociologists who recognize the power of societal forces but nevertheless want to use education as a means of challenging the status quo (see Whitty 1985: ch. 1). Unless we take an extreme Marxist perspective on the conditions necessary for a radical deconstruction of dominant models of production (including ideological production) we should be careful not to slip into the academic trap of automatically rubbishing all mainstream attempts to address issues of 'race' and racism in schools. This is particularly the case where critics, after the event, reduce teachers' efforts to just another means of 'social control'. The deliberate motivation behind most school-based attempts at multicultural and/or antiracist education is libertarian to some degree. If the unintended consequence is control this *must* be recognized – but not as an end point. There can be more to research than simply identifying the failings of school-based work; research can constructively engage with school- and community-based attempts to change the status quo. If the attempts fail, as academics we can be of aid in several ways. Identifying how and why innovations fail is important, but so too is the attempt to identify possibilities for the future and highlight successes (even if the victories remain incomplete). It is in this spirit that Part Two of this book examines antiracist change in state comprehensive schools.

Part One begins, in Chapter 2, by focusing on policy debates. I trace the changing forms of racist discourse, paying special attention to the *deracialization* of contemporary education policy. I argue that the absence of racial terminology should not mask the racist consequences threatened by Conservative ideology and figured in policies that deploy concepts such as 'culture' and 'heritage' as proxies for 'race'. The culturalist imagery of Thatcher and Major is not far removed from the racial language of Powell and Churchill.

Chapter 3 is concerned with 'race' and racism in educational research. The chapter examines some problems and controversies that have surrounded attempts to investigate 'race' in the everyday lives of schools. A series of methodological critiques reminds us of the importance of these issues. Such concerns should inform more incisive research; currently they threaten to suffocate critical perspectives. In their concern for 'proof', there is a danger that some observers may oversimplify the realities of racism and privilege a narrow and conservative version of social science.

Chapter 4 concludes the first part of the book by reviewing advances in the theorization of 'race', culture and identity. Traditional models of right/ left and black/white are giving way to a more sophisticated understanding of the complexity of identity politics. Simultaneously, doctrinaire 'munici- pal' and 'moral' forms of antiracism have been exposed as essentialist and, at times, racist. The chapter reviews recent crises in antiracist thinking (relating to the Rushdie affair and the Burnage report) and concludes that a more dynamic, *critical antiracism* is required. This provides the theo- retical groundwork for the analysis of school practice in the second part of the book.

Chapter 5 introduces the case study material by describing the schools which feature in Part Two. I adopt a micro-political perspective which views schools as *arenas of struggle* (Ball 1987: 19, original emphasis). The chapter looks at how antiracist work began in each case study school, highlighting strategic differences and similarities. A striking finding is that senior management support and the work of a small, committed 'core' group of staff were identified as essential first steps in each school.

Chapter 6 examines how the core groups sought to involve a wider range of colleagues in their work, seeking active links with local commu- nities and addressing the whole school. A crucial issue concerns the need to balance taking an active lead (pressing for change) against the fear, and resistance, of colleagues who are often ambivalent, sometimes opposed. The chapter highlights the painful and uncertain nature of the change process. Staff have to be worked *on* (through training activities) and *in* (via consultation). One of the most surprising and potentially powerful findings concerns the role played by students, who emerge as instrumental in rais- ing the status of antiracism within the schools.

In Chapter 7 the focus shifts from the whole school to the classroom. I review the gains, problems and tensions between antiracism *across* the curriculum (as part of subject teaching) and antiracism *on* the curriculum (as part of a separate programme). Experience in one case study school suggests that a combination of the two approaches may be the most fruit- ful strategy. Over a period of years a course in 'people's education' has been developed, gradually building into a remarkable forum where stu- dents (of different social class and ethnic backgrounds) explore their own experiences and feelings about 'race', racism and racists.

Part Two concludes, in Chapter 8, with a more detailed exploration of student perspectives. The chapter questions the familiar image of students as relatively powerless within schools and argues for a more sensitive and sophisticated approach to questions of *white* ethnicity. Students play a crucial role in developing and sustaining antiracism in the case study schools. Their active involvement in antiracism produces high expectations of teach- ers, who will be found wanting where they adopt narrow 'moralistic' approaches – especially if they seem to label white students as automatically racist or as the only ones capable of racism.

Sociology and the text: a word about words

> a turgid and polysyllabic prose does seem to prevail in the social sciences. I suppose those who use it believe they are imitating 'physical science', and are not aware that much of *that* prose is not altogether necessary . . . Such lack of ready intelligibility, I believe, usually has little or nothing to do with the complexity of subject matter, and nothing at all with profundity of thought . . . To overcome the academic *prose* you have first to overcome the academic *pose*.
>
> (Mills 1959: 239–40, original emphasis)

Despite the years that have passed since Mills wrote these words, social science writing is still dogged by dense and jargon-laden styles. Much sociological writing is just too complicated for non-sociologists. Without prior knowledge of specialist terms and debates, the reader is often denied access to a wealth of sociological theory and insight, simply because they cannot 'speak the language' of academic sociology. This is a serious problem because it helps prevent sociological research fulfilling its potential to influence the real world. It also strengthens one of the uglier stereotypes of sociologists – as self-obsessed, posturing academics with little regard for the people they use as subject matter (see, for example, Bradbury 1975).

Sociology, like other sciences, has developed, and continues to multiply, a specific vocabulary. Sometimes, of course, this is a necessary part of the sociological enterprise; breaking with familiar interpretations and making new and valuable connections between aspects of the social structure and the lives of people (as individual actors and/or as members of various social groups). Sometimes existing and/or familiar terms are simply not adequate for the specific meaning that we, as social scientists, wish to denote. Additionally, there is the question of *style*. As one of the foremost British sociologists notes:

> whilst it is the case that anything can be said in simple sentences – that is, there is no necessary relation between grammatical form and cognitive function – it is unlikely that everything can be said with equal facility and felicity.
>
> (Bernstein 1990: 119)

A central tenet of Basil Bernstein's sociology is that the very form of language used in educational settings works against the interests of certain groups (notably working-class children) (Bernstein 1971; 1974; 1975; 1977; 1990). Yet sociologists have been remarkably slow to turn their analysis on themselves and recognize the ways in which sociological discourse defines many people as outsiders, privileging sociologists and excluding others. This does not happen by accident and there are many forces at work here – not simply the vanity of authors. As sociologists, the first question we should perhaps be asking is, how is power implicated in the forms of sociological discourse?

As I noted, dense and jargon-laden sociological writing has been around for a long time, and shows no sign of retreating. One reason for this has to do with how we claim status as social scientists. This was brought home to Howard Becker (an eminent sociologist) when, during a writing seminar for graduate students, he encouraged them to say what they meant without dressing it up:

> [A student exclaimed] 'Gee, Howie, when you say it this way, it looks like something anybody could say.' You bet.
>
>   We talked about that. Was it what you said that was sociological, or was it the way you said it? Mind you, [in editing a sample piece of writing] we had not replaced any technical sociological language. That had not been the problem (it almost never is). We had replaced redundancies, 'fancy writing', pompous phrases ... We decided that authors tried to give substance and weight to what they wrote by sounding academic, even at the expense of the real meaning.
>
> (Becker 1986: 7)

As a sociologist I approach educational contexts with a particular set of interests, which prompt questions about how people view themselves and others; how power works through social interactions and bureaucratic procedures; how change is socially constructed and reconstructed. These are the key questions for this book. In addressing them I try to remain sociological while, as far as possible, doing without unnecessary linguistic complexities. This may not endear me to certain factions within sociology, but I hope it will enable non-sociologists to benefit from the analysis.

part one _____

'Race', research and policy _____

two

Discourse and policy

race is a fluid, transforming, historically specific concept parasitic on theoretic and social discourses for the meaning it assumes at any historical moment.

(Goldberg 1993: 74, original emphasis)

Its defence of 'Englishness', of that way of 'being British' or of the English feeling 'Great again', is a key to some of the unexpected sources of Thatcherism's popularity. Cultural racism has been one of its most powerful, enduring, effective – and least remarked – sources of strength.

(Hall 1988: 132)

Traditional understandings of 'race' and racism are no longer adequate. We must rethink 'race'. The nature of the relevant issues is both complex and changing: simple, fixed understandings of what constitutes 'race' and racism leave us ill prepared for critical analysis of contemporary society in the late twentieth century.

The 1990s have seen the *deracialization* of social policy. Issues of 'race' and racism, so prominent in the early 1980s, figure little in contemporary policy debates. In the field of education, in many local authorities, the 1980s witnessed a rush to formulate multicultural and/or antiracist policy statements (Troyna and Williams 1986). Additionally, a Government sponsored Committee of Inquiry reported twice on 'race' and education, marking the first establishment recognition that racism was a factor in the educational experience and achievement of ethnic minority students (Rampton 1981; Swann 1985). The latter even argued, albeit crudely and with little success, that multicultural and antiracist concerns should influence any 'good' education.

The Conservative educational assault, which began in earnest in the late 1980s, has changed all that. 'Race' has been swept from the policy agenda. And yet simultaneously issues of 'culture', 'heritage' and 'nationhood' have taken on renewed importance as a central strand in Conservative ideology.

These developments have direct consequences for 'racial' and ethnic inequality, in education and other fields of social policy. New conceptual tools are necessary if we are to understand critically the form, power and consequences of these developments.

In the first part of this chapter, therefore, I examine the role of *discourse* as a conceptual tool in the analysis of contemporary politics and social policy debates. This prepares the ground for an analysis of 'race' and ethnicity as central factors in Conservative political ideology. Although the language of debate has changed (substituting 'culture' for 'race', 'heritage' for 'colour') the superficial deracialization of 'the new racism' (Barker 1981) cannot disguise the links between 1960s Powellism and the crusade to defend the 'essential' England/Britain that features so strongly in contemporary politics.

In the final section of the chapter, I specifically focus on the operation of deracialized discourse in recent education policy. Although 'race' is hardly ever mentioned, current policies directly affect the experiences and opportunities available to minority students. The deracialized discourse of current education policy does more than disguise existing inequalities, it sustains and promotes racism.

Discourse, power and 'race'

Discourse as a conceptual tool

> How we are seen determines in part how we are treated; how we treat others is based on how we see them; such seeing comes from representation.
>
> (Dyer 1993: 1)

The way that things are represented (whether through talk, text or visual images) is always open to multiple interpretations. Nevertheless, certain interpretations carry greater authority/legitimacy than others, as a result of the way the representation is constructed and the context within which it is experienced (cf. Barthes 1972). Certain representations may be 'encoded' such that possible interpretations are effectively limited to a range of 'preferred' readings (During 1993a; Hall 1990). Hence, representations do not simply *reflect* (in some neutral way) a particular thing (object, person, group); they *construct* or support a particular idea of that object.

Interactionist sociology has always emphasized the importance of symbols and meaning, as essential components in understanding how social life is shaped and experienced (Blumer 1965; 1976; Mead 1934). The rise of Cultural Studies, as a particular branch of social science concerned with the study of contemporary culture, however, has added new concepts and approaches to this field.[1] One reflection of this is a concern with the nature and operation of *discourse* (talk and text), which has assumed a central place in much social science work over the last decade or so (cf. McCall and Becker 1990).[2]

As Stuart Hall notes, 'Not only is discourse always implicated in *power*; discourse is one of the "systems" through which power circulates' (Hall 1992a: 294, original emphasis). Discourse is, therefore, never neutral. The ways in which social objects (people, groups, institutions, nations) are constructed in discourse is never merely descriptive. The very act of 'encoding' (Hall 1990) via a particular discourse has consequences for the speaker/writer, the audience and the subject of the discourse:

> any discourse concerns itself with certain objects and puts forward certain concepts at the expense of others.
>
> (Macdonell 1986: 3)

> A discourse is a group of statements which provide a language for talking about – i.e. a way of representing – a particular kind of knowledge about a topic. When statements about a topic are made within a particular discourse, the discourse makes it possible to construct the topic in a certain way. It also limits the other ways in which the topic can be constructed.
>
> (Hall 1992a: 291)

Above all, then, discourse concerns the use of language as part of the exercise of *power*:

> Discourses are, therefore, about what can be said and thought, but also about who can speak, when, where and with what authority. Discourses embody meaning and social relationships, they constitute both subjectivity and power relations. Discourses are 'practices that systematically form the objects of which they speak . . . Discourses are not about objects; they do not identify objects, they constitute them and in the practice of doing so conceal their own invention' (Foucault 1977: 49). (Ball 1990a: 17).

Although the link with social representations theory in social psychology is plain (cf. Bhavnani 1991; Moscovici 1961; 1984), the concept of discourse is frequently associated with the work of Michel Foucault (especially 1972; 1980). However, it has sometimes been used in ways that are not limited by the particular context of Foucault's writing. Indeed, as Jennifer Gore argues, it is entirely in keeping with Foucault's style of work that the concept be taken up and used as a tool or 'gadget' of method, without being locked into some wider 'Foucauldian' analysis that is held accountable 'to the letter' of his work (Gore 1993: 50). It is in this way

		'Race' equality is genuinely implicated in the issues at stake?	
		Yes	No
'Racial' categories deployed in the discourse?	Yes	A	B
	No	C	D

Figure 2.1   'Race' and discourse: a matrix

that most British writers have sought to apply discourse analysis in the field of education (cf. Ball 1990b; 1993).

By analysing the role of 'race' and ethnicity in policy discourse, we are able to trace a dynamic, and often complex link between issues of racism and key policy pronouncements. We are able critically to deconstruct policies that claim (often explicitly) to be unconnected with 'race' while simultaneously granting legitimacy to a particular and racist definition of 'us' (the 'real' British, the heart of the nation) as opposed to 'them' (outsiders – such as 'alien' ethnic minorities – and the enemies within – political, social, sexual and gendered 'power minorities'). In this way, discourse offers a means of analysing the conjunction between political ideology and commonsense (Bhavnani with Collins 1993).

Before examining the detail of 'race' and racism in contemporary education policy discourse, we should be clear about some key terms. In the next section, therefore, I wish to clarify briefly the range of possible discursive positions regarding 'race' and education policy.

'Race' and policy discourse

Whether a discourse makes direct use of 'racial' images/language is not, of itself, important. What matters is who uses the discourse, the role of 'race' within it (explicitly and implicitly) and its consequences for the representation of the existing social formation. Hence a 'deracialized' discourse (where 'race' plays no obvious role in the central organizing concepts) is, by definition, no better or worse than a 'racialized' discourse (where racial categories are deployed in a prominent and explicit fashion). This is part of the equation, but a crucial second variable concerns the significance of 'race' and ethnicity in relation to the particular issue or group(s) addressed by and positioned within the discourse. Put another way, we must ask whether the issues at stake in the discourse have clear implications for 'race' and ethnic equality. This produces a matrix of four possible combinations, represented in Figure 2.1.

We can now look at the nature of each of these discourses in turn.

Racialized discourses appear both in cells A and B. They are discourses

'Race' equality is genuinely
implicated in the issues at stake?

		Yes	No
'Racial' categories deployed in the discourse?	Yes	legitimate racialization	spurious racialization
	No	spurious deracialization	legitimate deracialization

Figure 2.2 'Race' and discourse: a typology

that make 'explicit use of racial categorization and evaluation' (Troyna 1993a: 29). In type A, 'race' and ethnic equality is directly implicated in the issues at stake in the discourse. Barry Troyna cites support for ethnic monitoring as an example of this form of 'benign racialization' (after Reeves 1983) where discourse must be racialized in order to address the central issues. In such cases the racialization of discourse is *legitimate*.[3] In contrast, if matters of 'race' and ethnic equality are not genuinely implicated in the key issues (as in cell B) then the discourse is racialized on *spurious* grounds. An example of spurious racialization is the deliberate and strategic use of racial categories as a means of recasting crime statistics (see Carr-Hill and Drew 1988).

The distinction between legitimate and spurious racialization can be adapted in relation to *deracialized discourses*, where 'race' is not deployed explicitly.[4] Where 'race' and ethnic equality are not implicated in the relevant issues it is legitimate that the discourse should be similarly deracialized (type D). There is always the possibility, however, that a deracialized discourse may operate in damaging ways if it addresses issues where 'race' and ethnicity *are* genuinely implicated. Here, the deracialization is spurious (type C).

After a brief flurry of activity in the 1980s (especially at the level of the local state), much British political and education policy discourse has now returned to a deracialized format. This does not mean, however, that issues of 'race' and ethnic equality are not directly implicated in current policy developments. Rather, notions of history, culture, religion, nationality/nationhood, language and 'way of life' have come to act as 'proxy concepts' allowing policies to adopt a superficially deracialized format while directly addressing issues of relevance to existing (and future) racial inequalities (Troyna 1993a: 28). An example is to be found in the debates concerning the 1993 Education Act.

The white paper, *Choice and Diversity*, stated that 'Proper regard should continue to be paid to the nation's Christian heritage and traditions...' (DFE/WO 1992: para. 8.2). The deployment of key 'proxy concepts' is clear in the appeal to 'the nation', 'heritage' and 'traditions'. These themes were taken up and expanded during the Bill's progress through Parliament. Lady Olga Maitland (Conservative) stated:

> We should not allow non-believers to undermine our traditions ... It is a tragedy that the teaching of the Christian faith has become woefully neglected in the face of multiculturalism which is promoting minority faiths at the expense of Christianity.
>
> (quoted in CRE/Runnymede Trust 1993)

This discourse constructs ethnic minority communities as outsiders ('non-believers') who present a direct challenge to 'our' traditions and faith. The notion of a shared British *culture* (religion and tradition) acts as a proxy for the idea of separate 'races'. Indeed, during the entire second reading of the Bill (taking up around 90,000 words in *Hansard* and often focusing on questions of religion in schools) the words 'race', 'racial' and 'racism' were never spoken (CRE/Runnymede Trust 1993).

This example would be of limited importance were it an isolated or extreme incident; unfortunately, this is not the case. The discursive construction of minority communities as a threat (using deracialized concepts of culture and heritage) is a common feature of much contemporary policy debate. Indeed, this reflects a particularly important theme in modern Conservative political ideology. It is a theme that has been struck with most vigour by Enoch Powell (and more recently Winston Churchill), but it has been replayed and embellished by the New Right and endorsed by successive Conservative Prime Ministers. The significance of this theme goes beyond the ideological make-up of a single political party because it has consequences for the construction of 'race' and ethnicity in common sense discourse: it allows for, indeed promotes, racist thinking, policy and practice under the guise of deracialized discourses about 'nationhood' and 'heritage'.

Racism and Conservative ideology

> Power in contemporary society habitually passes itself off as embodied in the normal as opposed to the superior (cf. Marcuse 1964).
>
> (Dyer 1988: 142)

What's new about 'the new racism'?

In a study of developments in British Conservative ideology, Martin Barker identifies what he terms, 'the new racism':

> It is a theory that I shall call biological, or better, pseudo-biological culturalism. Nations on this view are not built out of politics and

economics, but out of human nature. It is in our biology, our instincts, to defend our way of life, traditions and customs against outsiders – not because they are inferior, but because they are part of different cultures.

(Barker 1981: 23–4)

Although Barker notes that 'it is by no means totally new' (p. 24), he argues that 'the new racism' is important because it breaks with old notions of racial superiority and inferiority – substituting instead, the key notion of *cultural difference*. This approach claims not to be racist because 'race' plays no part in the discourse. The 'new racism' presents itself as concerning culture, nation and human nature:

You do not need to think of yourself as superior – you do not even need to dislike or blame those who are so different from you – in order to say that the presence of these aliens constitutes a threat to our way of life.

(Barker 1981: 18)

This has become one of the central strands of New Right thinking. As Stephen Ball notes, a discursive appeal to unity, naturalness, order and standards has been seen as a characteristic of Thatcherism's appeal to 'authoritarian popularism' (Hall 1983). The new racism fits neatly into this wider discursive package:

In all this family and nation, morality and law are bound together in a discursive unity. The 'naturalness' of the traditional family, of fixed gender roles and 'normal' sexuality, of family loyalty and allegiance, fit neatly to the 'naturalness' of national loyalty, of order and place, of historic continuity. And out of this comes a 'natural' fear and suspicion of 'outsiders' and the rejection of alien values which undermine social cohesion.

(Ball 1990a: 40)

Although Margaret Thatcher has fallen from the prominent role she once had, 'the new racism' (like much that was characteristic of Thatcher*ism*) is alive and well in 1990s Britain. Indeed, if we stand back from the surface features of current deracialized policy discourse, it is possible to trace clear links all the way back to Enoch Powell – the politician most responsible for the tenor of racialized politics in the late 1960s and 1970s. Much of what is new about 'new racism' can be conceptualized as a modification of well established, racist, ideas. The discourse of the New Right and contemporary Government policy is not playing a new tune, simply a variation on an old, established – and popularist – theme.

Powell–Thatcher–Major: variations on a racist theme

> Thus is racism theorized out of the guts and made into commonsense.
>
> (Barker 1981: 23)

John Solomos (1991) has charted the changing form and content of discourses about 'race' and politics since the Second World War. Solomos begins by reviewing Enoch Powell's public statements on 'race', noting their immense significance as a watershed in the racialization of British politics:

> the emergence of Powellism as a political phenomenon helped to re-define the terms of political discourse about racial relations in British society during the late 1960s and 1970s.
>
> (Solomos 1991: 22)

Powell successfully racialized political discourse to such an extent that both Labour and Conservative governments took additional steps to limit immigration as a conscious attempt to placate the perceived fears to which Powell appealed (cf. Solomos 1989: ch. 3; Troyna 1988a).

Solomos identifies two key themes in Powell's public interventions on 'race':

Numbers: the idea that minority populations were large (too large) and expanding: as a result of both immigration and high birth rates.
Cultural threat: Powell argued that the 'social and cultural fabric of British society was likely to be undermined by the presence of migrants from a different cultural, racial and religious background' (Solomos 1991: 23).

This discourse asserted the existence of an essential, shared British culture in which ethnic minorities had no role, and to which they posed a threat. The discourse irretrievably locates ethnic minorities as outsiders (wherever they are born, whatever their views and experiences). The discourse constructs an idea of Britishness, more specifically *Englishness*, that defines whites as insiders and all others as a threat:

> The West Indian or Asian does not, by being born in England become an Englishman. In law he becomes a United Kingdom citizen by birth; in fact, he is a West Indian or Asian still . . . Time is running against us and them. (Powell, quoted in Smithies and Fiddick 1969, reprinted Solomos 1991: 23–4)

This quotation demonstrates racialized discourse in action. The terms 'West Indian' and 'Asian' come to signify more than ethnic origin, they are recast as racial signifiers of inherent difference. Englishness is asserted as a quality that such 'races' can never attain, wherever they happen to be born and to live their lives. The difference between 'us' and 'them' is irreconcilable because it is part of our very nature. The links with the 'pseudo-biological culturalism' of 'the new racism' are clear.

Solomos notes several parallels between Powellite discourse and the New Right discourse of contemporary Conservative politics. Building on Barker's notion of 'the new racism', he argues that an important aspect of New Right discourse in this field is 'the tendency to obscure or deny the meaning and implications of the deployment of race categories' (Solomos 1991: 27). While 'the new racism' presents suspicion of 'outsiders' as a 'natural' – not a racist – response, other aspects of New Right discourse continue to paint a specific and dangerous picture of minorities, although now deploying deracialized terms as proxy concepts. Two key themes emerge in New Right discourses: first the image of inner cities as 'black enclaves' where minority youth flout 'British' law and order. Second, a presentation of minority communities as an 'enemy within' threatening the moral and social fabric of society (Solomos 1991: 26).

Inner cities as lawless Black enclaves
Inner city areas and populations have come to occupy an important place in Conservative ideology. A range of stereotypes has been attached such that 'inner city' is often used as a general signifier for lawlessness, immorality and decay. Indeed, inner cities are sometimes constructed in Conservative discourse as not really a part of Britain at all, at least not part of what genuinely marks that country out as special. Take, for example, the views of William Whitelaw (Home Secretary and later Deputy Prime Minister to Margaret Thatcher). Whitelaw was Home Secretary at the time of the 1981 riots. In his memoirs, he recalls that period, and describes the solace he found at his country home:

> I remember sitting out after supper on a beautiful hot summer evening, looking at the fields and trees of Burnham Beeches. It was a perfect, peaceful English scene. Was it really in the same country as the riot towns and cities which I had visited that week? Was it really in the same vicinity as parts of London a few miles away which were at that moment full of troubles? Surely, I thought, this peaceful countryside represents more accurately the character and mood of the vast majority of the British people.
>
> (Whitelaw 1989, quoted by Newsinger 1992: 86)

The people and issues caught up in 'the riot towns and cities' are thus distinguished from 'the vast majority of the British people'. In this way, the inner cities can be safely contained (and condemned) without threat to the 'real' England.

The threat to 'our' moral and social fabric, 'our' culture, 'our' way of life

This strand of New Right discourse has been revitalized in the 1990s, especially building on the increased political mobilization of South Asian communities. The protests of Islamic groups against Salman Rushdie's book, *The Satanic Verses* (1988), and against white racism (Samad 1992) have signalled a new 'Muslim assertiveness' (Modood 1992) that the media and politicians have been quick to seize on as symptomatic of a dangerous 'illiberal' (non-British) intolerance and lawlessness (cf. Le Lohe 1989). Robin Richardson captures this stereotype well when he describes press responses to the establishment of 'the Muslim Parliament':

> In the current constellation of Western moral and cultural views, Islam is perceived and pictured as monolithic and homogeneous; literalist and fundamentalist in its uncritical, unscientific and anti-modernist approach to religious tradition and scripture; intolerant and authoritarian in its internal structures, particularly in its control of women and daughters, and with regard to human rights and freedoms ... and ungrateful to, and unappreciative of, Western ways and wisdom.
>
> (Richardson 1992: 2)

In addition, although such stereotypes specifically target Muslim groups, they are widely attached to any South Asian group, irrespective of particular ethnic, religious or political background. During the Gulf War, for example, these stereotypes were conflated with additional notions of both ethnic and political 'Otherness' such that: 'All Asians are "Pakis", and "Paki" passes as a synonym for mad Muslim. And all Muslims are Iraqis' (Sivanandan 1991: 87).[5]

The treatment of Islamic groups (by politicians, the media and the New Right) is a particular example of the broader attack on all non-white communities as a threat to 'our way of life'. The former chairman [*sic*] of the Conservative party, Norman Tebbit, struck an identical theme in public statements opposing any extension of British citizenship rights to Hong Kong residents:

> these islands are already overcrowded ... great waves of immigration by people who do not share our culture, our language, our ways of social conduct, in many cases who owe no allegiance to our country was, and is, a destabilising factor in society ... If we are not going to see social upheaval arising from religious and cultural and ethnic differences, then we have more than enough to do to integrate existing communities without adding to that burden or exacerbating existing problems.
>
> (quoted in Runnymede Trust 1990: 1–2)

The Powellite themes of overcrowding and threat to 'our culture, our language, our ways of social conduct' are plain: it is revealing, however, that by 1990 even someone with such extreme views nevertheless found it necessary to talk in terms of culture and ethnicity, rather than use overtly 'racial' language.

The deracialized talk of a cultural threat to 'our way of life' has penetrated beyond the extremes of Conservative politics and now occupies a central place in much political discourse.[6] Given the central importance of 'the new racism' to the Thatcherite project, it is no surprise that Margaret Thatcher always reaffirmed her pre-election views on the threat of 'swamping' – again returning to Powellite themes in a deracialized discourse about culture:

> people are really rather afraid that this country might be swamped by people with a different culture. And, you know, the British character has done so much for democracy, for law, and done so much throughout the world, that if there is a fear that it might be swamped, people are going to react and be rather hostile to those coming in.
> (Margaret Thatcher, January 1978: quoted in Barker 1981: 15)

This view played a part in Thatcher's speech to the 1987 party conference – a conference, of course, where reform of state education was one of the central themes. The following extract demonstrates how several elements of New Right ideology are mutually supporting so that an attack on 'extremist' teachers and poor educational standards gains strength by deploying images of inner city decay and the promotion of 'abnormal' sexualities. It is particularly revealing to note how educationists' attempts to confront racism are summarily dismissed – embodying the 'discourse of derision' (Ball 1990a) that paints antiracism as a 'loony tune' (Troyna and Carrington 1990):

> Too often our children don't get the education they need – the education they deserve. And in the inner cities – where youngsters must have a decent education if they are to have a better future – that opportunity is all too often snatched away from them by hard-left educational authorities and extremist teachers. Children who need to be able to count and multiply are learning anti-racist mathematics – whatever that might be. Children who need to be able to express themselves in clear English are being taught political slogans. Children who need to be taught to respect traditional moral values are being taught that they have an inalienable right to be gay.
> (Margaret Thatcher, October 1987: quoted in Ball 1990a: 49)

John Major, of course, has tended to use less dramatic – and less effective – discourse. Nevertheless, classic elements of New Right deracialized themes remain. In his first speech on 'race' equality as Prime Minister, for example, Major argued for 'more effective integration in the United Kingdom socially, culturally and economically' (John Major, September 1991: quoted in Runnymede Trust 1991: 5). In 1993, talk of the *United Kingdom* gave way to a romantic vision of *Britain*.[7] In a speech on European union, Major argued that 'the best of Britain', its 'distinctive and unique' character would remain. He continued:

> Fifty years from now Britain will still be the country of long shadows on county grounds, warm beer, invincible green suburbs, dog lovers and pools fillers and – as George Orwell said – 'old maids bicycling to holy communion through the morning mist' and – if we get our way – Shakespeare still read even in school. Britain will survive unamendable in all essentials.
>
> (Major 1993: 9)

The casual joke at the expense of the education system (towards the end of the quotation) is reminiscent of his predecessor's derision of educational standards and curriculum content half a decade earlier. But more important is the image of an 'essential' and 'unamendable' Britain – a Britain that is clearly white and (except perhaps for the 'dog lovers and pools fillers') overwhelmingly suburban/rural and middle class.

New racism/old racism: the significance of deracialized discourse

John Major's characterization of the 'essential' Britain gives expression to a powerful and racist construction of 'the nation' – one that excludes people of minority ethnic background. Major (like Thatcher before him) plays a variation on the themes originally struck by Enoch Powell. The crucial difference is in the deracialized nature of the discourse – a difference that was used to dramatic effect by Winston Churchill (descendant of the wartime leader) in his attempt to revive old-style Powellism:

> He [Major] promises us that fifty years on from now, spinsters will still be cycling to communion on Sunday mornings – more like the muezzin will be calling Allah's faithful to the high street mosque.
>
> (Winston Churchill, May 1993: quoted in
> Runnymede Trust 1993b: 2)

The discursive use of 'British' – as a proxy for white – has now become a familiar part of contemporary political discourse.[8] As Paul Boateng – one of the country's first ever black MPs – told the Speaker's Commission on Citizenship, talk of 'Britishness' often carries deeply racist connotations:

> There are very many areas in our country where people who talk about citizenship, and who talk about citizenship within a context of

Britishness, are the very people who are likely to harass your daughter and your wife as they go to school or as they go out shopping, and are the very people who are likely to lob a brick through your window, to put a fire bomb through your letterbox.

(Boateng 1989)

In 1990s England discursive constructions of 'Britishness' have become so shot through with racism, that even openly racist organizations, such as the neo-Nazi British National Party (BNP), have adopted the code.

On 16 September 1993, the BNP won a seat on the Tower Hamlets council in London (by a majority of just seven). The party's national organizer, Richard Edmonds, declared that 'We stand for truth. We stand for Britain. We stand for justice'. In his victory speech Derek Beackon, the BNP councillor, stated:

> The British people are no longer prepared to be treated as second class citizens in their own country. The British people have had enough. We are going to take our country back.[9]

The BNP campaign slogan ('Rights for Whites') betrays the BNP's interpretation of 'the British people'. I am not suggesting, of course, that the Conservative Party are directly comparable with neo-Nazi groups such as the BNP: what I am suggesting, is that deracialized discourse is inherently no better than the open racism of Powellism; that despite its deracialized form, the 'new' racism serves the same ends as the 'old' racism. Major's deracialized image of an unchanging Britain is no less racist in its construction of the 'nation' than Thatcher's 'people' who are afraid of being swamped or Powell's 'Englishmen'. These discourses construct ethnic minorities as non-British (less openly but at least as effectively) as the BNP's definition of 'the British people'.

The use of what I have called 'spurious deracialization' has become so commonplace that we all understand the code. Studs Terkel's exploration of 'race' in America reveals the same situation: 'All of us, black and white, know what it's about . . . It is the speech of a beleaguered people, or those who see themselves as such' (Terkel 1992: 4). Spurious deracialization is important because it offers a smokescreen of respectability to racist constructions. The BNP's rhetoric is less subtle (and less successful) than that of Thatcher and Major, but in many ways they are playing a similar game. The significance of spurious deracialization, however, goes beyond this 'smokescreen' effect.

Deracialized notions of culture, language, heritage and the nation construct a policy terrain in which 'race' equality is effectively removed from the agenda. Hence, the High Court (and later the Court of Appeal) dismissed a complaint, by the CRE, against Cleveland LEA's decision to accept a white parent's objection to a multi-ethnic school. The court interpreted her objections in terms of language and culture (rather than 'race'). In a letter to the local authority, the parent (Jenny Carney) had stated:

> I don't think it is fair for her to go through school with about four white friends and the rest Pakistan . . . I don't think it's right when she comes home singing in Pakistan. I know they only learn three Pakistan songs, but I don't want her to learn this language . . . I want her to go to a school where there will be the majority white children not Pakistan.
>
> (quoted in Vincent 1992: 429)

In analysing the case and its consequences, Carol Vincent argues that the judge 'appeared to accept that although "racial grounds" had influenced Ms Carney, her actions were primarily inspired by a desire to ensure that her daughter was not taught "a foreign language at a time when she needed to read and write her own language"' (Vincent 1992: 434). In this case deracialization was mobilized to deny the legitimacy of 'race' – where the Commission for Racial Equality was arguing that Cleveland's decision had consequences for 'race' equality. This is perhaps the most dangerous consequence of spurious deracialization. The ability to deny 'race' any legitimacy in a debate, and thereby leave the way clear for practices that have racist consequences, regardless of their deracialized façade. This is precisely the danger posed by the deracialization of current education policy.

Racism and the deracialization of education policy

In this section I analyse the deracialized discourse that characterizes contemporary education policy. In particular I focus on policy in the 'new era', heralded by the massive reforms of state education imposed by successive Conservative governments, under Margaret Thatcher, especially through the Education Reform Act (ERA) 1988, and John Major (notably in the Education Act 1993, which supports and extends the 1988 Act).

Elsewhere I have described the initial development of education policy in relation to cultural diversity in England and Wales (Gillborn 1990: ch. 6). After an early period where it was assumed that minorities would simply *assimilate* into the 'British way of life', there was an *integrationist* phase. Political discourse accepted the distinctiveness of minority communities, yet policy sought to continue the defence of existing structures and practices behind a rhetoric of 'colour blindness'. From the late 1970s official rhetoric was of *'cultural pluralism'*, embodying a recognition (and sometimes a celebration) of cultural difference and a limited commitment to equality of opportunity as part of an avowedly meritocratic system. Throughout these different 'phases', issues of 'race' and racism rarely took centre stage in education policy. David Kirp (1979) characterized British policy on 'race' and schooling as 'doing good by doing little'; his optimism has been criticized by several commentators who warn that 'doing little' in policy might amount to 'doing nothing' in practice. In several local authorities, especially those with significant ethnic minority populations, the 1980s saw a brief period when 'race' and ethnicity became prominent categories in education policy-making. Unfortunately, many of the changes remained superficial (see Troyna 1993a; Troyna and Williams 1986). Where progress was made, this was soon threatened by national reforms.

Thatcherism and education: 'race' and policy post-1988

The Education Reform Act 1988 marked the beginning of a distinctive new phase in British education policy. It had taken the Thatcher governments the best part of a decade to turn their attention fully to education, but when they did, the plans were startling. The 1988 Act established the legal framework for the imposition of a centrally defined 'National Curriculum'; the introduction of a national system of testing at certain 'key' ages (seven, 11, 14 and 16); the delegation of funds away from local authorities; and even made provision for new kinds of school (City Technology Colleges and Grant Maintained schools).

As Geoff Whitty has noted, the reforms embodied apparently contradictory elements of Conservative ideology. On the one hand, there was a 'neo-conservative emphasis on tradition, authority and national identity/ security', seen in the idea of a National Curriculum: on the other hand, there was a simultaneous 'espousal of neo-liberal free market economics', seen in moves to open up direct competition between schools (Whitty 1990: 23). This contradiction, however, is far from fatal. Indeed, as Whitty argues, from a New Right standpoint the combination offers a way forward because 'the overt ideology of the curriculum needs to be addressed directly before the "hidden curriculum" of the new structure is sufficiently developed to do its work' (Whitty 1992: 302).[10]

The place of 'race' and ethnic equality amid these reforms has always been uncertain. Several writers and pressure groups expressed deep concern at the ethnocentric character of the original 'reform' proposals (see Haviland 1988). At first 'multicultural issues' were officially characterized as a cross-curricular *theme* (DES 1989: para. 3.8). Later in the same year this changed to a cross-curricular *dimension* (NCC 1989) – a category that carries less force in terms of specific curricular implications (Gillborn 1990: 169–70).

Suspicion that 'race' issues were being removed from the agenda was confirmed by the fate of a working party, established to make specific recommendations on 'multicultural' issues in the National Curriculum. Speaking at the annual conference of the National Anti-racist Movement in Education, Beverley Anderson (a prominent Black writer/broadcaster and member of the National Curriculum Council (NCC)) stated that:

> she did *not* see the national curriculum as a device for diluting multi-cultural and anti-racist education in the 1990's, – she considered it could be a way of spreading good multicultural practice to all schools in a systematic way (Anderson 1989).
>
> (Tomlinson 1989: 130, original emphasis)

The 'Multicultural Task-Group' submitted its full report in June 1990. Despite an earlier commitment, however, the NCC never published the report (Tomlinson 1991).[11]

The status of 'race' as a legitimate policy issue was further undermined by the Education Act 1993. The preceding White Paper, '*Choice and Diversity: A New Framework for Schools*' (DES/WO 1992), was widely interpreted as an attempt to first, tie up loose ends from the 1988 Act, and second, rescue some of the measures that were failing – most notably the system allowing schools to 'opt out' of LEA control and assume Grant Maintained (GM) status (*Times Educational Supplement*, 31 July 1992).

Although different people now inhabited the key jobs (John Major had replaced Margaret Thatcher as Prime Minister and John Patten was the latest Secretary of State for Education) the official discourse remained constant. From an ideological position where *competition* is the key, the very notion of *equality* can be discredited by means of a discourse of derision:

> The Opposition like to talk about equality in education, but they do not mean equality, they mean uniformity. They mean pushing children together, en masse, to be treated exactly the same . . . We have successfully cast adrift the attachment to uniformity and conformity – those by-words of the left-wing education establishment that characterised our education system during the 1960s and 1970s and often did such damage to many in a generation of school children. We have replaced those by-words with some of our own – choice, diversity and, above all, standards.
>
> (John Patten, Secretary of State for Education, opening the second reading of the Education Bill 1992: quoted in CRE/Runnymede Trust 1993)

While the dominant discourse has remained constant, during the late 1980s and early 1990s the role of 'race', and related issues of 'racial' and ethnic equality, has been reconstructed in a variety of ways. The process of deracialization has involved several interwoven strands, which marginalize 'race' issues and effectively deny 'race' a legitimate place on the policy agenda.

The deracialization of education policy

The new racist concern with British/English (white) nationhood and cultural identity (discussed earlier in this chapter) plays an important role in the spurious deracialization of education policy. The discourse assumes an apparently inclusive character: hence, John Major's opening remarks in the 1992 education White Paper assert: 'The Government are determined that *every* child in this country should have the very best start in life' (DFE/ WO 1992: iii, emphasis added). Unfortunately, the proposals tend to assume a unitary conception of 'every child', just as they assume a particular view of 'parents' and 'commonsense' – one based firmly on Rightist principles of market competition. The White Paper says nothing about 'race' inequalities and, so far as ethnic diversity is concerned, is at pains to emphasize 'the nation's Christian heritage and traditions' (DFE/WO 1992: para. 8.2). The discourse appears *inclusive*, therefore, yet seems specifically to *exclude* certain minority groups.

In terms of education policy, two further dimensions of the deracialization process can be identified. First, there is a tendency to subsume 'race' amid other categories. This robs 'race' of any special status and denies its claim to attention. Second, the consistent failure/refusal to conceive of racism as anything but a small-scale problem of individual ignorance and 'prejudice'. By denying that racism is a widespread problem, and defining out the possibility that structural factors are implicated, this discourse takes a minimalist position that defends the (racially inequitable) status quo. It is worth examining each of these in a little more detail.

Subsuming 'race' into other categories
The final report of the Committee of Inquiry into the Education of Children from Ethnic Minority Groups (Swann 1985) included a section on education policy and matters of ethnic diversity. The report was especially critical of official statements that located minority 'needs' within 'the overall context of disadvantage' (Swann 1985: 214). Nevertheless, on the day of the report's publication, the then Secretary of State for Education and Science, Sir Keith Joseph, continued the trend by stating that:

> under-achievement is not confined to the ethnic minorities . . . [Our] policies apply to all pupils irrespective of ethnic origin. As they bear fruit, ethnic minority pupils will share in the benefit.
>
> (*Hansard*, 14 March 1985: col. 451)

This process of denying 'race' and ethnicity any special significance was later epitomized by a Minister of State at the DES under Joseph's successor, and architect of the 1988 Act, Kenneth Baker:

> the whole of this problem is perhaps changing with time and one perhaps cannot go back to something which was thought through . . . and presented in a time and in an era which is very different from today. One of the Government's main thrusts has been to tackle inner city problems, and that is one of the more effective ways if I might say so, for many of the suggestions that came through in the Swann Committee.
>
> (Angela Rumbold speaking just over three years after the publication of the Swann Report: quoted in Blair and Woods 1992: 36)

Government education policy at the time of the 1988 Act, therefore, was based on a view that equated 'race' and ethnic issues with 'inner city problems'. Swann's attempt to champion 'Education for All' (a limited policy of multicultural education with some antiracist features) was rejected as belonging to a different era. The pattern, therefore, is clear: issues of 'race' and ethnicity can safely be denied any special legitimacy; if there is a problem, it will be rectified by existing policies that address other – more important – issues. Minority groups will share in the benefits just like everybody else. The theme has been repeated by John Major:

> The government's education reforms directly addressed [African Caribbean parents'] concerns, the Prime Minister said. The national curriculum guaranteed that every child received a 'broad, balanced and relevant curriculum', while the Parents' Charter would especially help members of ethnic minorities who felt disadvantaged by lack of information about schools and lack of opportunity for involvement in their children's education.
>
> (Runnymede Trust 1991: 5)

By denying 'race' any special status in education (and other areas of social policy) this discourse undermines the position of individuals and groups who seek to address 'race' issues. If 'race' has no special status, then anyone who claims otherwise is not only wrong, but likely to be stirring up trouble (probably deliberately). This position is clearly illustrated in discourses that attack any individual or group that attempts to promote antiracist practice. In an attack on the 'mania' of antiracism, Russell Lewis argues that:

> The race relations industry has a momentum of its own. Those within it who do genuinely believe in the gospel they preach have every incentive to show proof that race relations are getting worse, for that makes their message all the more urgent. Others are not concerned

with highlighting racial problems in order that they may be more quickly solved, but are actually in the business of promoting social strife.

(Lewis 1988: quoted in Leech 1988/89: 12)

Hence, any attempt to adopt a racialized discourse may be condemned as the work of political zealots (preaching a false 'gospel'), or as a self-serving strategy by members of an 'industry' whose 'business' is the promotion of unrest.

Defining out the problem: racism as personal prejudice
A final aspect to the spurious deracialization of contemporary education policy has to do with the very notion of 'racism'.

Conservative discourse defines racism in terms of individual prejudice. It is a view that is repeatedly reinforced by the state, for example, in Lord Scarman's report on the 1981 Brixton riots (Scarman 1981). Here 'prejudice is constituted as an individualized, exceptional phenomenon, automatically exonerating society as a whole' (Henriques 1984: 62). This view holds:

> that there are racists in Britain and laws to combat their discriminatory behaviour should be enforced; but that there is nothing inherently or institutionally racist about the structure of society and accusations along these lines should be summarily discarded.
>
> (Troyna 1993a: 30)

It is accepted, therefore, that some white people (a small minority) harbour irrational prejudices against ethnic minorities, but this is seen as a personal failing, a result of ignorance, that should be handled carefully so as not to provoke any 'backlash'. This view effectively defines out of existence the possibility that impersonal rules and traditions, the very structures of society, might act in 'racist' ways. Any attempt to challenge this minimalist conception of racism is dismissed as guilt-inducing subversive propaganda (Honeyford 1989).

This minimalist perspective on racism can be seen at work in the Report of the Elton Committee of Enquiry, *Discipline in Schools* (Elton 1989). The report acknowledges evidence of 'racist attitudes among pupils' (para. 4.91) and even 'a few teachers' (para. 6.67). It argues that 'group differences' should not be ignored (para. 6.58) but cautions against any 'dogmatic' solutions (para. 6.61). The committee's preferred approach is a limited form of multiculturalism that stresses cultural diversity and mutual tolerance.

> Head-on confrontation is likely to be counter-productive. It may alienate as many pupils as it wins over. We believe that using the curriculum

to emphasise the importance of tolerance and respect for other cultures is a more productive approach.

(Elton 1989: para. 4.91)

Hence, racism is reduced to personal prejudice and ignorance: nowhere is it considered as a dynamic and complex facet of school life (in which routine institutional procedures and teacher expectations may be deeply implicated).

Deracialized discourse and racist practice: the case of African Caribbean exclusions

Previous sections have explored the key elements that make up the deracialized discourse of contemporary policy debates. I have argued that the spurious deracialization of current Government policy not only fails to recognize racism, in all but the most crude and limited way, but actually sustains and extends racism by denying legitimacy to racialized analyses and protests. At this point it is useful to bring these ideas together through an analysis of education policy in action. The case in question concerns the 1993 Education Act and amendments that the Government made while the Bill passed through Parliament. The changes illustrate the nature of 'race' in current education discourse and illustrate its racist consequences; in this case ignoring the racialized character of present patterns in school exclusion.

One of the main innovations in the 1993 Act is the establishment of a Funding Agency for Schools (FAS). This body administers the payment of funds to Grant Maintained schools and, under certain circumstances, shares or takes over local authorities' duties with regard to the provision of school places. Initially it was not certain that the FAS would be subject to the requirements of the Race Relations Act 1976 (CRE 1992a). After strong lobbying, however, the Government accepted that this was appropriate and agreed to amend the Bill accordingly (CRE/Runnymede Trust 1993).

The recognition of the Race Relations Act 1976 does not accord with some New Right commentators' distaste for bodies like the CRE – a leading part of the 'race relations industry' (Lewis 1988). Nevertheless, this move is in keeping with neo-conservative paternalism and the minimalist position on racism, where legislation against racist excesses *is* seen as a proper exercise of state power.

A second area where the Government amended the Bill concerned exclusions from school – an issue of huge concern to African Caribbean communities. Exclusions are a disciplinary mechanism by which students can be barred from attending school, ranging from exclusion for a day or so,

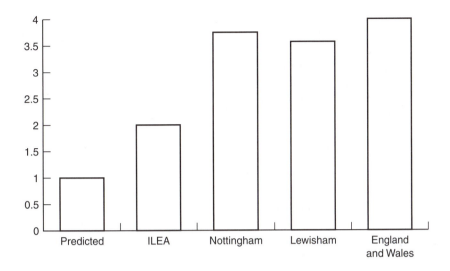

Figure 2.3 The over-representation of black youth in exclusions from school

through to permanent removal from the school's roll. Whenever data on exclusions are analysed by ethnic origin a consistent pattern of disadvantage emerges (see Figure 2.3).[12] In the now abolished Inner London Education Authority (ILEA), in 1986/7, 'Afro-Caribbean' students accounted for 14 per cent of all pupils, but made up more than 30 per cent of all exclusions (*Times Educational Supplement*, 9 September 1988). That is, more than twice as many African Caribbean students were excluded than would have been predicted based on their representation in the school population. More recent data paint an even bleaker picture. In Nottingham, between September 1989 and April 1990, 'Black' (i.e. African Caribbean and 'mixed race') students made up just over 6 per cent of the secondary school population, but accounted for almost 25 per cent of pupils 'involved in exclusion procedures' (Nottinghamshire County Council 1991: 21). In Lewisham, between the summer term 1990 and spring term 1991, 'Black Afro-Caribbean' students made up 25 per cent of all exclusions from secondary school, but were estimated to account for around 7 per cent of the pupil population (Lewisham 1991: Table 3). The first ever nationwide survey of exclusions (limited to permanent exclusions only) confirmed that 'Afro-Caribbean pupils appeared to be disproportionately represented within the excluded pupil population (8.1% of the overall total)' (DFE 1992: 3). When compared with the estimated proportion of African Caribbean students in the school population (2 per cent: Runnymede Trust 1993a: 6), this means that *four times as many African Caribbean students were permanently excluded than would have been predicted, all other things being equal.*

The DFE's statement on the over-representation of African Caribbean students, therefore, confirms earlier fears about exclusions in certain local authorities. The significance of the DFE's data, however, is that their figures refer to *all* reported permanent exclusions across England and Wales: based on returns to the National Exclusions Reporting System (NERS).[13]

The NERS data also offer a crude indication of the damage that permanent exclusion does to students' educational careers: *two out of every three students who are permanently excluded fail to secure a place in another mainstream school* (DFE 1993a: 4). The over-representation of African Caribbean students in exclusion figures is, therefore, extremely serious. The DFE's own statistics suggest that exclusions are operating in a racialized fashion, such that African Caribbean students are disproportionately denied even basic access to educational institutions – let alone substantive access to educational opportunities within schools.

In some areas the exclusion of African Caribbean students has reached crisis proportions. The Nottingham figures (detailed above) amount to 11.2 per cent of the entire 'Black' (African Caribbean and 'mixed race') population of that county's secondary schools: that is, *in less than a full academic year, more than one in ten of Nottingham's Black students were 'involved in exclusion procedures'.*[14] In contrast, only around one in fifty white and 'Asian' students were involved (see Figure 2.4).

Although the Government's own data confirm fears about a crisis of African Caribbean exclusions, the deracialization of contemporary policy discourse ensures that the issue of racism remains unexplored. The Department for Education has begun to address the rising number of exclusions, but 'race' has been almost completely absent from the documents. In April 1993, as the Education Bill moved through Parliament, the DFE issued a press release announcing a 'new deal for "out of school" pupils' (DFE 1993a). The package of measures included several amendments to the Bill and a commitment to issue 'guidance to schools' at a later date. The amendments placed a duty on local authorities to 'secure the education of pupils otherwise than at school' and concerned the management and aims of 'Pupil Referral Units'. 'Race', ethnicity and racism were not mentioned, despite the fact that official figures, appended to the press release, repeated the finding that African Caribbean students were disproportionately subject to permanent exclusion (DFE 1993a: 4). Later the same year a draft circular on exclusions was issued (DFE 1993b). This time the African

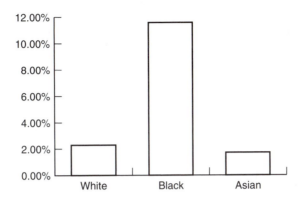

Figure 2.4 Involvement in exclusion procedures by ethnic background (Nottingham)

Caribbean over-representation was acknowledged in the main body of the text: it received a single paragraph (two sentences) amid 40-odd pages of other material. The circular advises headteachers to 'ensure that they apply disciplinary procedures objectively and consistently across all ethnic groups' (DFE 1993b: circular 3, para. 33).

Whatever lies behind the figures, therefore, the Government's amendments and guidance on exclusions almost totally ignore 'race' as a relevant issue. Except for a cursory mention (which echoes the minimalist view of racism as personal prejudice) the issue is lost amid the deracialized discourse, leaving the crisis to continue unchecked. In this way, the deracialized discourse protects the racialized and racist operation of the education system.

Conclusions

In contemporary political discourse, people's understanding of 'race' and racism is as important as ever, although its precise form and usage vary. 'Race' is no longer limited to the extreme forms of racialized politics. The supposedly *renegade* views of Enoch Powell and Winston Churchill, whose statements on 'race' drew official reprimands from their political superiors, are actually reflected in *mainstream* policy debates. Yet this is a complex linguistic territory: we have to understand the power and dynamics of *discourse* before we can fully critique the racist operation of concepts that are specifically *de*racialized.

In adopting discourse as a conceptual tool, I have argued that the use of racialized and deracialized language is only part of the equation. We must also ask whether racial inequality is implicated in the issues that are at stake in a particular discourse. The distinction between *spurious* and *legitimate* (de)racialized discourses rests on a combination of these factors.

I have traced three main themes in the spurious deracialization of contemporary education policy. First, a 'new racist' obsession with national identity and culture. By defining ethnic 'others' as a threat to the unity of the nation, this discourse mobilizes deracialized concepts (language, history, culture, etc.) towards racist ends.

Second, the discourse subsumes certain 'race' issues within wider deracialized concepts, such as 'disadvantage' and 'the inner cities'. In this way critical analyses of racial inequality are denied legitimacy. Anyone who attempts (legitimately) to racialize the discourse may be dismissed as a political extremist or self-serving member of the 'race relations industry'.

The third theme in the spurious deracialization of education policy is the minimalist and individualistic definition of racism, as a personal issue of ignorance and prejudice. This position defines out of existence any systematic bias in institutional structures and norms.

The deracialization of education policy has crucial and damaging consequences. It has created, for example, a situation where 'language' and 'culture' may be used to justify a choice of school along 'racial' lines; and where the systematic exclusion of African Caribbean students can remain as a footnote to official debates.

By effectively removing 'race' from the policy agenda, deracialization leaves the way clear for each new development to operate in racially inequitable ways. A further example is the Conservative attack on teacher training institutions, which aims to place most initial teacher education in the hands of schools. The emphasis on the craft knowledge of practising teachers is expressed as a victory for 'commonsense' over elaborate and ineffective educational 'theory'. Yet these moves threaten to create exactly the conditions that will sustain and extend existing disadvantages, for example, as a result of the stereotyped beliefs about certain ethnic groups that can form part of the craft (commonsense) knowledge of teachers (see Gillborn 1990).

Decisions about the legitimate role of 'race' and ethnicity in policy debates are not easy, but a critical awareness of the dangers of deracialized discourse is essential. Deracialized talk of 'culture', 'language' and 'nation' can have racist consequences. In the next chapter, I argue that exactly the same kind of danger awaits researchers who fail to challenge commonsense and practitioner-based assumptions about 'race' and ethnicity.

three _____

Racism and research _____

> Methodology is too important to be left to methodologists.
>
> (Becker 1970: 3)

The leap from the realm of policy and politics (in the previous chapter) to the world of academic research (in this) is not as great as many suppose. Among the many common issues are the problems of representation and the use of discourse to construct minority students as other.

This chapter examines the problems that arise in relation to the conceptualization of 'race' and racism in educational research. How researchers think about 'race' influences the design of their projects, the kinds of data they collect, the analyses they conduct, and the conclusions they draw.

The chapter begins with an examination of quantitative approaches to 'race' and education. For many years research in this field was synonymous with large-scale surveys of academic achievement. The late 1980s and the 1990s have seen significant advances in quantitative research but the work still suffers from an inability to explore adequately the complex and sometimes hidden nature of 'race' and racism in schools. These issues are examined via the treatment of racism in *The School Effect* (Smith and Tomlinson 1989) – a large-scale quantitative study of multi-ethnic comprehensives. *The School Effect* is unusual in attempting to go beyond a concern with academic attainment and directly address the school experiences of minority students.

Qualitative research is seen by some as a more sensitive means of researching 'race' and racism. It has been argued, for example, that such work is more attuned to the intricacies of power and selection in schools. Qualitative approaches, however, do not offer a panacea to the problems of research in this field.

Several ethnographic studies of multi-ethnic schools have suggested that teachers play an active (though usually unintentional) role in the processes that structure the educational opportunities of minority students. However, a series of methodological critiques (by a small group of writers) has developed into a cumulative project which challenges the validity of this work. The ensuing controversy highlights key problems about standards of evidence and ways of theorizing 'race' and racism in empirical research. The bulk of this chapter examines the controversy. In particular, I focus on the protagonists' conflicting assumptions and conceptual frameworks. I try to identify the consequences of the methodological project (both intended and unintended), and conclude that the critiques embody a conservative notion of social research. It is a project that defines racism in crude and limited ways; defends the status quo; and employs a sociological discourse that pathologizes minority students in general, and African Caribbean young men in particular. The controversy highlights important lessons for all those concerned with empirical research on 'race' and racism, not least in terms of the need to challenge taken-for-granted assumptions which might reproduce wider inequalities in the racial structuring of educational opportunities.

Researching racism in schools: quantitative approaches

There is a long tradition of quantitative research in British sociology. Indeed, for most of its history the sociology of education has been dominated by work that places a premium on statistical data and analysis. A particular approach, known as 'political-arithmetic', underpinned several classics of British sociological research (e.g. Douglas 1964; Glass 1954; Goldthorpe et al. 1980; Halsey et al. 1980):

> the political-arithmetic tradition . . . has a double intent; on the one hand it engages in the primary sociological task of describing and documenting the 'state of society'; on the other hand it addresses itself to central social and political issues.
>
> (Halsey et al. 1980: 1)

This attempt to wed a scientific respect for statistical facts with liberal social and political concerns, typified much early research on social class and educational opportunity. Similar assumptions eventually found expression in work on 'race' and ethnicity in education.

After a long period of neglect, the late 1970s and early 1980s witnessed a growth in research in this area. The work primarily sought to quantify how minority students were performing in education, with a view to identifying possible sources of inequality. Arguments about the possible 'underachievement' of African Caribbean students were especially prominent. The quality of the research, however, rarely matched the importance of the issues. Data on minority students was often aggregated in ways that lost sight of significant historical, cultural, political and social differences. Social class (strongly associated with educational achievement) was rarely taken into account. Samples were constructed with little or no regard to national patterns of migration and settlement. The result was a series of studies that painted a partial, and possibly misleading, picture of minority achievement (Kysel 1988; Mabey 1986; Maughan and Rutter 1986; Rampton 1981; Swann 1985).

The 1990s have seen important advances in quantitative research in this field. Findings, based on the first ever nationally representative sample of minority students, indicate that their achievement is more complex (and possibly more encouraging) than suggested by earlier work (Drew and Gray 1990; 1991; Drew et al. 1992). In addition, new statistical techniques have encouraged more ambitious attempts to understand the interaction of different variables in relation to students' school achievements and patterns of attainment over time. The development of multi-level modelling (Goldstein 1987) has been especially important, underpinning several studies that have attempted to measure schools' 'effectiveness' for different groups of students – including those of minority background (Mortimore et al. 1988; Nuttall et al. 1992; Nuttall and Varlaam 1990; Smith and Tomlinson 1989; Thomas et al. 1993).

Quantitative studies of 'race' and ethnicity in education, therefore, have given prominence to questions of academic achievement and progress.[1] The studies are at their strongest when charting general patterns of success/failure, but begin to come unstuck when questions are asked about *why* the patterns have come about. Quantitative research has been singularly unsuccessful in describing the *processes* that underlie students' experience of school. The nature of the problems can be explored by briefly considering a quantitative study that explicitly tried to address such issues.

The School Effect, by David Smith and Sally Tomlinson (1989), reports a study of twenty multi-ethnic comprehensives (conducted between 1981 and 1988). The project was unusual among quantitative studies in seeking not only to record differences in progress and achievement between ethnic groups, but also to 'describe *processes* underlying school success' and to 'describe the educational *experience*' of minority students (Smith and Tomlinson 1989: 28, emphasis added). In judging students' experiences of school, the researchers were limited to two main sources of data: first, a questionnaire that sought 12 and 13 year-old students' views on matters such as friendship choices, participation in school activities and their receipt of praise and blame in class. Second, the researchers drew on interviews with parents that covered the parents' view of their children's progress and happiness in school. No systematic classroom observation was undertaken.

The researchers found few parents who criticized schools on 'racial' grounds (p. 62) and noted that minority students were relatively highly motivated:

> children from ethnic minority groups actually have more positive feel-ings about school in the second year than white children. These findings suggest that difficulties children would notice, such as racial hostility at school, are rare, or that children have learnt to live with them. This is strongly confirmed by the survey of parents...
>
> (Smith and Tomlinson 1989: 106)

On the basis of their data, the researchers concluded:

> there was little indication of overt racism in relations among pupils or between pupils and staff... there is no evidence that racial hostility at school is an important factor for 12 and 13-year olds.
>
> (Smith and Tomlinson 1989: 63 and 305)

Smith and Tomlinson's conclusion, on the lack of racism in their sample of schools, has been criticized for several reasons. Writers have objected to the unexplained emphasis on *overt* racism; the assumption that parents would know whether their children were subject to racial harassment in school (and that they would share that knowledge); and the existence of a simple link between receipt of harassment and academic motivation (Gillborn 1990; Gillborn and Drew 1992; Troyna 1991a; Troyna and Hatcher 1992). Indeed, a qualitative study of one of Smith and Tomlinson's sample schools (Gillborn 1990) came to very different conclusions, arguing that racism was very much a part of the minority students' school lives (more on this below).

In considering the confidence we can have in Smith and Tomlinson's conclusion we have to judge the kinds of data that were generated, the questions that were asked of it, and the assumptions that underlay the research. Where the collection of quantitative material opened up previ-ously unexplored areas the study produced many important findings; for example, in relation to language teaching (Smith and Tomlinson 1989: ch. 7), variations in school/teacher expectations (ch. 13) and the complexity of achievement between and within different ethnic groups (ch. 16). In respect of racism (as a potentially complex and sometimes 'hidden' quality of school life), however, the project's data were poor and the analysis simplistic. The most important point is that *The School Effect* was not designed to address racism as a major aspect of students' school lives. It is not safe, therefore, to assume that the *lack* of evidence of racism can itself be interpreted as *evidence* of a lack of racism. Put another way, the study did not set out to investigate racism, so we should be careful about how we interpret its failure to find it. The fact that racism does not show up in *The School Effect* may tell us more about the project than the schools involved.

The problems raised by the treatment of racism in *The School Effect* highlight important issues for quantitative research in this field. Here was a survey-based project, which uncharacteristically aimed to go beyond broad patterns of attainment to understand educational processes and student experiences. Its failure to get to grips with racism may be symptomatic of a wider problem facing quantitative research in this field (Gillborn and Drew 1992; Troyna 1991a). Qualitative research, however, also has an uneven record. Indeed, a controversy about standards of evidence in work on teacher racism highlights the fact that research methods (quantitative and qualitative) are only part of the picture. At the heart of the controversy lies a fundamental dispute about the nature of racism and the critical character of sociological research. These are crucial issues for sociology and the rest of this chapter focuses on the debate in detail. Before examining the particular claims and counterclaims, however, it is necessary to contextualize the debate by reviewing some previous qualitative studies of multi-ethnic schools. Of special significance is the history of research into conflict between white teachers and African Caribbean students.

Researching racism in schools: qualitative approaches

Studies of white teacher/black student conflict

The 1970s and 1980s saw qualitative research established as a major strand in British sociology of education (cf. Burgess 1986; Woods 1983). Although these developments borrowed a great deal from American studies (Hammersley and Woods 1984) important differences emerged in terms of the particular issues that attracted sociological interest. As was the case with quantitative work, for too long matters of 'race' and ethnicity were conspicuously absent from the UK research:

> It is entirely in keeping with respective sets of national preoccupations that North American scholars should more frequently represent a situation of cultural pluralism, while their British counterparts represent local manifestations of class conflict . . . the study of ethnic differences has not figured prominently in the British literature.
> (Atkinson et al. 1988: 236 and 243)

Writing in 1988 Paul Atkinson and his colleagues were only able to cite a handful of qualitative research papers concerned with ethnicity; including Driver (1979), Fuller (1980) and Furlong (1984).[2] Needless to say, the situation has changed. There is now a growing body of qualitative work that addresses issues of 'race', ethnicity and education in the UK. A particularly significant development has been the publication of a series of ethnographic studies of multi-ethnic secondary schools. Research by Cecile Wright (1986), Máirtín Mac an Ghaill (1988), Peter Foster (1990a) and myself (Gillborn 1990) represented the first sustained attempts to chart the realities of life in secondary schools where 'race' and ethnicity were accorded a central place in the analysis. With the notable exception of Foster's work (to which I return shortly) these ethnographies share several common features. They:

- Make extensive use of observational and interview data to explore the daily character of life in multi-ethnic comprehensive schools;
- Focus on interactions between white teachers and minority students, especially as they relate to academic selection and matters of school discipline;
- Chart the students' progress in terms of survival and accommodation strategies within school contexts that are (whatever the institutions' rhetoric) experienced as hostile by many ethnic minority students.

Additionally, both Mac an Ghaill and I consciously address the significance of 'racism'. We go beyond individualistic analyses of personal 'prejudice' to examine how racism operates as a complex and multifaceted aspect of school life: one that links the wider structures of power in society with the minutia of classroom experience and control.

This research has been complemented subsequently by work in primary schools (Troyna and Hatcher 1992; Wright 1992a and b) and as part of a wider study focusing on black young women (Mirza 1992).

Each of these studies claims to be 'ethnographic'. Although they give little attention to their theoretical and methodological antecedents, they each give priority to understanding the dynamics of students' experiences via the analysis of multiple types of qualitative data (especially by observation and interview). They suggest that, even where well-intentioned white teachers are conscientious and committed to equality of opportunity as an ideal, they may nevertheless *act* in ways that unwittingly reproduce familiar racial stereotypes, generate conflict (especially with African Caribbean young men) and perpetuate existing inequalities of opportunity and achievement. As Mac an Ghaill notes:

There may be no conscious attempt to treat black youth in a different way to white youth, but the unintended teacher effects result in differential responses, which work against black youth ... There was a tendency for Asian male students to be seen by the teachers as technically of 'high ability' and socially as conformist. Afro-Caribbean male students tended to be seen as having 'low ability' and potential discipline problems.

(Mac an Ghaill 1988: 3–4 and 64)[3]

Teacher expectations can lead to inequitable treatment. Classroom observation, for example, has suggested that African Caribbean students are frequently singled out for criticism even where several students (of other ethnic backgrounds) share in the conduct (Gillborn 1990: 30–31; Wright 1992a: 16–19).

In my study of 'City Road Comprehensive', an inner city secondary school in the Midlands,[4] I noted teachers' tendency to perceive a threat to their authority in many routine dealings with African Caribbean students. The vast majority of City Road teachers were genuinely committed to the ideals of equal opportunity, yet in practice they tended to generalize that conflict with an African Caribbean student was indicative of a more deep-seated rejection of authority, typical of African Caribbeans *as a group*. This view is captured in the following quotation, for example, where a female teacher implies that while verbal abuse is not uncommon in City Road, only African Caribbean students are capable of physical assault:

> I've never been assaulted by a white kid.
> I've been thrown against a wall by a pupil and it was a black kid.
> I've been called a 'Fucking slag' but I've only ever been *hit* by a black kid.

African Caribbean students were seen to represent both a more frequent, and a more severe, challenge to teachers' authority. This 'myth' became an accepted (though largely unspoken) part of teachers' 'craft' knowledge – their idea of 'how it really is'. One of its consequences was that any sign of apparent disobedience by an African Caribbean student might be dealt with harshly so as to 'nip in the bud' any further problems. Additionally, actions that conveyed the students' sense of ethnicity – their identity as black young people – were often interpreted by teachers as a sign of aggression or the wrong 'attitude'. When teachers acted on these perceptions they increased the potential for further conflict, especially where students drew attention to what they saw as unfair treatment. Strikingly similar processes of labelling and increased teacher–student conflict have been documented by Cecile Wright in primary and middle-school classrooms (Wright 1992a and b).

In contrast to this body of work, Peter Foster's study of a multi-ethnic school in the North of England ('Milltown High'), challenges the view that racism is a subtle and widespread influence on the lives of minority students.

Peter Foster on 'Milltown High'

In his book, '*Policy and Practice in Multicultural and Anti-Racist Education*' (1990a) Peter Foster looks at the development of 'multicultural and anti-racist education' policy in a school. He also considers how students were differentiated into hierarchically set teaching groups and explicitly addresses the question of racism in the school. The most striking of Foster's conclusions is that 'ethnic minority students enjoyed equal opportunities with their white peers' (Foster 1990a: 174). Foster's work is the only published ethnography of a British school where racial inequalities are not highlighted as a major issue despite the author having made 'race' a central problematic of the research.

The distinctiveness of Foster's conclusions was rapidly picked up by others in the field. Smith and Tomlinson (1989: 63) drew comfort from the lack of 'racial antagonism' in Milltown High, a finding that they contrasted with previous work on racial harassment and used to support their own conclusions on the issue (see above). In reviewing qualitative research on 'race' and schooling, Peter Woods also drew attention to the contrast with previous work. Rather than using Foster to question the accuracy of others, however, Woods sought an explanation in the nature of Foster's case:

> Why should this school be so different from those studied by Wright and others? Assuming the methodologies were comparable, there were some significant differences. Foster's school served a community with a long history of co-operation. It had a most liberal organization. Its staff had a high level of awareness about 'race', and were actually implementing an anti-racist programme. Above all, perhaps, it was most generously staffed ...
>
> (Woods 1990: 100)

Woods' points are well made and allow for the obvious possibility that (despite different findings) Foster and the other ethnographers of multi-ethnic schools have each accurately represented the realities of life in their chosen cases. Unfortunately, when Foster's account is scrutinized, it is difficult to sustain such a conclusion: his failure to critically deconstruct teachers' racialized assumptions is especially significant.

A careful reading of Foster's book reveals a good deal of *prime facie* evidence of the racial structuring of educational opportunities in Milltown (see Connolly 1992). One of the most obvious examples is the over-representation of African Caribbean males in low status teaching and examination groups:

In the English Department:
a number of students who were defined as 'bright enough' were ruled out because of their record of past behaviour. Interestingly these students were nearly all Afro/Caribbean boys, which perhaps accounts for the fact that there was only one Afro/Caribbean boy in the top English group in that year.

(Foster 1990a: 143)

In Science and Humanities:
The Science teachers then created their male class of 'difficult' students, the majority of whom, in the 1985–6 fourth year, were Afro/Caribbean, and the Humanities department selected a 'remedial' group of 'those who need most help'. Again the majority were Afro/Caribbean boys.

(Foster 1990a: 144)

Despite an acknowledged 'tendency for Afro/Caribbean boys to be under-represented in high status groups' (p. 145), Foster finds no cause for concern. He notes Wright's (1986) work on the negative consequences of teachers' labelling black students as troublemakers but defends the process in Milltown High:

They [African Caribbean boys] did seem less likely to secure places in high status groups . . . often for behavioural reasons. However, such a criticism [as Wright's] is, in my view, unjustified. It seems to me that both academic ability and motivation (which is, I would think, most reliably indicated by past behaviour and work output) are important in deciding which students are likely to make best use of a place in a high status group, and this is what teachers must decide.

(Foster 1990a: 145)

In fact Foster does accept that their over-representation in low status groups may have exposed a greater proportion of African Caribbean young men to low teacher expectations:

My rather tentative conclusion is that boys, especially Afro/Caribbean boys, were slightly disadvantaged . . .

(Foster 1990a: 147)

Unfortunately, this 'slight' disadvantage falls from sight quite quickly; a few pages later a new chapter begins with the bold statement:

There was no evidence that ethnic minority students were disadvantaged by the internal practices and procedures of Milltown High School.

(Foster 1990a: 151)

Foster, therefore, recognizes that the distribution of African Caribbean young men was not equitable, but defends this on the basis that their 'past behaviour' did not suggest they would 'make best use of a place in a high status group' (p. 145). Because he does not provide typical examples of this 'past behaviour' the reader is unable to judge whether the issue was really as clear-cut as Foster suggests, or may have included cases of the kind of racialized disciplinary control described by Cecile Wright (1992a and b) and myself (Gillborn 1990).[5]

I return to Foster's empirical study later, for the time being, however, it is sufficient to recognize that his ethnography suggests a rather uncritical reading of 'racial' issues in a secondary school. As a reviewer commented:

> what we appear to get here are the observations not of an academic entering an unfamiliar world and largely influenced by a critical perspective, but those of a teacher on secondment still inherently sympathetic to the views of teachers.
>
> (Hannan 1993: 96)

Foster's description of Milltown High – on the surface at least – confirms the patterns of racialized control and selection that have been highlighted by a succession of qualitative studies. What sets Foster apart is his conclusion that the processes were legitimate. Having reached this conclusion, Foster followed the publication of his book with a succession of articles that attempted 'to understand the discrepancy between his findings and those of other researchers in the field' (Hammersley 1993b: 430). In the following section I examine the development of this project.

A project of methodological criticism: a controversy about racism and research

Since 1990, Peter Foster has published a series of papers, each focusing on one or more qualitative studies that have claimed to produce evidence of racial injustice in educational settings. Foster's conclusion, *without exception*, is that the work fails to stand up to his scrutiny. Regarding Carrington and Wood (1983), for example, Foster suggests they 'have selectively interpreted much of their data in order to fit their case' (Foster 1990b: 341). Similarly my own work is dismissed as 'implausible' and my 'empirical claims, like those of Mac an Ghaill [1988], are unsubstantiated and unconvincing' (Foster 1992b: 94). In one paper it is asserted that my analysis 'rested on only one example' (Foster 1993a: 548).

These judgements are especially interesting because I consciously drew on a range of both qualitative and quantitative data. My study of City Road uses interview material (from conversations with teachers and students); observational notes and audio recordings of school life in a variety of contexts (such as classrooms, corridors and in the assembly hall); and data from school documents (such as students' personal record files and the school 'punishment books'). When drawing these different sources together I tried to be aware of potential queries or alternative explanations. In examining teachers' disproportionate criticism of African Caribbean young people, for example, I used data from my own observations, from sentence completion questionnaires, from school records and from interviews. In the latter case, I was careful to include the views of high achieving white students to establish that 'an awareness of teachers' frequent criticism and control of Afro-Caribbean pupils was not restricted to the Afro-Caribbean pupils themselves or to their more "disaffected" white peers' (Gillborn 1990: 32).[6]

Foster finds these data 'unconvincing'; others have found them a good deal more persuasive (cf. Eggleston 1991; Klein 1993; Marland 1990; Tomlinson 1992). The key point here is not whether there is a single 'correct' verdict on my, or anyone else's, research. Rather, it is vital to note that Foster's reading of others' work *always* finds evidence of teacher racism to be unconvincing. Typically he moves from a micro-level critique (say of a single piece of data) to a full-blown rejection of the research in its totality. Whatever the variety of data, Foster seems to find nothing of worth in these studies.

Foster has been joined in his critique by Martyn Hammersley and Roger Gomm.[7] Martyn Hammersley is a prolific writer on social science methodology. His recent work has addressed a series of concerns about the nature and validity of qualitative research (e.g. Hammersley 1990; 1991; 1992b) – part of what John Brewer (1994) terms 'the ethnographic critique of ethnography'. Work on 'race' and ethnicity plays little or no part in Hammersley's books: his writing here seems to have developed as an extension of his previous critiques (e.g. Hammersley 1992a) – notably echoing his objections to feminist methodology (Hammersley 1992c; 1994) – and as a response to those who have criticized Foster (Hammersley 1993b; Hammersley and Gomm 1993). Roger Gomm's involvement with this debate began with a critique of a quantitative paper, on the disadvantaged position of South Asian students in a school's system of setting and examination entry (Gomm 1993).[8] Taken as a whole this work amounts to a sustained project that undertakes the systematic critique of research on the racial structuring of educational opportunities:

> They have taken on the mantle of 'methodological purists'. Their purpose is to explicate the allegedly dubious empirical grounds on which claims of racial inequality in education have been mounted.
>
> (Troyna 1993b: 167)

It is important to recognize that the papers by Foster, Hammersley and Gomm add up to more than a collection of unconnected critiques. They carry additional weight as a *cumulative* series: a series targeting research that claims to have identified some of the processes by which racism is implicated in the patterning of racial disadvantage in schools (see Figure 3.1).

Foster, Hammersley and Gomm's methodological critiques of research on racism and schooling raise many important issues. Of particular significance are the consequences of their position for the way that researchers

Study suggesting racism-racial injustice in an educational setting	Methodological critique(s)
Green (1983; 1985)	Foster (1993b)
Wright (1986)	Foster (1990b)
Mac an Ghaill (1988)	Foster (1992b)
Gillborn (1990)	Foster (1992b)
Troyna (1991b)	Gomm (1993)
Gillborn and Drew (1992)	Hammersley & Gomm (1993)

Figure 3.1   A methodological project

conceptualize 'race' and racism in empirical research. In the rest of this chapter I explore these issues as they arise through the intended and unintended consequences of their work.[9]

Intended consequences of the methodological project

In this section I want to consider briefly the conscious aims and objectives of the 'methodological purists', as laid out in their own writings.

The pursuit of truth: plausibility and credibility: politics and research

Throughout their various critiques, Foster, Hammersley and Gomm set out their central task as the pursuit of knowledge. Some postmodern critics would challenge the assumption that there is any 'objective' truth beyond the multiple readings (texts) produced by different actors (cf. Baudrillard 1983; Clifford and Marcus 1986). However, the 'purists' goal is in keeping with the approach taken by the writers whom they attack: most (including myself) have to date retained a vision of science and empirical enquiry underlain by what Norman Denzin critically describes as 'a "realist" conception of the social – there is an obdurate world out there' (Denzin 1992: 158).

Put simply, the methodological project's first intended goal is 'to subject empirical studies to critical scrutiny' as a necessary part of 'the aim of empirical research in education . . . to increase our knowledge of how the educational system works' (Foster 1991: 165). So far, so good. But a major problem emerges when this 'critical scrutiny' translates into a debate about whether a case is 'proven beyond reasonable doubt' (Foster 1990b; 1991). This suggests the possibility of identifying a critical mass of evidence, beyond which a case should be accepted as proven, but where anything less is rejected. Such an approach is 'authoritative, closed and certain' where a more helpful approach might seek to open up the complex and contingent nature of social processes (see Ball 1994).

In their attempt to find an authoritative guide to what constitutes proof 'beyond reasonable doubt', Foster, Hammersley and Gomm appeal to 'methodological common sense' (Hammersley 1993a: 339), but risk simply reifying one set of assumptions over another:

> The problem of what constitutes adequate evidence for us to judge a claim valid is one that faces all of us once we abandon foundationalism. Elsewhere, I have outlined a proposed solution, suggesting that claims and evidence must be judged on the basis of two considerations: plausibility in relation to knowledge we currently take as beyond reasonable doubt, and credibility in relation to judgments about the likelihood of various sorts of error (Hammersley, 1991, Chs. 3 and 4; 1992, Ch. 4).
>
> (Hammersley 1993a: 340)

According to this view disagreement about the plausibility and/or credibility of a study, should be decided in relation to assumptions 'that we expect to be accepted as beyond reasonable doubt by other members of the research community' (Hammersley 1993b: 439). In practice Foster, Hammersley and Gomm tend to apply crude and absolutist notions of plausibility and credibility, which reflect a view of the UK in general, and schools in particular, that fails to engage with critical theory. As Caroline Ramazanoglu notes (in her response to an attack on feminist methodology) Hammersley adopts a position that fails to problematize the question of 'who has the power to judge what is relevant':

> His sense of the superiority of reason over political commitment is to be validated in the good sense of scholarly colleagues. The way in which he takes his conception of rationality for granted allows him to justify his position in terms of his personal judgements...
>
> (Ramazanoglu 1992: 208)

What seems plausible and credible to some, might appear to be wildly optimistic, or even politically motivated propaganda, to others. The criteria for plausibility and credibility cannot be divorced from the assumptions of the individual critic, whose views may reflect particular political, methodological, class-based, gendered and racialized assumptions. Yet Foster, Hammersley and Gomm seem to assert their independence from such concerns, trusting an idealized community of academics to settle rationally any disputes that arise.[10] Their position, especially the talk of 'proof', neglects the degree of uncertainty that characterizes all social science research. Qualitative data are always open to alternative explanations; the amount and type of evidence we produce may make our analyses more or less convincing – but there is no fixed line between proven and unproven:

In the empirical sciences there is never compelling proof there is only plausible proof.

(Becker 1980, quoted in Verhoeven 1989: 145)

no set of guidelines or conditions will ever be sufficient to rule out alternative explanations. At best an ethnographer (like all social scientists) can only persuade the reader to agree that the explanation is a plausible one, but not that it is the *only* plausible one.

(Brewer 1994: 243, original emphasis)

The methodological critique, therefore, rests on a simplistic reading of the issues surrounding plausibility and 'proof' in the social sciences. Also of relevance here is the way the critics draw a contrast between their own purely scientific goals and the political motives that might taint the work of others in the field:

The overriding concern of researchers is the truth of claims, not their political implications or practical consequences.

(Hammersley 1993b: 438)

For me, the point of research is to produce knowledge, not to transform the world, or to achieve any other practical result.

(Hammersley 1994: 293)

In this way a stark binary division is suggested: the imputation is that research which deliberately engages with the political character of all knowledge (Ramazanoglu 1992: 207) is antithetical to good scholarly practice. In response to feminist critics, Hammersley discusses his perspective on this, making clear that he equates political motivation with partiality in the research act. The argument is simple; if you are politically motivated, and hope to use research (directly or indirectly) toward political ends, the chances are that you will compromise your position as a scientist. On the question of 'important differences between research and political activity', Hammersley states:

in political activity it is often not sensible to mention relevant information that could weaken one's case; and, on occasion, we may feel that deception and manipulation are justified. By contrast, such tactics are not reasonable in a research context. This is because the aim here is to discover, through empirical investigation and rational discussion, which conclusions are sound and which are not, and why.

(Hammersley 1994: 294)

Hence, research and political activity are defined as mutually exclusive, with the non-political researcher firmly placed on the moral high ground. Hammersley (1993b) appeals to similar ideas when he portrays Foster's critics as forced to reject academic rigour where it conflicts with their political stance. The result presents antiracism (and all who are identified with it) as irretrievably biased and closed to evidence.

Reflecting on problems in sociological writing, Peter Woods warns against building a 'straw person', where 'in an attempt to highlight one's own argument and increase its purity and force, one may construct an apology of an opposing one which does not really exist' (Woods 1986: 184). Hammersley falls into this trap when, in his paper 'Research and "antiracism": the case of Peter Foster and his critics', he judges it 'neither possible nor necessary' to 'reconstruct the actual views of Foster's critics'. Instead, he discusses 'what critics of this kind *could* say' (Hammersley 1993b: 430, original emphasis), deriving these arguments from a definition of antiracism 'in common usage' (no supporting references are offered). According to this view, antiracism is a closed ideology that includes 'specific ideas about the nature, distribution, and origins of racism and about how it must be dealt with' (Hammersley 1993b: 446). Such a position, of course, would have no need of research since its devotee's would already 'know' both the problem and the solution. It is a position that contrasts with that of many prominent writers in this field, but does echo familiar media presentations of antiracism which 'still the voices of those, like myself, who tried to say that there was no body of thought called antiracism, no orthodoxy or dogma, no manual of strategy and tactics, no demonology' (Sivanandan 1988: 147). Hammersley acknowledges that his description is an abstraction, but he doubts that this matters very much:

> It is also true, of course, that 'anti-racists' differ about many issues, but for the purposes of my task in this paper these differences are probably not significant.
>
> (Hammersley 1993b: 446)

The methodological project is presented, therefore, as concerned purely with scientific rigour and truth. In contrast, those who seek to counter their attacks are presented as politically motivated and consequently non-academic and not trustworthy.

The defence of teachers and 'what we know' about multi-ethnic schools

This much is clear: research on 'race' and ethnicity in education, like any other branch of science, must be open to critique. The 'methodological purists' have every right to be critical of research. The main problem with their project lies in its persistent attempt not only to raise problems, but to go beyond this, to conclude that there is no good reason to believe that minority students are unfairly disadvantaged by school-based processes and the actions of teachers:

We see our methodological assessment as having positive value in these ways. It has provided a defence against unjustified claims based on inadequate evidence which often, in our view, serve to victimise teachers. It has also made a contribution to the development of knowledge by clarifying what we know, beyond reasonable doubt, and what we do not know, about 'race' and in-school processes...

(Foster 1993a: 550)

The 'defence' of teachers, therefore, is given a central place in the methodological project. Yet this invokes a simplistic reading of previous research. Most of the work Foster criticizes seeks to understand teachers' actions and perspectives as they are created and modified through multiple interactions in complex organizational settings. True, much of this work is critical, but none amounts to a blanket condemnation of teachers as a group. Teachers have led many antiracist initiatives and most writers assign them a crucial role in moving towards a more equitable education system (cf. Epstein 1993; Nixon 1985; Siraj-Blatchford 1994; Troyna and Hatcher 1992). To portray critical research as 'victimization' risks constructing a dangerous dichotomy between work that is either *for* or *against* teachers. Such a position leaves little room for progress.

Peter Foster does not spell out 'what we know, beyond reasonable doubt, and what we do not know, about "race" and in-school processes'. Because of the nature of their project, the methodological critiques are mostly constructed in negative terms – questioning others' views rather than establishing any new insights. In the following section I examine, in greater detail, the ways in which Foster, Hammersley and Gomm's methodological project may play an unintended role in defending and sustaining existing racial inequalities.

Unintended consequences of the methodological project

This section deals with the unintended consequences of the methodological project. That is, consequences that may not be part of Foster, Hammersley and Gomm's conscious agenda (and may even conflict with their avowed aims) but arise as a result of their critical project.

My discussion of these unintended consequences must be prefaced by a reminder. I have already accepted that work on 'race' and ethnicity, like any other empirical research, must be open to critical scrutiny. Indeed, every study cited so far, including my own, suffers from one weakness or another: there is no such thing as the perfect field study. My concern here is that Foster, Hammersley and Gomm go beyond the bounds of useful or constructive criticism. They move from micro-level critiques to the rejection of the entire body of work. In so doing, their methodological project threatens critical research in the sociology of education; it denies the nature and extent of racism in schools, defends the status quo and, ultimately, reifies an uncritical and deeply unsociological vision of science as an apolitical activity. Of crucial importance is the limited understanding of racism that informs the analysis. The next section shows how, even if we take an avowedly apolitical stance, research inevitably forces us to make decisions (e.g. about conceptual issues) which might unwittingly reproduce the very assumptions that shape existing inequalities.

Defining and seeing racism in schools

In his study of Milltown High, Foster defines racism as:

> practices which restrict the chances of success of individuals from a particular racial or ethnic group, *and* which are based on, or legitimized by, some form of belief that this racial or ethnic group is inherently morally, culturally, or intellectually inferior.
>
> (Foster 1990a: 5, original emphasis)

This definition enshrines a classic notion of racism that includes both (1) discriminatory action *and* (2) a 'racial inferiority/superiority couplet' (Mac an Ghaill 1988: 3). This is a crude and limited notion of racism: it defines out of existence the possibility of 'unintentional' or institutional racism, where individuals and organizations act in ways that are discriminatory in their effects, though not in intention (see Eggleston et al. 1986: 12–13; Gillborn 1990: 8–10; Klein 1993: 12–14).

Subsequently, Foster has attempted to clarify the methodological purists' position on racism. He describes as 'grossly inaccurate' the suggestion that his research defined out the possibility of institutional racism:

> I devoted a considerable amount of attention in my book to investigating school practices which might indirectly disadvantage ethnic minority students (see Foster 1990a: 6–8, 174–6) . . . The definition of racism used in my book has not underpinned our subsequent work; most of our concern has been with evidence about more indirect, institutional forms of discrimination.
>
> (Foster 1993a: 549)

Unfortunately, their subsequent work does not specify any alternative definition of racism. Additionally, in Foster's empirical study, there is evidence that he granted his own understanding of racism priority over the views of his research subjects. When African Caribbean students accused teachers of racism, for example:

> When pressed further these boys found it difficult to specify exactly what they meant and to give examples of incidents which they felt showed 'prejudice' . . . Occasionally the hostility of Afro/Caribbean students was expressed using the vocabulary of 'racism', but such accusations rarely specified incidents that were racist in terms of the definition I have used.
>
> (Foster 1990a: 135 and 136)

Accusations of racism, therefore, were not reflected back onto a critical examination of teacher–student interactions, but rather interpreted as a sign of the students' 'hostility'. This apparent disregard for student perspectives is surprising. A useful approach would have been to clarify the kinds of incident that students perceived to be 'prejudiced' or 'racist' and to explore the consequences for teacher–student interaction. Unfortunately, Foster simply rejects the students' views as failing to meet *his* preferred definition.

It is regrettable that Foster, Hammersley and Gomm have failed to specify a definition of racism that they would accept as a basis for empirical research on 'indirect, institutional forms of discrimination'. If we knew the standard against which data were to be measured it might be easier to achieve broad consensus about what is 'plausible' and 'credible'. Foster's earliest understanding (racism = discriminatory action + a sense of racial superiority) remains the only definition to have been specified in their work.

The sum of Foster, Hammersley and Gomm's methodological critiques is an inescapable (though implicit) conclusion about the extent of racism in schools. Since all existing evidence fails to meet their personal standards of plausibility and credibility, they effectively reduce the 'more indirect, institutional forms of discrimination' to nothing more than a theoretical possibility:

> They ['racial' inequities in within-school processes] may, of course, exist, but, as our work has demonstrated, this has not been convincingly established.
>
> (Foster 1993a: 551)

In this way, the methodological project goes beyond its intended goal of '*clarifying* what we know, beyond reasonable doubt' (emphasis added). Despite their failure to specify the kinds of evidence they would accept regarding indirect/unintended racism, the critics feel secure in rejecting all existing attempts. Institutional racism is thus reduced to a mere theoretical possibility. The consequence is an implicit denial that racism exists as a fundamental characteristic of the lived experience of ethnic minority school students.

Sociology and the status quo

In view of a public perception that frequently links sociology with a fashionable, but ultimately superficial, brand of 1960s radicalism (cf. Bradbury 1975), it is easy to forget the discipline's conservative roots, often characterized by elitism and a central concern with order and stability (Hamilton 1992). This is a far cry from the critical perspective described by Mills (1959) and given centre-stage in much British sociology of education:

> The practice of sociology is criticism. It exists to criticize claims about the value of achievement and to question assumptions about the meaning of conduct . . . to examine, to question, to raise doubts about, to criticize the assumptions on which current policy, current theory and current practice are based.
>
> (Burns 1967: 358 and 366–7, quoted in Burgess 1986: 10)

This does not mean that sociologists must blindly criticize for its own sake; rather, that a critical sociological perspective will tend to produce new insights that challenge taken-for-granted assumptions.[11] Classic functionalism aside, whatever our particular school of thought or favoured 'grand-narrative' we should surely be cautious about sociological work that presents the existing status quo as an equitable or natural state of affairs, since such arrangements usually emerge as anything but equitable in research that penetrates surface assumptions. Most importantly, Foster, Hammersley and Gomm seem not only to accept current practice as equitable, but actually to *privilege* current practices; granting current practices and assumptions a protected status until evidence can be produced that will convince them 'beyond reasonable doubt' that something is wrong:

> Drawing attention to the limitations of research studies in this area may serve to defend the school practices which were attacked, but if practices in the schools studied were equitable and fair (and the research studies concerned did not establish that they were not), then this seems reasonable (especially as the schools concerned have little opportunity to reply). Indeed, it seems unfair and unwise to criticise current practices unless there is reasonable evidence that such practices are deserving of criticism.
>
> (Foster 1993a: 551)

The onus of 'proof' is, therefore, placed squarely on the shoulders of those who seek to question the current distribution of opportunities and rewards. According to Foster's position even where African Caribbean males are consistently over-represented in low status teaching groups (as they were in his own empirical study) schools should not feel compelled to change the practices that produce such a racially structured hierarchy.

The arguments here echo the debate concerning IQism and the 'null hypothesis' (Kamin 1974: 175–6). That is, in the absence of conclusive 'proof' there is a judgement to be made about the course of action with the least damaging potential. Hence, the most sensible approach to the nature/nurture debate about 'intelligence' is to assume no significant role for genetic heritability; if this belief is correct we avoid needlessly condemning countless young people to a second-class education and wasting incalculable human (and economic) potential. Alternatively, if the hypothesis is false we will have wasted resources on those who could not take full advantage. It is a value judgement that places human suffering and inequality against immediate economic concerns.

There is a parallel question concerning the extent of racism (overt, institutional or unconscious) in schools. If we accept existing evidence as sufficient cause for concern and begin to question current practices then hypothetically we risk wasting time and energy trying to address inequalities that are not significantly influenced by schools. Alternatively, we can accept the status quo and risk knowingly perpetuating massive educational and economic inequalities.

Racism and sociological discourse

It is not necessary to accept the entire body of post-structural and post-modern theory to recognize the importance of discourse as part of the operation of power in society. An analysis of the political nature of discourse is especially relevant in the field of 'race' and ethnicity – where even the most basic categories are continually contested (cf. Bulmer 1986; Cross 1989).

Foster, Hammersley and Gomm's critiques deploy a particular discourse of methodological purity that, like all discourse, 'limits the other ways in which the topic can be constructed' (Hall 1992a: 291). Notably they close down certain pedagogic, research and policy alternatives. This is clearest where Foster asserts the supremacy of 'basic societal and educational values' central to the operation of schools in 'liberal, democratic, industrial societies' (Foster 1992b: 96). But it is also present, and potentially most powerful, as a thread that is woven throughout their discussion of possible ('more plausible') explanations for data that others interpret in terms of racism. Their analyses are presented as founded in academic neutrality – a concern simply to identify alternative possible explanations – yet their discursive effect is to construct minority students in terms of *difference*; they become a strange and threatening other – the bearers of chaos and destruction (cf. Said 1978). Here the methodological purists come dangerously close to the kind of new racist discourse analysed in the previous chapter. In trying to account for conflict between white teachers and African Caribbean students, for example, Peter Foster suggests the 'social structural situation of Afro/Caribbean communities' as a major factor (Foster 1990b: 343). When challenged to defend this assertion, he is careful to reject the idea that school processes play *no* role, while simultaneously appealing to images of alienation and disorder that firmly locate the source of any conflict as lying outside the school:

> There is also, of course, quite a lot of evidence which documents the general alienation of some Afro/Caribbean young people and their 'resistance' to aspects of mainstream British society (see for example Dhondy, 1974; Hall et al., 1978; Pryce, 1979; Scarman, 1981; Cashmore and Troyna, 1982). It seems a reasonable possibility that sometimes this alienation and resistance spills over into the school situation. My own experience of teaching in three multi-ethnic schools supports this ... I think that there may be a general tendency for Afro/Caribbean students *on average* to be less well behaved in schools.
>
> (Foster 1991: 168 original emphasis).

Foster returns to the same theme in a later critique.

> If, for example, different cultural norms result in students from a certain group being more noisy, aggressive, inattentive, prone to classroom disruption, or disrespectful of others, then teachers surely cannot, and should not, be expected to accept such behaviour just because it is the product of different cultural norms.
>
> I think there is a possibility that this may be the case with some of the cultural norms of certain Afro/Caribbean students – especially those associated with male, youth, subcultural forms.
>
> (Foster 1992b: 96)

Speculation about '*some* Afro/Caribbean young people', '*average*' differences in behaviour and '*certain* Afro/Caribbean students' is presented, therefore, as '*reasonable*' cause to reject critical analyses that view teachers as actively implicated in the racial structuring of educational opportunities.

Foster's speculations about African Caribbean students echo popular images of minority communities in general, and African Caribbean young people in particular, as other – as not really part of the nation; as outside 'mainstream British society' (1991: 168). This links directly with the issues I addressed in the previous chapter. The new racist political discourse is here reworked using the language of scientific neutrality as a means of denying the political and social implications of the discourse (and the assumptions which sustain it).

As I have noted (above) Foster, Hammersley and Gomm's methodological project, on 'race' research, invokes an image of scientific neutrality that is explicitly depoliticized. This view cannot accept that science, rules of evidence, and judgements about 'plausibility/credibility' might, like schools themselves, be 'deeply implicated in forms of discourse, social relations, and webs of meaning that produce particular moral truths and values' (Giroux 1991a: 507). In this way the discourse of methodological purism is implicated in the defence of the racist practices at the heart of this debate. Specifically, from a standpoint of professed academic neutrality, it is a discourse that emphasizes cultural difference and serves to pathologize minority students in general, and African Caribbean males in particular.

Conclusions

> What varieties of men and women now prevail in this society and in this period? And what varieties are coming to prevail? In what ways are they selected and formed, liberated and repressed, made sensitive and blunted?
>
> (Mills 1959: 13)

Questions of power and social critique are central to the survival of sociology as a living and dynamic discipline. The imperative to question the taken-for-granted should not be sacrificed on the altar of methodological purism. Every piece of empirical work must, of course, be subject to critical scrutiny: this is one of the primary means of advancing sociological method and theory. This scrutiny, however, should itself remain true to the critical spirit of the sociological imagination: 'Avoid the fetishism of method and technique' (Mills 1959: 246).

In this chapter I have explored some of the difficulties facing those who seek to research the role of 'race' and ethnicity in educational settings. It is impossible to address all the relevant issues in a single chapter;[12] in keeping with the theme of the book, I have focused on issues arising from the way that researchers conceptualize racism and antiracism.

How a researcher thinks about 'race' and ethnicity influences the design of their project, the kinds of data they gather, and the analyses they conduct. In the first part of the chapter I looked briefly at a well-known quantitative study of multi-ethnic comprehensive schools (Smith and Tomlinson 1989). Most quantitative projects can be criticized for their failure to engage with the complex social processes that lie behind the broader patterns of educational progress and achievement. In contrast, *The School Effect* deliberately set out to address such issues. Unfortunately, the kind of data gathered offered a particularly limited snapshot of the perspectives and experiences of teachers and students. The researchers lost sight of these limitations when concluding 'there is no evidence that racial hostility at school is an important factor for 12 and 13-year old children' (Smith and Tomlinson 1989: 305). Their data were simply too limited to warrant such a conclusion.

Some writers (myself included) have suggested that qualitative research, with its attention to multiple participant perspectives, social interaction and power within institutions, is more suited to the exploration of 'race' and racism in schools. A recent methodological project, critiquing research on 'race' and schooling, calls this idea into question.

Critiques by Peter Foster, Martyn Hammersley and Roger Gomm challenge the conclusions of several studies of multi-ethnic schools. They are especially damning of researchers who claim to identify school-based processes that inadvertently disadvantage members of one or more ethnic minority groups. A prominent theme in these critiques, and in Foster's empirical work, has been the defence of teachers against accusations of unintended racism, especially in their disciplinary control and criticism of African Caribbean students. I have tried to summarize the main characteristics of this methodological project and highlight the serious problems associated with it. I have argued that in their concern to scrutinize research on the racial structuring of educational processes, Foster, Hammersley and Gomm lose sight of the critical dimension that is central to sociological work. Their methodological project enshrines judgements about the plausibility and credibility of evidence as if they were apolitical matters of fact, rather than the product of a particular (class-related, gendered and culturalist) perspective.

Additionally, the methodological project has a number of important unintended consequences. First, it reduces institutional racism to the status of a mere theoretical possibility. It results in a position that effectively denies teacher racism any major role as an explanatory (or even descriptive) concept in relation to the lived experience of minority students.

Second, Foster, Hammersley and Gomm's methodological critiques privilege the status quo. The burden of empirical proof is placed on those who seek to question current practices and assumptions. This produces a static and deeply conservative notion of social science, one that might ultimately be driven to focus on relatively safe and uncontentious issues (where 'proof' and 'evidence' could command widespread support).

Finally, the methodological project embodies a conception of science that is blind to all but the most crude operations of power and politics. By denying that scientific discourse is itself implicated in the processes of cultural production and reproduction, the 'methodological purists' offer a prescription for sociology that is at best ethnocentric, at worst racist. That is to say, by privileging the values, expectations and assumptions of the dominant ethnic group these authors (whatever their conscious intent) may defend processes that systematically serve to disadvantage minority groups.

Such a position is not inevitable. Sociology has an impressive history of challenging the taken-for-granted; piercing institutional and professional façades; subverting common stereotypes and prejudices. Research that applies qualitative approaches to urban settings has produced some of the most striking examples of this strand in the sociological imagination. The work of the Chicago school, and the many studies following in its wake (including much British research) is replete with powerful insights into people's experiences and lived careers. Criticisms of this work as 'voyeurism' (Denzin 1992) or novelty hunting (Hammersley 1992b) miss the point. These accounts produce new insights that undermine received wisdom about groups of people ('immigrants', 'mental patients', 'criminals', etc.) that are commonly constructed as unlike our 'normal'/'moral' (white/middle-class?) selves. In so doing, this work offers a possible subversion of dominant processes of labelling and social control.

This chapter, therefore, addresses fundamental problems facing researchers in this field – problems about the design of projects; the interpretation of data; the nature and role of academic discourse in a society shot through with 'racial' and ethnically specific assumptions. I want to conclude by emphasizing that a proper regard for rigorous methods and analysis should play a vital role in sustaining critical sociological research.

Earlier I noted the failure of certain studies genuinely to consider the meanings and interpretations offered by minority students. This points to the importance of one of the basic requirements of critical qualitative research; that, where possible, the perspectives of a range of participants should be sought and included in the analysis. This is vital, not because of a sentimental desire to fight for the 'underdog' (as some interpret Howard Becker (1967) to have argued) but rather because participants in 'subordinate' positions (for all they lack in formal training and institutional influence) sometimes understand more than their 'superiors':[13]

> it's using the view of the subordinate as a lever, a wedge, a way to find out things that you need to know to understand the organization fully. You are not accepting their point of view ... you know, there are some terrible people who are subordinates sometimes – politically speaking – it's not that they are such wonderful people. But they, after all, know more about certain things than the people above them ... I systematically question as a routine matter whether the people who run any organization know anything about it. I don't say they don't, I just say it's a question ... it's not that you do that for political motives you do it for scientific ones. But it has political consequence and the political consequence is almost invariably in the direction of anti-establishment.
>
> (Becker 1980)

Like any other perspective the sociological imagination may tend towards ethnocentrism, that is, the tendency to view things, and make judgements, based on familiar – culturally specific – knowledge and experience. The proper exercise of critical techniques and safeguards, however, should reveal alternative perspectives which, at their best, will challenge racism, because racism (ultimately) relies on mistaken views of human differences and competencies.

four

Theorizing identity and antiracism

> No discourse is inherently liberating or oppressive. The liberatory
> status of any theoretical discourse is a matter of historical inquiry, not
> theoretical pronouncement.
>
> (Sawicki 1988: 166, quoted by Gore 1993: 50, original emphasis)

Antiracism frequently appears in the media as a focus for scare stories
about 'loony left' authorities and the dangers of 'political correctness'.
Such coverage is usually wildly inaccurate. Nevertheless, it does at least
indicate that something called 'antiracism' has achieved a certain status in
the popular consciousness. In particular, for many people antiracism is
associated with politics at the level of the local state. The ways that policies have been developed and implemented under the antiracist banner
raise important questions about the future theory and practice of racism
and antiracism.

During the 1980s antiracism emerged as a notable presence in radical
anti-oppressive politics. In some local authorities antiracist campaigns and
organizations benefited from injections of public money. In education,
antiracists waged a war against racism and multiculturalism – perceiving
the latter as tokenism which failed to address the key structural forces
involved in shaping and sustaining racism (see Brandt 1986).

Always under attack from the political right, in the late 1980s and early
1990s antiracism has been the focus of increasing criticism from across the
political spectrum. Some liberal commentators question the finality of the
multicultural/antiracist dichotomy (Grinter 1985; Leicester 1986; 1989)
while others attempt a solution by splicing the two terms together (e.g.
Duncan 1988; Massey 1991; Taylor 1992). More significantly, critics on
the political left have also joined the attack. It has been argued, for example, that antiracist initiatives have reproduced existing fallacies about the
fixed nature of cultural groups, thereby inadvertently echoing New Right
analyses. For some, antiracism appears as a grand theory totally at odds
with the fractured, rapidly changing identity politics of contemporary society.

Certain forms of antiracism now stand accused (by the very people from whom *support* might be expected) of actually inflaming racism and racial violence. These debates, concerning left critiques of antiracism, form the basis of this chapter.

I begin by reviewing the theoretical arguments about the changing nature of 'race' and identity in contemporary 'postmodern' societies. This provides the conceptual foundation for many of the left critiques of antiracism that are explored in subsequent sections. In particular, I focus on criticisms of 'municipal' antiracism (at the level of the local state) and 'moral' antiracism (at the school level). In the final section, I outline the main lessons to be learnt from the left critiques, concluding that a more sophisticated 'critical antiracism' is both possible and necessary.

Who's who? Theorizing identity and difference

Recent developments in social theory challenge the most basic assumptions about the nature of human identity. These perspectives speak to a wide range of policy specialisms, including education. They offer a springboard for a new and radical critique of previous theorizing in the field of 'race' and ethnicity. The new approaches provide the background for a series of critical contributions to policy debates, which potentially offer a more sophisticated perspective on the development of effective antiracist strategies. Indeed, some suggest that antiracism itself is no longer tenable. These are crucial arguments. Before examining the detail of this work, however, it is necessary briefly to say something about its philosophical antecedents.

Postmodernity and postmodernism

> While it would be easy to dismiss postmodernism as simply a code word for a new theoretical fashion, the term is important because it directs our attention to a number of changes and challenges that are a part of the contemporary age.
>
> (Giroux 1991b: 62)

Over the last two decades or so, much social science writing has addressed debates about the significance of changes in the nature and meaning of the social world. The second half of the twentieth century, so the argument goes, has witnessed changes so fundamental that society has entered a substantially new period.

> What appears on one level as the latest fad, advertising pitch and hollow spectacle is part of a slowly emerging cultural transformation in Western societies, a change in sensibility for which the term 'post-

modern' is actually, at least for now, wholly adequate. The nature and depth of that transformation are debatable, but transformation it is.

(Huyssens 1984, quoted in Harvey 1989: 39)

This new era has been given a range of titles; depending on writers' particular political and/or theoretical stance, it has been described variously as 'postmodernity' (Baudrillard 1983; Harvey 1989; Lyotard 1984), late modernity (Giddens 1990), late Capitalism (Jameson 1984) and New Times (Hall and Jacques 1989). Although each term has been used to denote a particular understanding of the key characteristics of contemporary society, they are also sometimes used interchangeably (despite apparent contradictions). While this might look like conceptual sloppiness to some, to others it is entirely appropriate in a period where the 'modern' totalizing, neat and rational models of science and society (born of the Enlightenment in the eighteenth century) finally break down and fail. Within postmodernism there is:

> total acceptance of the ephemerality, fragmentation, discontinuity, and the chaotic . . . But postmodernism responds to the fact of that in a very particular way. It does not try to transcend it, counteract it, or even define the 'eternal and immutable' elements that might lie within it. Postmodernism swims, even wallows, in the fragmentary and the chaotic currents of change as if that is all there is.
>
> (Harvey 1989: 44)

Postmodernism, therefore, rejects 'modernist' grand narratives. In a wide range of fields (including art, architecture, film, literature, anthropology, music and sociology) postmodernism questions the basic assumptions about progress and structure that have long been taken for granted:

> postmodern criticism calls attention to the shifting boundaries related to the increasing influence of the electronic mass media and information technology, the changing nature of class and social formations in postindustrialized capitalist societies, and the growing transgression of boundaries between life and art, high and popular culture, and image and reality.
>
> (Giroux 1991b: 59)

A bewildering range of positions has been taken beneath the umbrella term 'postmodernism'; a thorough tour of these differences is unnecessary here, suffice it to say that ideas about postmodernism have become a major influence in contemporary social science (see Thompson 1992).

Predictably, the notions of postmodernity (describing a fundamentally new epoch in Western, even global, social relations) and postmodernism (a philosophical, artistic and/or academic movement) arouse great controversy. Part of the problem lies in the variety of, sometimes conflicting, ideas and arguments that have been labelled 'postmodern': 'the term is at once fashionable yet irritatingly elusive to define' (Featherstone 1988: 195). For some, postmodernism is no more than a fad, a cultural bandwagon, bereft of critical insights. Some versions of postmodernism conclude at an 'anything goes' level, where critical social science is reduced to a 'playful' reading of surface features, emphasizing change and diversity while, by definition, denying any deeper insight (Callinicos 1989; Green 1994). It would be premature, however, simply to reject out of hand all arguments   about   postmodernity.

Increasingly, theorists are using elements of postmodernism in ways that produce new questions and insights, but do not entail a complete rejection of previous analyses:

> while postmodern social theory is articulating real problems and posing important challenges to radical social theory and politics today, it is exaggerating the break, rupture and alleged novelty in the contemporary socio-historical epoch and is downplaying, and even occluding, the continuities.
>
> (Kellner 1988: 267)

> Modernism is far from dead – its central categories are simply being written within a plurality of narratives that are attempting to address the new set of social, political, technical, and scientific configurations that constitute the current age.
>
> (Giroux 1991b: 63)

These critical approaches to postmodernism represent an important development in contemporary theorizing; an approach that acknowledges the importance of new cultural, social and political formations but retains a concern to link with past theoretical achievements. Such approaches may offer a means of addressing changes in contemporary society without losing sight of the operation of power and oppression – as tends to happen in the most extreme forms of postmodernism (Skeggs 1991). Postmodernist analyses, with their concern to chart the multiple fracturing of social relations, for example, place great stress on the provisional nature of definitions of culture and identity. Although this can successfully break down assumptions about the homogeneity of majority groups, and the 'otherness' of minorities, it can also lead to a situation where the sheer diversity of form comes to mask deeper/more fundamental aspects of the social formation:

> postmodernism has a tendency to democratize the notion of difference in a way that echoes a type of vapid liberal pluralism. There is in this discourse the danger of affirming difference simply as an end in itself

without acknowledging how difference is formed, erased, and resuscitated within and despite asymmetrical relations of power. Lost here is any understanding of how difference is forged in both domination and opposition.

(Giroux 1991b: 72)

Here, Henry Giroux raises a vital issue. It is possible to acknowledge that social identities are formed in novel and changing ways, without rejecting all previous work as irredeemably 'modernist'. As Dick Hebdige notes, amid a variety of new and changing social categories and shifting identities, we still 'live in a world and in bodies which are deeply scored by the power relations of race and class, sexuality and gender' (Hebdige 1989: 89).

Postmodernity and identity

Distinctive features of the new cultural politics of difference are to trash the monolithic and homogeneous in the name of diversity, multiplicity, and heterogeneity; to reject the abstract, general, and universal in light of the concrete, specific, and particular; and to historicize, contextualize, and pluralize by highlighting the contingent, provisional, variable, tentative, shifting, and changing.

(West 1990: 203–4)

The fragmentation of social life (characteristic of postmodernity) has direct consequences for the way individuals think of themselves and others. The Enlightenment project, privileging order and reason, assumed a neatly focused, self-contained image of the individual as freed from the bounds of tradition and nature, able to make the world as they see fit. As Raymond Williams noted, from the late seventeenth century, philosophy (largely influenced by Descartes) 'proposed the thinking self as the first substantial area of knowledge – the *subject* – from the operations of which the independent existence of all other things must be deduced – as *objects* thrown before this consciousness' (Williams 1983: 309, original emphasis). Stuart Hall describes the Enlightenment idea of the individual (subject) as:

based on a conception of the human person as a fully centred, unified individual, endowed with the capacities of reason, consciousness and action, whose 'centre' consisted of an inner core which first emerged when the subject was born, and unfolded with it, while remaining essentially the same – continuous or 'identical' with itself – throughout the individual's existence. The essential centre of the self was a person's identity.

(Hall 1992b: 275)

This conception of a unified, '*centred*' human subject has become progressively harder to sustain throughout the twentieth century. Developments, not least in social theory (especially feminism), psychoanalysis and politics, have highlighted the multiple forces at work *on* and *through* the individual subject. As contemporary societies are increasingly fractured and 'dislocated' (Laclau 1990), so the boundaries between centre and periphery break down and a variety of subject positions are constructed. Individuals may see themselves through a variety of lenses, in ways that are not always consistent. The idea of self as simple and unitary ('centred') breaks down and is replaced by a '*de-centred*' subjectivity. Stuart Hall outlines a version of the 'post-modern subject' that, while simplified for the sake of clarity, captures well the essentials of postmodernist arguments about the fractured nature of identity:

> The fully unified, completed, secure and coherent identity is a fantasy. Instead, as the systems of meaning and cultural representation multiply, we are confronted by a bewildering, fleeting multiplicity of possible identities, any one of which we could identify with – at least temporarily.
>
> (Hall 1992b: 277)

As an example of how de-centred subjectivity has consequences for the politics of everyday life, Hall cites the controversy that surrounded the US Senate hearings of October 1991. Here a man nominated for the US Supreme Court was accused of sexual harassment by a woman who had previously worked as his subordinate. Both the complainant, Anita Hill, and the accused, Clarence Thomas, were of African-American ethnic background. Hall notes the many cross-cutting identifications that came into play in the reactions of the American public, media and social critics. Response to the issues fractured in ways that reflected the de-centring of contemporary identities. Opinion focused on a range of issues (reflecting class, gender, sexuality, 'race') yet none of these came to act as a sole locus (a centre) for debate:

> Some blacks supported Thomas on racial grounds; others opposed him on sexual grounds. Black women were divided, depending on whether their 'identities' as blacks or as women prevailed. Black men were also divided, depending on whether their sexism overrode their liberalism. White men were divided, depending, not only on their politics [Thomas was nominated for office by the Republican President George Bush], but on how they identified themselves with respect to racism and sexism. White conservative women supported Thomas, not only on political grounds, but also because of their opposition to

feminism. White feminists, often liberal on race, opposed Thomas on sexual grounds . . .

(Hall 1992b: 279–80)

Of particular significance here is the way that 'race' featured in the hearings. At the heart of the controversy lay an allegation of *sexual* harassment. We might, therefore, have predicted that the discourses of sexual and gender politics would dominate discussion of the hearings. By playing on the fact that African-American males have long endured a particular sexualized (as well as racialized) stereotype, however, Thomas made his 'race' a central issue – even though his accuser was of the *same* ethnic background:

> Clarence Thomas, in a later period of the Hearings, referred to the procedures as a 'high tech lynching for an uppity black' . . . he [also] used the metaphor of lynching very early on – in the final sentences of his opening statement. He states, there, 'I will not provide the rope for my own lynching or for further humiliation'. In drawing upon lynching, Thomas is not only presenting himself as a racialised victim but as a sexual victim too. This is because lynching connotes 'race' and sex simultaneously, for black men in the United States were often castrated when they were lynched by white people. Also, lynchings were presented as an appropriate sanction when there were allegations that black men had slept with white women . . . So Thomas brings about an image of himself as a racial and sexual victim.
>
> (Bhavnani with Collins 1993: 500)

The political consequences of de-centred subjectivities are also dramatically highlighted in the controversy surrounding Salman Rushdie's novel *The Satanic Verses*.[1]

Rushdie's book aroused deep religious anger among Muslims in many countries – and not only, or even mostly, among 'fundamentalists' or middle-class Islamic scholars.[2] In early 1989 protests escalated and, following the deaths of demonstrators in Pakistan and India, Iran's spiritual leader, Ayatollah Khomeni, passed a sentence of death on the author, forcing Rushdie into years of hiding.

For some observers, such as conservative whites, the Islamic responses to Rushdie's novel (whether threatening death from Iran or burning a book in Bradford) simply confirmed the barbarity of a 'fundamentalist', illiberal and pre-modern people. Such reactions brought together a range of stereotypes that embodied centuries of Western antipathy to the Islamic 'Other' (Said 1978) and found complementary discourses in 'the new racism' and its focus on 'British' values and traditions (see Chapter 2). Harder to predict, and sustain, were the responses of other minority groups, liberal and antiracist whites. Many people who, as a facet of their own political, 'racial' and/or ethnic identifications, were ordinarily sympathetic to the claims of minority ethnic groups, were uncertain about how best to react in this instance. The 'illiberal' response of a minority community threw into stark relief the complexity of contemporary identity politics:

> This issue is as important to the future of race relations as were the riots of the early 1980s. Just as they were an expression of community anger and put black people and their concerns on the political map, so the present ferment is of that magnitude for Muslims.
>
> (Modood 1989: 284)

For Tariq Modood, the Rushdie affair is of great importance in revealing the poverty of previous antiracist assumptions. Modood has been one of the most prolific and articulate critics of antiracism in recent years. Unlike the New Right, who see antiracism as a threat to order and 'Britishness', Modood is one of several critics who, while sharing the anti-oppressive goals of antiracism, have begun to question key aspects of its theory and (less often) its practice. Their 'New Left' critiques[3] build (sometimes explicitly) on the postmodern critique of the centred subject, rationality and a politics framed by any single dominant 'master identity'.

Antiracism and New Left critiques

Since the late 1980s, antiracism has come under increased attack from the left, as well as the right.[4] Most of the New Left critiques take as their focus the high profile 'municipal' antiracism practised by certain labour controlled local authorities, most notably the Greater London Council (GLC) (cf. Gilroy 1987).[5] The critiques cover a range of issues and frequently conflict on specific points. Additionally, there is a dominant concern with theory, which relegates antiracist *practice* to the sidelines. Some writers ignore practice altogether, while others only make brief reference to occasional examples. Nevertheless, any serious attempt to rethink the practice of education in a racist society must address the crucial conceptual issues raised by emerging left critiques of municipal antiracism. In this section I examine two of the most important contributions (those by Tariq Modood and Paul Gilroy) and consider how similar critiques have been applied in the field of education (most notably by Ali Rattansi and in the work of the 'Burnage' inquiry team).

Antiracism and the Rushdie affair

Tariq Modood has written a good deal about the position of British Asian Muslims, especially in relation to 'the Rushdie affair'. Through a variety of pieces (including academic papers, book reviews and newspaper articles) Modood has begun to develop a critique of much 'race' and 'religious' thinking in the UK (cf. Modood 1992). He is particularly critical of the emphasis on 'colour racism', arguing that this excludes minority groups whose most dearly felt identity concerns 'culture', not colour.

Modood takes as his target a form of antiracist local politics most clearly manifest during the 1980s in the work and political campaigns of the GLC. He describes the 1980s as a decade that:

> saw the rise of race professionals and theorists who marketed the idea of an Alabama-like Britain consisting of two races, whites and blacks, and of the latter as a potentially revolutionary underclass allied to feminism, gay rights, Irish nationalism and radical ecology. The politics based on these ideas, with the corollary that 'race relations' had to be redefined as 'anti-racism', came to prominence in the wake of the urban riots of 1981 and after, and reached a peak in the heyday of Ken Livingstone's rule at the GLC . . .
>
> (Modood 1989: 280–1)

In many ways, Modood's language echoes the New Right's discourse of derision, which attacks any attempt critically to address 'racial'/ethnic inequalities (see Chapter 2). Talk of 'race professionals' who 'marketed' their view, for example, smacks of the New Right's insinuation that bodies like the CRE are motivated by self-interest (Lewis 1988). Similarly, by using the word 'rule', to describe Ken Livingstone's period of office as elected leader of an elected local authority, Modood seems to echo stereotyped views of the GLC as an extremist 'loony left' authority (see Troyna and Carrington 1990). And yet Modood's central aim is not at all that of the New Right. On the question of 'freedom of speech', for example, he opposes both the aggressively secular stance of some neo-liberals and neo-conservative ideas about a legitimate Christian bias in British law. Modood questions the basis upon which liberals can accept a law against incitement to racial hatred while simultaneously using 'freedom of speech' to reject Muslim calls for changes in the blasphemy laws (Modood 1993). On the question of antiracist politics, Modood does not intend to discredit or abandon antiracism in its totality. Rather, he aims to highlight conceptual weaknesses as the basis for building a more 'mature' form of antiracism in the future (Modood 1990b: 95).

Theorizing 'race' and culture: against 'racial dualism'

Tariq Modood's central objection to the municipal antiracism of the 1980s is that it reads both 'race' and racism purely in terms of colour. This, he argues, leads to 'racial dualism', the view that the world consists of two groups; white and black. Not only does this ignore significant social, economic, religious and political differences (between and within ethnic minority groups), it also leads to a narrow definition of what counts as legitimate antiracist politics:

> Media interest, reflecting the social policy paradigm of the 1980s, has been narrowly circumscribed by racism and anti-racism: ethnic minorities are of interest if and only if they can be portrayed as victims of or threats to white society.
>
> (Modood 1989: 281)

Modood traces the part that this 'radicals and criminals' perspective played in stifling peaceful protest against *The Satanic Verses* – fuelling Muslim anger and encouraging 'the unfortunate but true conclusion that they would remain unheeded till something shocking and threatening was done' (Modood 1989: 282). He argues that a mature antiracism must develop a more sophisticated approach to the concepts of 'race' and ethnicity. Crucially, it must recognize that 'culture' is not a surface factor that can be dismissed as unimportant – as if minorities who do not see themselves in terms of colour are somehow deluded about where their true interests lie:

> neither they [Muslims] nor other religious-ethnic minorities will be understood unless current race philosophies are re-evaluated. The beginning of that understanding is the appreciation of the centrality of religion to the Muslim, and perhaps also to the Sikh and Hindu, psyche: that it is of far more importance and central to self-definition than 'race' or than can be allowed for by the black–white view of the world.
>
> (Modood 1989: 284)

Municipal antiracism's constant privileging of 'colour', therefore, means that it is bound to fail to connect with many minority populations:

> in terms of their own being, Muslims feel most acutely those problems that the anti-racists are blind to; and respond weakly to those challenges that the anti-racists want to meet with most force . . . We need concepts of race and racism that can critique socio-cultural environments which devalue people because of their physical differences but also because of their membership of a cultural minority and, critically, where the two overlap and create a double disadvantage.
>
> (Modood 1990a: 157)

Modood makes his points with eloquence and passion. His attack on municipal antiracism pinpoints several weaknesses in the kind of simplistic politicking that has sometimes characterized the local state's attempts to challenge racism. In particular, the failure to acknowledge ethnic *culture*, as a genuine and vital part of Asian identities, is revealed as a serious mistake in attempts to encourage political mobilization around antiracist concerns.

The absence of culture from many antiracist agendas reflects the bitter disputes between multiculturalists and antiracists in the late 1970s and 1980s (see Gillborn 1990: ch. 6; Solomos and Back 1994). In education, for example, multicultural approaches frequently emphasized the need for diverse cultural images which, in reality, often patronized minority students and reinforced white assumptions about exotic, distant and 'primitive' populations. In contrast, antiracists' explicit concern with political struggle and opposition to racism frequently labelled any concern for 'culture' as a short-sighted characteristic of multiculturalism that was destined to leave racist structures unchallenged (see, for example, Brandt 1986: 121). Modood's work demonstrates that culture cannot simply be ignored by antiracists who seriously wish to address a range of minority groups.

The historical reasons for antiracists' unease about the political and epistemological status of ethnic cultures, however, should not be forgotten. Indeed, while Tariq Modood criticizes antiracism for failing to engage with issues of culture, Paul Gilroy has attacked it for accepting too readily 'the absolutist imagery of ethnic categories beloved of the New Right' (Cross 1990: 3). Gilroy's critique echo's Modood's concern to break down the simplistic assumptions that exposed much municipal antiracism to ridicule, while failing to connect with the lived experiences and struggles of some minority groups. At the same time, however, Gilroy takes a rather different position on the politics of culture within antiracism; a position that highlights the complexity of identity, 'race' and culture in contemporary Western societies.

Beyond municipal antiracism

Paul Gilroy's work addresses a diverse set of issues, frequently challenging received wisdom about 'race', racism, social policy and critical theory. His book '*There Ain't No Black in the Union Jack*' (Gilroy 1987) examines the changing meaning of 'race' and 'nation' in contemporary politics, and includes an examination of the antiracist campaigns of the GLC. This acts as the basis for a sustained critique of municipal antiracism and the simplistic analyses of racism and power which it embodies. These arguments were later developed in a pamphlet for the Runnymede Trust (Gilroy 1988) and reworked in an article entitled 'The end of anti-racism' (Gilroy 1990). The latter is an especially powerful piece which, despite sometimes losing sight of the author's own qualifications about the scope of the critique,[6] brings together Gilroy's views on the failure of municipal antiracism and the lessons that must be learnt.

Theorizing 'race' and culture: an anti-essentialist approach

Gilroy is especially critical of the conceptions of 'race' and racism which underlie municipal antiracism. He attacks the 'coat-of-paint theory of racism' which views racism as a blemish 'on the surface of other things' and never calls into doubt 'the basic structures and relations of [the] British economy and society' (Gilroy 1990: 74). Such an approach places racism outside key debates, seeing it as a complicating factor of marginal importance rather than a central concern. In contrast, Gilroy argues that racism must be placed 'in the mainstream', viewing 'race' and racism:

> not as fringe questions but as a volatile presence at the very centre of British politics actively shaping and determining the history not simply of blacks, but of this country as a whole at a crucial stage in its development.
>
> (Gilroy 1990: 73)

A constant theme in Gilroy's attack on municipal antiracism concerns its inability critically to deconstruct and oppose the new racism. He argues that 'it has been incapable of showing how British cultural nationalism becomes a language of race' (Gilroy 1990: 77). He argues for a wider and more dynamic understanding of 'race' and racism; one that foregrounds the socially constructed nature of 'racial' categories and draws attention to their historically constituted and specific nature:

> At a theoretical level 'race' needs to be viewed much more contingently, as a precarious discursive construction. To note this does not, of course, imply that it is any less real or effective politically.
>
> (Gilroy 1990: 72)

This analysis is familiar (see Chapter 2 and the discussion of de-centred subjectivities above), but Gilroy relates it to antiracist theory in a way that is both distinctive and vital to more effective antiracist practice. Specifically, he argues that municipal antiracism, despite its opposition to the New Right's culturalist politics, has itself come to accept a spurious ideology of 'culturalism and cultural absolutism' (Gilroy 1990: 82). This reflects several factors, not least the drive to support ethnic minority groups, and distinctive cultural activities, as a corrective to the deficit models proposed by New Right analyses.[7] By simply inverting the right's pathological view of minority culture, however, municipal antiracism repeats and sustains the culturalist analyses it seeks to oppose in different contexts. For example:

'Same-race' adoption and fostering for 'minority ethnics' is presented as an unchallenged and seemingly unchallengeable benefit for all concerned. It is hotly defended with the same fervour that denounces white demands for 'same race' schooling as a repellent manifestation of racism.

(Gilroy 1990: 81)

In these terms, the thinking that supports 'same-race' adoption and fostering is both *essentialist* and *reductionist*. Although born of anti-oppressive aims, it actually commits the same errors that typify the racist thinking it seeks to oppose. It argues that there is some innate quality that characterizes the essence of a particular 'racial'/cultural group. This 'sad inability to see beyond the conservation of racial identities to [the] possibility of their transcendence' reinforces assumptions about inherent difference between cultural groups and trivializes 'the rich complexity of black life by reducing it to nothing more than a response to racism' (Gilroy 1990: 81 and 83). Gilroy argues that just as they must adopt a more sophisticated understanding of 'race', so antiracists must break with limiting notions of 'culture' as in any way natural, homogeneous or fixed:

Culture, even the culture which defines the groups we know as races, is never fixed, finished or final. It is fluid, it is actively and continually made and re-made. In our multi-cultural schools the sound of steel pan may evoke Caribbean ethnicity, tradition and authenticity yet they originate in the oil drums of the Standard Oil Company rather than the mysterious knowledge of ancient African griots.

(Gilroy 1990: 80)

Gilroy argues, therefore, for a conception of culture and 'race' politics that recognizes the fluid, dynamic and highly complex character of the new cultural politics of difference (cf. Hall 1992c; West 1990). This is the clearest point of contact between Gilroy's analysis of municipal antiracism and later attempts to apply the insights of postmodern theory to antiracism in education.

Applying the New Left critique in education

In an edited collection entitled *'Race', Culture and Difference*, James Donald and Ali Rattansi bring together a series of pieces (including reprinted articles by Modood and Gilroy) which explore an 'anti-essentialist understanding of racial categories' (Donald and Rattansi 1992: 7). Culture, they argue, must be returned to the centre of debate, but in terms of an explicitly *'critical'* reading of the concept. That is, an approach that reflects 'theoretical advances' which 'make it impossible to think of culture as a finite and self-sufficient body of contents, customs and traditions' (Donald and Rattansi 1992: 1 and 5). In the first contribution to the book, Rattansi specifically applies this approach to the field of education.

Rattansi argues that 'now is a time to take stock and to reflect on the theoretical, pedagogic and political foundations of multiculturalism and antiracism' (Rattansi 1992: 11). Key sections of his paper deal with the importance of post-structuralism and psychoanalytic approaches as the basis for an 'alternative framework' which emphasizes the complex and contingent nature of 'race', culture and identity in contemporary society:

> I would argue that racialized and ethnic discourses and encounters have a tendency to be contradictory and ambivalent in character. These internal complexities are contextually produced and differentially deployed in particular situations and institutional locations. Racialized and ethnic discourses and encounters are also inevitably suffused with elements of sexual and class difference and therefore fractured and criss-crossed around a number of axes and identities.
>
> (Rattansi 1992: 37)

Similar arguments about the 'non-synchronous' interplay of class, 'race', gender and sexuality have been developed in the United States (cf. McCarthy 1990; McCarthy and Apple 1988). Avtar Brah's work, on the experiences and perspectives of Asian Muslim young women in Britain, reveals congruent patterns of 'a multiplicity of ideological, cultural and structural factors' (Brah 1993: 456). Her analysis draws attention to 'the intersections between gender, class, ethnicity, racism, religion and other axes of differentiations empirically and historically as contingent relationships' (Brah 1993: 441). These analyses share a concern to break down narrow essentialist and reductionist approaches to the study of 'race' and racism. As far as educational *practice* is concerned, however, the consequences of such an approach are far from clear.

Ali Rattansi claims that antiracism in education has 'produced only patchy evidence of success' (1992: 33) and eventually concludes that 'We need to move beyond both multiculturalism and antiracism' (1992: 41). The evidential basis for this conclusion is unclear: his critique is overwhelmingly concerned with *conceptual* issues. Rattansi has little to say about the details of curriculum and classroom practice: where he does address pedagogy, for example, it is on the basis of limited empirical evidence, with the main thrust being to criticize the supposedly rationalist *philosophy* of antiracist approaches.[8] Barry Troyna (1993a: ch. 7) argues that Rattansi and other critics (such as Cohen 1992) do a serious injustice to the range and variety of antiracist approaches.

Given our current state of knowledge, it is difficult to arrive at any secure judgement about the overall success or failure of antiracism in education: we simply know too little about what constitutes good antiracist practice. We do, however, have a clearer idea about what constitutes bad practice. The evidence for this arises out of tragedy at Burnage High School in Manchester (see below). Subsequently, the case has taken on wider significance so that it is often cited (by right and left alike) as final evidence of the failure of antiracism in education.

'Moral' antiracism and Burnage High School

On Wednesday 17 September 1986, Ahmed Iqbal Ullah (an Asian student at Burnage) was murdered in the playground by Darren Coulburn (a white peer). A subsequent inquiry, led by Ian Macdonald QC, investigated the background to the murder and presented a full report to Manchester City Council. In view of the Council's refusal to publish the report, and following widespread 'leaks' and misreporting in the popular press, the inquiry team itself decided to publish their findings (Macdonald et al. 1989). Rattansi describes their conclusions as follows:

> The committee of inquiry, composed of individuals with impressive antiracist credentials – Ian Macdonald, Gus John, Reena Bhavnani, Lily Khan – delivered a strong and, for some, an astonishing condemnation of the antiracist policies apparently vigorously pursued at the school, castigating them as doctrinaire, divisive, ineffectual and counterproductive.
>
> (Rattansi 1992: 13)

The inquiry team were highly critical of the particular form of antiracism that had been practised in Burnage; what they call *'symbolic'* or *'moral'* antiracism. It is a form of antiracism that is essentialist and reductionist in the extreme. 'Race' and racism are assumed to be dominant factors in the experiences of 'black' and white students, with the former cast as victims, the latter as aggressors. According to moral antiracism:

> since black students are the victims of the immoral and prejudiced behaviour of white students, white students are all to be seen as 'racist', whether they are ferret-eyed fascists or committed anti-racists. Racism is thus placed in some kind of moral vacuum and is totally divorced from the more complex reality of human relations in the classroom, playground or community. In this model of anti-racism there is no room for issues of class, sex, age or size.
>
> (Macdonald et al. 1989: 402)

The inquiry report documents the way that this approach combined with several other factors (including the style of management and 'macho' disciplinary atmosphere in the school) to increase tension and damage relationships (between school and community; between staff and students; students and their peers; teachers and their colleagues). While the report is damning in its criticism of Burnage's 'moral' antiracism, it is absolutely clear about the reality of racism and the need for more sensitive and sophisticated approaches to antiracism. Although this point was reflected in the first press coverage (in a local paper in Manchester), the national press took a rather different line.

The national press tended to represent the report as 'proof' that antiracism is a damaging extremist political creed: a 'dangerous obsession' which is, according to the *Daily Mail*, 'endemic to certain left-dominated authorities'. The *Daily Telegraph* went further, presenting Ahmed as a victim of antiracism rather than a white racist, by proclaiming: 'Anti-racist policy led to killing' (quoted in Macdonald et al. 1989: xx). In response, the inquiry team issued a press statement which repeated the specific criticism of Burnage, but made clear their continuing support for antiracist education policies:

It is because we consider the task of combating racism to be such a critical part of the function of schooling and education that we condemn symbolic, moral and doctrinaire anti-racism. We urge care, rigour and caution in the formulating and implementing of such policies because we consider the struggle against racism and racial injustice to be an essential element in the struggle for social justice which we see as the ultimate goal of education . . . We repudiate totally any suggestion that the anti-racist education policy of Burnage High School led . . . to the death of Ahmed Ullah . . . [W]e state emphatically that the work of all schools should be informed by a policy that recognises the pernicious and all-pervasive nature of racism in the lives of students, teachers and parents, black and white, and the need to confront it.

(reprinted in Macdonald et al. 1989: xxiii–xxiv)

Unfortunately this statement received relatively little coverage in the press. In education and academia also, the 'Burnage report' – though rarely read in detail – is frequently taken as an attack on antiracism itself. In the same way that Gilroy's attack on municipal antiracism can (mistakenly) be read as a wider attack on any policy under the 'antiracist' heading, so Macdonald and his colleagues' views on 'moral' antiracism are sometimes taken as an attack on the very idea of antiracist education. Ali Rattansi, for example, characterizes the report's importance as follows:

From within the movement, the publication of the Macdonald Report on the tragic events at Burnage High School has been widely interpreted as signalling the failure of the antiracist project in education.

If antiracism is to be effective in education, it is therefore necessary to take a hard and perhaps painful look at the terms under which we have operated so far.

(Rattansi 1992: 11)

In its attack on essentialist and reductionist analyses of 'race' and racism, the Burnage report shares several key features with other left critiques of antiracist theory and practice. Although the critiques have been generated by a range of writers, with diverse agendas, some important lessons can be learnt. Such conclusions, however, must be drawn with extreme care. In this field it is sometimes easy to lapse into rhetoric at the expense of analysis. If the left critiques are genuinely to contribute to effective action against racism, we must guard against the essentialism and reductionism that we criticize elsewhere.

Lessons of the New Left critique

Criticism, from whatever quarter, is a vital spur to the development of both theory and practice – but it must be used constructively. The left critique of antiracism does not amount to the death knell of everything under the antiracist banner. The first task, when evaluating the contribution made by New Left commentaries on antiracism, is to be clear about the limits of the critique. If we lose sight of the critics' specific targets there is a real danger that we might forfeit gains that have already been won. The left critique arises from the very quarter where antiracist practitioners would have expected support; for those struggling to make antiracism a reality in schools, such an attack – if overstated or misrepresented – might paralyse future developments by undermining practitioners' belief in their ability to do anything without falling foul of one theoretical position or another. *The first conclusion to be drawn from the New Left critiques, therefore, is that any talk of simply abandoning antiracism is premature.*

The left critiques of antiracism have tended to focus on two particular approaches; that is, 'municipal' antiracism (embodied in the GLC campaigns of the 1980s) and the 'moral' antiracism revealed by the Burnage inquiry. Each critic I have cited takes care, at some point, to distance themselves from an all out attack on the totality of antiracist theory and practice – unfortunately, the language of critique sometimes comes to dominate in a way that loses sight of this.

An attempt to balance specific criticisms with more general issues is exemplified in the work of Ian Macdonald, Reena Bhavnani, Lily Khan and Gus John (the Burnage inquiry team). Although their report is damning in its attack on 'moral' antiracism, it is admirably clear in its support for antiracism as a principle. Beyond this, the report begins to address central questions that must be considered in future practice. Their work demonstrates that a commitment to fighting racism does not require simplistic or patronizing approaches which force people into corners and deny the complexity of the real world. While such simplistic approaches might suggest eyecatching posters and memorable catch-phrases, they offer no basis for educational work in contemporary society.

The Burnage inquiry team, better than any other left critics, exemplify the need for balance and a careful eye towards the realities of life in the school and classroom. The reaction to their work (in the media, politics and parts of academia) highlights the problems of constructive critique in a field of practice that has so many opponents. Yet important lessons can, and must, be learnt. The left critiques, when kept in perspective, do not spell the end of antiracism as such; they offer the possibility of a more critical and effective antiracism. In the rest of this section, I will outline briefly what I take to be the major constructive elements arising from that work.

Beyond 'racial dualism'

One of the most important contributions to this field is Tariq Modood's attack on the 'racial dualism' that conceives of the world in stark black/white terms. It has been argued that such essentialism is sometimes 'necessary as a strategy of resistance . . . in certain political moments' (Epstein 1993: 17). Modood convincingly demonstrates the dangers of such an approach where it is adopted as a timeless/context-free paradigm for social analysis. He argues that racial dualism operates to restrict critical perspectives and denies legitimacy to groups and issues that do not fit the 'radicals and criminals' model.

This critique is especially valuable in facilitating analysis of cultural racisms. By breaking with the municipal antiracist fixation with colour racism, we are better placed to analyse and work against the many forms of racism that take culture, not colour, as a focal point. The need for such an approach has become especially pressing with the rise of the new racism. Nevertheless, there is danger here. The 'trend towards "global homogenization"', seen in the operation of global information and market systems, 'is matched by a powerful revival of "ethnicity"' (Hall 1992b: 313). This growing fascination with the local and 'ethnic', could collapse into a form of *ethnicism* where culture is not only recognized as *an* important factor in the structuring of social experience, but is taken as *the essential* category:

> Ethnicism, I would suggest, defines the experience of racialized groups primarily in 'culturalist' terms: that is, it posits 'ethnic difference' as

the primary modality around which social life is constituted and experienced. Cultural needs are defined largely as independent of other
social experiences centred around class, gender, racism or sexuality.
This means that a group identified as culturally different is assumed
to be internally homogeneous . . . [E]thnicist discourses seek to impose
stereotypic notions of 'common cultural need' upon heterogeneous
groups with diverse social aspirations and interests.

(Brah 1992a: 129)

This is precisely the kind of 'cultural insiderism' that Paul Gilroy is so
critical of within the local politics of municipal antiracism (1990: 80).
Here an ethnicized identity can be a passport to local finance but a barrier
to wider political action and alliances. Gilroy argues that ethnicism must
be resisted by foregrounding the dynamic and fluid nature of contemporary cultures, even those that are commonly represented as historically
fixed and absolute. This critical approach to culture is exactly what Donald
and Rattansi (1992: 1) call for. It is a view of culture that resists the simple
essentialist and reductionist analyses characteristic of ethnicism, and central to the new racism.

The new cultural politics of difference

An awareness of the dynamic and heterogeneous nature of contemporary
culture is a central element in analyses of postmodernity. Just as all cultures are 'continually made and re-made' (Gilroy 1990: 80) so *ethnicity* –
people's sense and expression of a particular cultural identity – is continually negotiated and recreated. Stuart Hall (1992c) draws attention to the
'new ethnicities' explored in some contemporary film and photography,
where the constructed and historically specific character of ethnicity is
highlighted – particularly in relation to the criss-crossing of 'racial', class
and sexual identities. Donald and Rattansi take up the same theme, listing
a series of artists who explore and articulate a variety of 'hybrid identities'
(1992: 5). The exploration of new ethnicities is not, however, restricted to
the realm of film and other formalized means of cultural production and
representation: *the fluid interaction of changing ethnic categories can be
seen in the youth club and playground, as well as the art gallery.* Social
research in urban areas has revealed young people's active engagement in
processes of 'cultural syncretism' (Back 1993: 230).[9] Here, 'race', ethnicity
and racism operate in complex, and often unpredictable ways. Elements of
'black' style and culture, for example, are colonized by white youth, especially where they address particular notions of masculinity and sexual
prowess (see Mac an Ghaill 1994). Additionally, white youth draw

distinctions between different minority groups, which reflect both local and national factors and sustain differing levels of racist abuse.

An awareness of the cultural syncretism at work in society (at both macro and micro levels) is necessary if the critical understanding of culture (required by New Left critiques) is to inform a more effective antiracism. We must ensure, however, that questions of power and oppression remain clearly in sight. For all the complexity and 'hybridity' of identity, local white 'loyalties' still can act to legitimate and protect openly violent (even murderous) racist gangs (cf. Centre for Multicultural Education 1993: part 1). A reminder, if one were needed, that 'race' and racism must not be lost sight of amid a postmodern concern for plurality and diversity. 'Race' and racism are alive and well, but taking new twists and turns to which our analytical frameworks must be sensitive.

The end of essentialism?

In his work on the politics of representation and ethnicity, Stuart Hall argues that there has been a major shift in the representation of black culture. He notes an 'end of innocence' heralded by the collapse of the 'essential black subject':

> What is at issue here is the recognition of the extraordinary diversity of subjective positions, social experiences and cultural identities which compose the category 'black'.
>
> (Hall 1992c: 254)

In the realm of antiracist politics this is a particularly important shift in thinking about 'race', because it clears the ground for a more sophisticated recognition of the diversity within and between groups that are subject to racism. It is an analytical shift that is exemplified in Modood and Gilroy's critiques of municipal antiracism and its attempt simplistically to invert racist stereotypes towards antiracist ends:

> You can no longer conduct black politics through a strategy of a simple set of reversals, putting in the place of the bad old essential white subject, the new essentially good black subject. Now, that formulation may seem to threaten the collapse of an entire political world. Alternatively, it may be greeted with extraordinary relief at the passing away of what at one time seemed to be a necessary fiction. Namely, either that all black people are good or indeed that all black people are *the same*.
>
> (Hall 1992c: 254, original emphasis)

This perspective is familiar as part of the Macdonald inquiry's criticism of the 'moral' antiracism at Burnage, where all whites were cast as racists.

This shift in thinking challenges essentialist approaches to racism and antiracism, and encourages a more critical approach; one that can now recognize the complexities of 'race' and racism as they are experienced in the real world. Tariq Modood, for example, acknowledges the depth and variety of racist attitudes held by some Muslims – despite their 'colour-blind' faith:

> The Quranic teaching is that people are to be valued in terms of virtue not colour or race. Muslims insist that there is no divinely favoured race and that the Quran is God's message to the whole of mankind ... Like all 'colour-blind' approaches [however] ... it is too weak to prevent racial and ethnic prejudice ... Arab racism is such that most Pakistanis would prefer to work in Britain than in Saudi Arabia for a higher income; racist humiliations from shop-keepers, taxi-drivers, catering staff and so on have become a regular feature of the pilgrimage to Mecca for the diverse ethnic groups of Islam. Asians have no fewer racial stereotypes about whites and blacks than these groups have about Asians or about each other.
>
> (Modood 1990a: 158)

By acknowledging what Hall calls 'the end of the essential black subject', antiracist theorizing is better placed to make sense of the myriad forms and practice of racism in contemporary society. If they are to avoid 'moral' antiracism and gain the confidence of students (of all ethnic backgrounds), for example, anyone attempting to operate antiracism within a school will have to acknowledge that *'racism and ethnocentrism are not necessarily confined to white groups'* (Rattansi 1992: 36, original emphasis).[10]

Racism, contingency and process

Donald and Rattansi see the exploration of new ethnicities as central to a new politics of identity:

> This represents neither the old multicultural celebration of diversity, nor a naive postmodern embrace of an endless multiplication of cultural identities.
>
> (1992: 5–6)

But this new 'critical rethinking of the relationship between culture, "race" and politics' has yet to find a secure balance between first, recognizing the dynamic and changing character of 'racial' and ethnic categories, and second, retaining a concern for wider patterns in the social formation, especially those linking structure to the operation of power and oppression.

Ali Rattansi, for example, argues that the term 'racism' should be restricted to certain forms of *discourse* (1992: 36).[11] He seems to view the term 'racial discrimination' as a convenient catchall for *actions* that have negative consequences for members of minority ethnic groups. Unfortunately, 'racial discrimination' tends to carry implications of conscious intent and individualizes the analysis, so that discussions of action are placed outside wider analyses of social structural factors. Rattansi's 'alternative framework', therefore, assumes a fairly clear-cut distinction between discourse and action. But the dynamics of racism are too complex for such a schema: new racist discourses of the nation can have direct consequences for local discourses of belonging/otherness, and for aggressively racist actions – including racially motivated harassment, and even murder (Back 1993; Centre for Multicultural Education 1993). *Racism operates through petrol bombs, knives and boots, as well as discourse.*

In the classroom, racism can find powerful expression through disciplinary procedures, often despite the good intentions of white teachers who would reject crude notions of racial inferiority (see Chapter 3). To understand how racist *discourses* interact with routine *actions* that are racist in their consequences (though not intent), qualitative researchers frequently utilize the concept of *process* (cf. Gillborn 1990; Mac an Ghaill 1988; Wright 1986). This may now have a wider use as critics seek to marry a recognition of new and complex forms of racism, to a concern to chart deeper patterns of power and oppression.

Michael McCall and Howard Becker (1990) seek common ground and constructive differences between the approaches of symbolic interactionism and cultural studies. They argue that *process* offers a valuable way forward. *Contingency*, McCall and Becker observe, is a 'point many workers in cultural studies want to emphasize' (McCall and Becker 1990: 6) – as I have shown already, a concern with contingency features in several New Left analyses of 'race', ethnicity and difference (cf. Brah 1993; Gilroy 1990; West 1990). By adopting a sociological perspective, particularly one informed by symbolic interactionism, the concept of process allows us critically to consider 'race' and racism as historically contingent, without abandoning our commitment to identify deeper structures:

Nothing *has* to happen. Nothing is fully determined. At every step of every unfolding event, something else *might* happen. To be sure, the balance of constraints and opportunities available to the actors, individual and collective, in a situation will lead many, perhaps most, of them to do the same thing. Contingency doesn't mean people behave randomly, but it does recognize that they can behave in surprising and unconventional ways. The interactionist emphasis on process stands, as Blumer insisted, as a corrective to any view that insists that culture or social structure determines what people do.

(McCall and Becker 1990: 6)

Put simply, the idea of process makes analytical space for contingency without reducing everything to a random plurality of differences – avoiding the 'naive postmodern embrace of an endless multiplication of cultural identities' feared by Donald and Rattansi (1992: 6). In further studies of the operation of 'race' and racism, therefore, it may be especially fruitful to adopt a broadly interactionist perspective; one that utilizes the potential insights of attention to social process. This kind of approach has to be alive to the complex reworking of ethnicity and identities in contemporary society while maintaining the ability to recognize and critique the continued (though changing) operation of 'race' and racism.

Critical antiracism

Not all postmodernism celebrates diversity and superficial change at the expense of more penetrating and insightful analyses. Just as authors have begun increasingly to utilize postmodernism, without becoming slaves to it (cf. Aronowitz and Giroux 1991; Hall 1992b), so the critiques of municipal and moral antiracism, provide the basis for a more critical form of antiracist theory and practice.

Paul Gilroy, for example, builds his critique of municipal antiracism on a recognition of the complex and diverse nature of difference and identity in contemporary society; characteristically, however, he does not lose sight of 'race' and racism as crucial facts of life. Gilroy sustains a concern with the lived experience and daily struggles of 'black' people – resolutely maintaining the political significance of a label that transcends 'culturalist' tendencies towards ethnicism. Although Gilroy strikes a challenging note in his critiques of antiracism, there is no suggestion that the issues should be recast in a way that marginalizes racism, or reduces 'race' to just another entry on a list of potentially important subject identities: 'race' and racism are of crucial significance for all.

Similarly, although Gilroy raises fundamental questions about the project of municipal antiracism, he builds on this to offer signposts towards more sophisticated approaches. In looking to the future of anti-oppressive struggles and antiracist theory, Gilroy suggests that any attempt to produce 'a general theory of anti-racist politics may itself be a misplaced and fruitless activity' (Gilroy 1987: 149). Like other grand narratives, such a 'general theory' will fail in the face of the rapidly changing and multifaceted nature of identity in contemporary society. This marks the end of municipal antiracism as a viable analysis and basis for action. This conclusion does not, however, signal the end of antiracist politics in any general sense. Rather, it suggests the need for a more sophisticated approach; one that recognizes the multiple sources and politics of identity, resists essentialist and reductionist analyses, and engages with the reality of 'race' and multiple racisms:

> I propose that we reject the central image of ourselves as victims and install instead an alternative conception which sees us as an active force working in many different ways for our freedom from racial subordination. The plural is important here for there can be no single or homogeneous strategy against racism because racism itself is never homogeneous. It varies, it changes and it is *always* uneven.
>
> (Gilroy 1990: 83, original emphasis)

This is a deceptively simple formulation. Gilroy's rejection of the label 'victim', challenges essentialist and deficit stereotypes while simultaneously acknowledging the variety of ways in which racism is actively resisted. He recognizes the dynamic, complex and 'uneven' character of racism, and goes further, arguing that multiple and contingent forms of racism, require multiple and contingent forms of struggle.

In the absence of any 'one right way', the responsibility is with all of us to work against racism, and to remain self-critically aware of the tendency for unintended consequences to reproduce the very inequalities we seek to dismantle. In particular, we must realize, first, that no strategy is ever likely to be completely successful, and second, that an effective strategy in one context, may fail in another context or at another time. It is with these limits in mind that the second part of this book should be read.

Conclusions

Antiracism has always been under attack. Predictably, the first critics included a mixture of the conservative New Right and liberals. The former set out to 'defend' (assert) a mythical homogeneous 'British' (white) culture; the latter viewed antiracism as a harsh, undemocratic attempt to challenge the modest gains made in the name of multiculturalism. During the late 1980s and early 1990s, however, a New Left critique has evolved. The very source from where antiracists might have expected most support, has begun to generate doubts about the basic assumptions of antiracist theory and practice.

In this chapter I have examined the left critique of antiracism, mainly focusing on writers who have resisted the pull of extreme, and naive, postmodernism. This is not to say that postmodernist theory has nothing to contribute; indeed, the postmodern de-centred subject is a key to understanding the importance and complexity of contemporary identity politics. Although some postmodernism is rightly attacked as a self-serving exercise in self-aggrandizement, devoid of real substance, a *critical* awareness of 'the postmodern condition' is vital. Episodes like the Hill/Thomas Senate hearings in the United States, and the international furore surrounding *The Satanic Verses*, cannot be understood within traditional models of right/ left and black/white politics.

I have argued that in considering the New Left commentaries on antiracism it is vital to keep sight of the limits of the critique. Certain forms of antiracism have been discredited; the failure of 'municipal' and 'moral' antiracism, however, does not require the abandonment of all work under the antiracist banner. Indeed, the best critiques offer guidance about the future form of a more sophisticated critical antiracism.

A critical and reflexive antiracism cannot be constrained by the narrow politics of 'racial dualism', which denies the importance of culture and cultural racisms; but neither must it lapse into an ethnic absolutism that mirrors the New Right's ethnicist discourse. Cultures are never fixed; the dynamic relations between changing ethnic categories are reflected in every-day interactions, including the school-lives of young people. An awareness of the new cultural politics of difference offers a lens on the racism at work between and within various minority communities – a reality often denied by previous antiracist analyses. An awareness of hybrid identities and 'cultural syncretism', however, should not blind us to the continuing power of traditional 'racial' dichotomies – categories that have genuine currency in countless contexts and can still prove fatal.

In looking to the future of antiracist theory and practice, therefore, the left critiques highlight the need for a reflexive, self-critical approach. We must learn from mistakes, but maintain 'race' and racism as indispensable concepts in our attempts to understand and change the processes which influence and restrict the lives of all people in a racist society. There are unlikely to be any approaches that will be totally successful; even strategies that prove effective in practice, may not be transferable elsewhere or re-sistant to changing forms of discourse and interaction over time. It is on this basis that the following analysis of antiracist change in English sec-ondary schools should be read. By adopting an interactionist approach I am consciously seeking to expose the complex issues that face schools attempting to find rigorous, but workable, approaches to antiracism. The teachers and students, whose efforts and experiences form the basis of the next four chapters, have not discovered any magic formulas; they do, however, provide a wealth of invaluable insights on the workings of 'race' and racism in schools. Their experiences speak to all those concerned with 'race' in education, whether theorist, practitioner or – best of all – that combination of both to which critical antiracism strives.

part two

'Race' and educational practice

The politics of school change __

> Conflict and change are inevitably interlocked as any redistribution of
> power and privilege will be sought by some and resisted by others.
> (Kelly 1969: 69, quoted by Ball 1987: 78)

Over the next four chapters I examine the processes of antiracist change
in secondary schools. Building on interviews with teachers and students, I
aim to chart the realities of change in schools that have attempted to
deconstruct and oppose the racism that permeates so much of life in contemporary Britain.

In this chapter I summarize the character and location of the main case
study schools: Mary Seacole Girls'; Garret Morgan; and Forest Boys'. The
schools are located in different parts of England and serve student
populations of markedly different compositions in terms of social class,
ethnic background and gender. Nevertheless, in each school the moves
towards antiracist change were initiated by a small 'core' group of committed teachers, supported by their headteacher and senior management.
The chapter concludes by exploring the similarities and differences in the
style of work adopted by these core groups.

The next chapter investigates how the core groups sought to influence
the work of their colleagues more generally, on a whole-school basis. This
includes a section on the core groups' continuing actions to sustain and
extend antiracism in the face of changes in national education policy.

The final two chapters in this part of the book move beyond the realms
of policy-making and implementation, and into the classroom. First, I
examine the status of antiracist work within the curriculum. In particular,
I focus on the experiences of teachers and students involved in a programme of anti-oppressive teaching in Seacole. This is followed by a chapter that surveys the range and complexity of student perspectives on
antiracism in the case study schools. I consider the important role that
students continue to play in the development of antiracism, and examine

both the theoretical and practical issues raised by white students' experiences in antiracist schools.

The micro-political perspective

Before looking at the case study data, it is necessary to say something about the theoretical position that underpins the research. It is a perspective that views schools as sites of micro-political struggle. Stephen Ball draws particular attention to the role of conflict in school life:

> I take schools, in common with virtually all other social organizations, to be *arenas of struggle*; to be riven with actual or potential conflict between members; to be poorly co-ordinated; to be ideologically diverse. I take it to be essential that if we are to understand the nature of schools as organizations, we must achieve some understanding of these conflicts.
>
> (Ball 1987: 19, original emphasis)

In this book I adopt a micro-political approach to the analysis of change and decision-making in schools.

This perspective focuses on relations between different groups and individuals within the school; people that hold a range of positions within the organization and may have widely different views of themselves, their roles and the school that they all work in. The micro-political approach gives *power* a central place in the analysis. It is recognized that while, officially, the headteacher holds ultimate power within a school, countless others have the potential to influence events in ways that demonstrate their own practical (as opposed to formal/institutional) power. This perspective also allows for a more sensitive and flexible analysis of the relations between power at the macro level (of education policy) and the micro level (school change and management). Policy reforms do not simply *dictate* the managerial nor pedagogic character of teachers' work, but they can have an effect in countless ways. A micro-political perspective can illuminate how, for example, numerous factors (some specific to the school; some concerning the local community; others defined by legislation) can converge to encourage the adoption of more autocratic and hierarchical procedures – even where previous practice would have seemed antagonistic to such a shift (Gillborn 1994). At the same time the perspective highlights the spaces within which national reforms may be reinterpreted, even subverted, at the local level:

> schooling and teachers' work cannot be defined solely within the stultifying parameters of policy. Policies are not totalizing, they do not

address every eventuality, they do not specify every act, they do not speak meaningfully to all settings.

(Ball 1994: 177)

In the following chapters, therefore, I am concerned to understand how a group of committed teachers can come to influence the development of whole-school policy and practice, despite the inertia of their colleagues, most of whom are at best ambivalent, at worst opposed, to antiracist change. A finding that may surprise some readers is that students emerge as a key group in the changes. In this sense, students are a powerful group within schools – not powerful in the familiar sense of a group with recognized authority, but powerful in their ability (under certain circumstances) to challenge taken-for-granted assumptions and make heard alternative voices.

The micro-political perspective on school life (which gives a central place to conflict and power) contrasts with 'organizational science' or 'managerialist' approaches, which tend to assume reason and consensus. The latter conceive of schools as places where the majority can be won over to a particular course of action through reason and debate, backed by the legitimate authority of the headteacher. These models of school organization continue to find support:

> Whilst politicking does exist in schools, and can be a very effective initiator of change, our research shows that *change can be and often is planned in schools in a less self-centred and more rational manner.* The Heads of Department at Summerfield High who were discussing the adoption of a formula system for the allocation of capitation did not seem to be unduly disturbed by whether their own departments would come out better or worse under a new system... Senior management can give staff confidence if it is seen to believe that groups of staff can bring about change. For this not to lead to a haphazard collection of unco-ordinated change, *it helps if... there is a shared view of the priorities of the school, and hence of the direction for change.*
>
> (Torrington and Weightman 1989: 89, emphasis added)

This quotation presents schools as rational places where people can reasonably be expected to act in selfless ways if it is for the good of the school: as defined by 'a shared view of the priorities'. This does not match the picture produced by sociologists who have used qualitative approaches (especially interviews and observations) to chart the day-to-day life of schools (e.g. Bowe et al. 1992; Burgess 1988; Gillborn 1994; Powney and Weiner 1991; Riseborough 1981; Wolpe 1988). It certainly does not hold much promise when considering antiracism in schools.

The whole idea of addressing inequality in education has come under fire as part of the drive to introduce market forces into education; heightening competition and accentuating difference. Anti-oppressive moves have been attacked both explicitly (by the reforms' architects: see Chapter 2) and more indirectly (as a consequence of wider changes). For example, the reforms have led to an intensification of teachers' work. Many are concerned simply to cope and survive – let alone take on new challenges that are not demanded by legislation. In addition, 'race' continues to be seen as a sensitive, even contentious, area that many people (including teachers, governors and local politicians) would prefer to avoid (Taylor 1992: 26, 30–1). While most teachers may be sympathetic to ideals of equality, and relatively few are openly hostile to minority students and their communities, in the current climate antiracism is unlikely to feature very high on most teachers' list of priorities.[1] This is the context in which antiracism must currently operate. It is a context in which a micro-political analysis is essential if we are to understand the range of conflicts thrown up by antiracist change.

In the following chapters I examine the experiences of teachers and students in schools that have begun to adopt antiracism as an essential part of their ethos – a day-to-day reality in practice, not merely a rhetorical position to be trotted out when convenient. None of the schools have been totally successful – perhaps none ever are – but their experiences reveal a great deal about the problems and possibilities of change in a school system that continues to operate in racialized ways.

The schools

The following analysis, of antiracist change in secondary schools, draws primarily on the experiences of two schools. Both began concerted moves towards antiracist changes in the mid-1980s. By the time of the research fieldwork (1992) they had achieved real progress and a confident sense of their own identity as antiracist organizations. The schools are located in very different geographical areas, which have experienced contrasting histories of economic development and recession. In addition, they serve a diverse range of students and local communities, in terms of both ethnic and social class backgrounds.

Mary Seacole Comprehensive

An LEA maintained girls' school in a large Midlands city, Seacole serves around 550 students from the ages of 11 to 16.

The student population is extremely diverse. Just under half are of South Asian background, mostly with family origins in Pakistan and northern

India. The principal religious faiths are Islam and Sikhism. Around a third of students are white, with roughly 18 per cent of African Caribbean ethnic background. The school also includes a small number with Vietnamese, Greek and Italian ethnic backgrounds.

Like most industrial centres in the English North and Midlands, the city suffered rising unemployment during the late 1980s and early 1990s. This is reflected in the student population. Around three-quarters of the students come from economically disadvantaged areas; half are entitled to free school meals.

As the city's only maintained girls' school, historically Seacole has played an important part in the life of the various South Asian communities in the City. From as early as the 1970s, for example, many Muslim parents made special attempts to get their daughters on the roll (including moving house into what was then a clearly defined catchment area). The school has since changed sites and now relies wholly on parental choice from across the city. Most students travel to school on public transport.

Garret Morgan Comprehensive

Located in a small and relatively prosperous city in the English South East, Morgan is a mixed comprehensive school, serving 500 students from the ages of 11 to 18.

The student population is predominantly white. However, the school traditionally draws a small but significant group of students from ethnic minority groups, especially the city's long established Bangladeshi community. In the late 1980s ethnic minority students accounted for around 15 per cent of the roll. As the number of white students has increased over recent years, however, the relative proportion of minority students has fallen to around 10 per cent.

Located on the edge of the city, Morgan recruits from a wide area, with half the students travelling from smaller towns and villages in the surrounding area, others from the centre and outskirts of the city itself. Although the Bangladeshi community suffers a disproportionately high rate of unemployment, generally unemployment is low. Less than 10 per cent of students are entitled to free school meals.

These two schools formed the core of the research fieldwork for this study. The analysis is also informed, however, by earlier work on a boys' school in the English North.

Forest Comprehensive School

I visited Forest boys' school as part of an earlier study of approaches to discipline in inner city schools (Gillborn et al. 1993). The school had 550 students on roll and drew around 95 per cent of them from the city's South Asian communities, mostly Muslims with family origins in Pakistan. The school had undergone fairly rapid changes in its student population and, elsewhere, I have examined in detail how a new headteacher attempted to change the staff's assumptions about the students, their needs and their parent communities (cf. Gillborn 1992a; Gillborn et al. 1993, ch. 6).

Forest school was important to me, because it raised a series of issues that informed the design and analysis of this study. Additionally, in this chapter I include data from Forest where it helps to illuminate issues in the other case study schools or present the issues in somewhat different circumstances.

The remainder of this, and the following three chapters, are based largely on my research in Seacole and Morgan. Before getting to grips with the school-based data, however, it may be helpful briefly to outline the conception of change that underlies this account.

Theorizing school change

Schools have always had to cope with change. Indeed, the ability to respond to changing local circumstances, and to initiate new programmes and approaches, has long been seen as an essential part of any good educational system. In recent times, however, there have been unprecedented calls for change (often linked to statutory requirements) that have affected every state maintained school in England and Wales. Throughout the late 1980s and early 1990s successive pieces of legislation have demanded change at the school level, often tied to mechanisms that hold schools 'accountable' via published reports and crude performance indicators, such as the so-called 'league tables' of examination results (first published nationally in 1992).

In this context the management of change has become a major concern. In particular, the notion of *whole-school* change has assumed a central position in much policy and academic discourse. Building on the fact that piecemeal innovations often produce more problems than they solve, and are vulnerable to stagnation or reversal at a later date, it has become customary to advocate change that influences every facet of school organization and is supported through the actions of all staff. The concern for whole-school change also reflects a desire to retain some sort of consistency and coherence within a system that seems increasingly to push towards fragmentation (Nixon 1991). There is fragmentation *between* different 'types' of school and between schools competing for the same students in a locality: in addition, there is internal fragmentation *within* schools, as the requirements of the National Curriculum and linked assessment systems reinforce a partitioned and clearly differentiated system of school subjects.

The notion of whole-school change is, however, rarely subjected to proper critical scrutiny. David Reynolds (1989: 38) may be correct in arguing that 'a large variety of current *whole-school* policies . . . are an inefficient waste of time and resources' (original emphasis). There is no doubting the need for change to be effected on a school-wide basis if it is to make a significant impact on traditional patterns of student experience, success and failure. But there is no magic formula; no blueprint as to what successful whole-school change looks like in the day-to-day life of teachers and students. Simply addressing all participants in a school is not enough. To bring about change in reality (as opposed to rhetoric) requires an engagement with the forces that shape routine interactions inside schools.

The fact that fundamental change cannot be simply programmed into schools, as if they were machines, has been established over several decades, and through a variety of attempted innovations in curriculum content, teaching styles and school organization. This experience forces us to face the difficult problems posed by institutional inertia and established traditions (Rudduck 1991) and micro-political struggles between different individuals and interest groups (Ball 1987). *Whole-school change is, therefore, a goal, not a strategy.* To aim for whole-school change says something about the scope of the enterprise, but nothing about the means by which the changes can be won. And *won* they must be.

By definition, change threatens the existing status quo – there will always be people who perceive themselves as potential 'losers' in such circumstances (Watson 1986). Change threatens people's view of themselves and their role in the school. Change is, therefore, about the *power* of one or more groups to influence the shape of the institution – possibly against the wishes of others; sometimes even in the face of open hostility. This is the basic recognition at the heart of the micro-political perspective, and the starting point for this chapter.

By stressing the uncertain and complex nature of change, however, the micro-political perspective raises problems for those engaged in describing and analysing change through text. There are computer media that allow you (the reader) to begin at any point and to decide your own path through a variety of material held on a database. That is not possible in a book. Qualitative researchers, faced with a mass of field data on interconnecting and complex social processes, are often acutely aware of the limitations of this form of presentation:

> It once led my colleague Blanche Geer to wish for a way to write what she had to say on the surface of a sphere, so that nothing would have to come first . . . The image of writing on a sphere exactly captures the

insoluble nature of the problem, as people usually define it. You can't talk about everything at once, no matter how much you want to, no matter how much it seems to be the only way.

(Becker 1986: 59)

When describing how people and/or particular institutions have changed over time, the obvious (and usually irresistible) solution is to organize the account chronologically – dealing with events and problems in the order that they originally occurred. This is sometimes the only way that readers can understand how the participants came to interpret situations in particular ways. Unfortunately, such a presentation can lead to a kind of evolutionary perspective, as if each event were somehow a necessary and/ or logical 'stage' or 'phase' in a process of personal and/or institutional development.

This is a particular problem for qualitative researchers examining change, because the conventions of linguistic and textual presentation can work against the basics of our analysis. Qualitative research, especially that which adopts a micro-political perspective, subverts 'commonsense' fictions that present change as a linear, rationally organized process. School change rarely happens as neat, self-contained chains of cause and effect. Yet, the very act of presenting the change process through text, which must be sequentially ordered, imposes a particular 'logic' on the events that belies the uncertainty and stress of the processes as they are experienced by participants. This should be remembered while reading the accounts of change in this and following chapters which, I hope, nevertheless retain something of the pain and uncertainty that accompany the real thing.

Getting started

Student and community influences

Forms of antiracist and/or multicultural education have now taken root in a number of schools and colleges where there are few, if any, students of minority ethnic background (see Epstein 1993; Gaine 1987; Massey 1991; Tomlinson 1990; Troyna and Selman 1991). It is still the case, however, that most developments in this field have been pioneered in schools that serve ethnically diverse populations (Klein 1993). It is not surprising, therefore, that the presence of African Caribbean and Asian students was the first factor behind the progress made in the schools covered by this research project. As the head at Seacole remembers:

the first roots began to be put down, and that was the sheer fact of the ethnic background of the girls who were coming to the school.

(. . .) So the first thing that made you think was actually seeing girls and meeting with families that you realised that there was something more to them than just a family who wanted their girl to go to Seacole, that there was a whole history and richness of culture and a background that had to be taken on board.

In Seacole work on 'race' and ethnicity began quite slowly. There were some moderate changes in the late 1970s and early 1980s, but it was not until the mid-1980s that concerted efforts, and rapid development, really got underway. In contrast, some schools perceive the pressures to be more immediate and face more accelerated demands for change. Forest Comprehensive, for example, underwent significant changes to its student population over a relatively short time. Having witnessed a growth in the number of Asian students during the 1970s, the school was nevertheless unprepared for a dramatic increase throughout the 1980s that left white students in the minority. The head feels that many teachers felt 'de-skilled' by the range of linguistic and social needs that the children brought with them. The issues involved both ethnicity and social class:

the school's population was getting to the point where there was 60 to 70 per cent ethnic minority students. And the really interesting shift was that it was a different kind of youngster that was coming in. These were families who had not necessarily come from areas of any kind of affluence; families who didn't have experience of formal schooling before coming here; families who had been in rural, very poor areas of northern Pakistan [now] living in fairly poor and inadequate and overcrowded housing within the city centre.

When appointed, in the late 1980s, the head at Forest inherited a staff who were:

utterly bewildered by what they had seen happen and couldn't understand why it had happened (. . .) At my very first staff meeting here one of the staff said to me, 'The trouble with this school is we have got the wrong children here'. And that was the pervading feeling.

The literature on 'race' and education in the UK already provides several examples of schools where an increase in ethnic diversity is seen (by some teachers) as leading to a decline in standards of discipline and achievement. Research by Cecile Wright (1986) and Máirtín Mac an Ghaill (1988), for example, highlights how far relations between students and teachers can deteriorate when existing stereotypes are left unchecked. In Forest, as in the other schools described in this research, the actions of the headteacher and a 'core' of committed and knowledgeable staff proved crucial to change within the school. It must be noted, however, that the role of minority students and their communities does not end with their numerical presence in the schools and their immediate localities.

African Caribbean and Asian students play key roles throughout the story of these schools. Their voices have influenced policy, challenged taken-for-granted assumptions and ensured that teachers retain a constructive sense of exploration. They remind all those involved (from headteacher through to part-time ancillary staff) that, because issues of 'race' and ethnicity are so complex and dynamic, we are always working towards better solutions: it is never time to stop thinking or questioning.

At Seacole, as the student population began to change, the teachers found themselves dealing with a range of issues they had not previously encountered. The present head of technology remembers that accusations of racism played a key part in forcing him to rethink his assumptions:

> The school I had been in before I came here was 100 per cent white and my knowledge of Asian culture in particular was nothing at all (. . .) So there was the problem of the Asians and the Black girls and not suddenly saying something or doing something which they perceived as being wrong or against them (. . .) [A group of girls] would walk into registration late, for instance, every single day. So you would shout at them, 'Go and sit down there, and don't disrupt the rest of the group when you come in'.
>
> *'Oh, you are being racist because we're black'.*
>
> So immediately from that it is, 'Well, am I?'
>
> So it immediately puts a doubt in and then you think, 'Am I approaching it wrong?' And just from that the whole thing starts to open up from there and you think, 'All right, I was approaching it correctly, but nevertheless I ought to start looking into it in a wider sense.'

For this teacher, the accusation was an important turning point, prompting him to become actively involved with colleagues who were trying to understand more about the range of issues thrown into relief by the school's diverse student population. Not all teachers respond so constructively. Some, for example, reject any suggestion that their own actions, or the customs of the school, might no longer be appropriate. These teachers frequently hold deficit views of minority students – seeing them as fundamentally different, and as a source of problems. A teacher at Garret Morgan recalls:

> During one breaktime [a teacher] looked out of the window and said, 'Look at all those kids over there, they never mix with anyone else.' And he was pointing at the Bangladeshi kids. And that made me aware of, maybe that was a reflection (as I felt there was in the

school) of a general *'us'* and *'them'* attitude. That something was needed to break that barrier down and develop a bit more awareness. (. . .) *They* were the problem because *'they* don't mix.' 'Why do they sit in class and talk in their own language? And in the dinner queue? And why do they play together all the time? What's their problem?'

Ironically, such negative expressions can themselves have positive outcomes. Here, spurring a colleague to action, in view of sentiments that he felt were racist and indicated how much had to be changed. The teacher continues:

Hearing how a member of staff – who was thought to have quite a bit of status and kudos in the school – and was coming out with these statements . . . I was quite flabbergasted because they were verging on racism, in my view at the time. I didn't say that to him but I thought, 'something is wrong here. Something has got to be done'.

Managing for change: establishing a core group

I deal in pockets of people. Because in the whole staff arena it is merely driving some people further into corners.
                              (The headteacher, Forest Comprehensive)

This study suggests that, as with many revolutions, when encouraging schools to rethink their approach to 'race' and ethnicity, it is necessary to have a small but committed 'core' group working for the changes. The precise composition of the group seems relatively unimportant; even in my small sample there was a range of different groupings and ways of working. The support of the headteacher, however, was a common element. This confirms previous work that highlights the strategic importance of headteachers (Ball 1987; Burgess 1983; 1988; Mortimore et al. 1988; Weindling and Early 1987). Without the support of the headteacher, any group that seeks to change the taken-for-granted assumptions of a teaching staff will face a difficult, if not impossible task. The headteacher's support may not be sufficient to guarantee progress, but it is probably a necessary precondition for major self-generated change.

In Garret Morgan Comprehensive a previous headteacher played a central role in setting up a small group who would begin to think through some of the issues raised by the increasing ethnic diversity of the student population. Similarly, in Seacole, one of the headteacher's first decisions on her appointment was to settle an ongoing dispute about the school's dress code – allowing Muslim students to attend school in non-western clothes (e.g. shalwar kameez) if they wished. Although this was only a small step, it clearly signalled that the school would now change in response to the ethnic diversity of its student population. Having made this strategic move, the head was then happy to take a less directive role, leaving a voluntary core group to lead discussion within the staff.

In Forest Comprehensive the situation was rather different, with some staff showing open hostility to the changing student population. The headteacher responded by making explicit her opposition to racism and by establishing precedents that overturned some school traditions (such as a ban on the use of community languages) which were incompatible with antiracism. Nevertheless, here too the head used a small group of staff as the first means of trying to change the culture of the school. Speaking three years after her arrival, the head is candid about the reasons for adopting this strategy:

> I have *tried* not to force people into corners, to give them opportu-
> nities to develop and change. In some cases I have been successful and
> in quite a lot I haven't. Now there is a view I suppose (I have talked
> to people about this) that somebody could have come in and operated
> very differently. I think it would have blown this place apart (. . .)
> There are people who would quite welcome this school getting [nega-
> tive and damaging] media attention;
> <head mimics an outraged voice> *'People out there ought to know
> what it is like in here.'*
> I have got some staff who would be happy to see this school close.

In Seacole the core group originally consisted of six members of staff who met regularly after school to discuss their own uncertainties and seek ways forward. A deputy headteacher and a colleague employed as part of the school's Section 11 provision came to take on the central roles in the group; this built partly on their existing commitment to the field, and on others' view of them as having a more advanced grasp of the issues. Similarly, in Morgan the core group again consisted of about half a dozen teachers: they came together in response to a staffroom notice inviting interested people to an open meeting. Both groups recognized a need for more information and support from beyond the confines of the school. In Morgan, the teachers began a long process of searching out relevant docu-ments from schools and local authorities that they knew had begun work on 'multicultural' and/or 'antiracist' education. At that point they were keen to see what kinds of structures and policies had been elaborated elsewhere. They hoped to find examples of good practice that they could adopt directly, as well as highlight areas that might need further development.

Seacole's core group invited outside speakers to address them on a range of issues. Sometimes this was a useful source of new ideas and, just as important, provided support when morale was low. The speakers confirmed that there was no magic formula to improvement in this field, and helped the group to become more self-critical. This was not always a comfortable process. Some of the earliest contacts with prominent members of the African Caribbean and Asian communities, for example, were more challenging than most anticipated. A member of the core group recalls:

> We were doing all we could to try and develop the race side of the school and suddenly we got all this flack. (. . .) a leader in the Black community, one that a lot of the Black girls looked towards (. . .) he came in to talk to the staff. But there was a lot of conflict at one stage because it seemed to us that he was forcing forward his views without taking into account how they could be actually put into practice. And that flared up for a little while and then it sort of died down again as we had more meetings and more discussions . . .

Handled badly, incidents like this might strike a death blow to developing work in the school. In Seacole, however, there were people who were prepared to engage with the arguments from both sides: recognizing that the staff needed to be supported and encouraged, but that community members might view their early work as piecemeal, or even patronizing. These teachers kept up a skilful balance of supporting the core group, while simultaneously maintaining the pressure to review their work and assumptions.

The teachers involved in the early core group discussions now recall the experience with pleasure, remembering meetings where people could genuinely share personal worries without the fear of ridicule or attack. When a new teacher joined the school, with experience of antiracist work outside education, she became a key resource for the core group. She helped to reassure members and encourage moves beyond a multicultural position (concerned with differences in culture and 'lifestyle') towards a more oppositional (antiracist) stance:

> I had been a youth worker for 10 years in the city centre (. . .) to come into a school which obviously was taking note of the importance of racism awareness was a relief to me because I had worked so long in the front line, working with black young people and Asian young people in the city. So I was very impressed by that. (. . .) in the early days it was learning how other cultures live and, you know, very much of that. But then that developed into racism awareness and this school has gone through the importance of knowing the cultures . . .

New members of staff were seen as a significant resource for the group. Even where they had no direct experience to draw on, fresh from teacher training their enthusiasm could be a valuable asset. More importantly perhaps, it was an opportunity for the group to help shape the views of people who might potentially be part of the school's future for many years to come. As one teacher remembers:

> I felt that I didn't contribute a lot because I had just started (it was when I was a probationer) and I said things every now and again but was still unsure. But I enjoyed it because I learned a lot from what they were saying.

Besides recruiting new members of staff, the core group in Seacole also began to 'headhunt' from the wider staff body. The initial small group of volunteers knew other teachers who shared some of their concerns but who, for a variety of reasons, did not feel that they had the time or confidence to join the group. By seeking out such colleagues, and encouraging them to attend meetings occasionally, the core was able to expand its influence among teaching staff. A similar pattern developed at Morgan, except that here the micro-political intent was much more deliberate. One of the first members of the core group at Morgan recalls a sense of unease at the absence of certain curriculum areas:

> It seemed to be weighted at that time towards the communications and the humanities. Scientists, I think, at that time were not represented. So we decided that perhaps it would benefit if we could get a volunteer. And it wasn't *a lot* of arm twisting, you know, a volunteer came in and made a very positive input.

At Garret Morgan the core group seem to have been much more aware of micro-political issues than at Seacole. The priority at Seacole was to establish a core, then slowly recruit members wherever they could. On a day-to-day basis the Section 11 teachers were especially influential. In contrast, the Morgan group were concerned to avoid any possibility of being marginalized within the school: they consciously set out to create a separate identity and to involve someone from each subject department. The head of Section 11 in Morgan states:

> We, as Section 11 people, have tried to operate within the school system so that the mainstream teachers take over systems, and organizing systems, like racist complaints and things like that. It is because we didn't want to feel that Section 11 postholders were the ones who dealt with anything that appeared to be racist.

In Morgan issues such as racist harassment are now dealt with by the 'Equal Opportunities Committee' – a body that has evolved out of the core group. The head of the 'EO' committee has been one of the strongest forces for change in the school and it was his decision to push for departmental representation from the start. This reflects both the length of his experience as a teacher (having seen several initiatives destroyed by departmental interests) and something of the particular character of the school, where individual departments have established more clearly defined identities than is the case at Seacole. He feels that the strategy has been partly successful; change has occurred as a result of issues and materials that volunteers have taken back to their specialist departments. Nevertheless, the struggle continues:

> We got responses from [some] areas saying, 'Well how can we have multicultural Maths?' And things like that. But fortunately, at the time, they have always had support within those departments for Bangladeshi students and therefore the teachers involved [in the core group] would take along material and show them; 'Look. It is possible'. And the Maths department were very amenable to that and they have taken it on board. Individual members of the science department have actually taken on board some of those points and are very co-operative. But what we are getting at is, philosophically I think, some departments (even the ones I mentioned) are still prepared to see that as just a lower priority than other priorities that are coming up (. . .) I think those are the areas where I have always felt there has been a tacit, 'Oh yes, we will give a nod of the head but we won't actually *do* a great deal'. Because basically, maybe politically, they don't really fully agree with the whole thing.

The core group at Garret Morgan, therefore, began working on the rest of the staff almost immediately; recruiting 'volunteers' from each area who would relate the group's work to separate departments and act as a conduit for subject specific materials and advice. As the quotation above shows, this is a strategy that continues to the present. In Seacole, however, moves to influence the staff beyond the core were rather more measured. They illustrate several important points about the micro-politics of 'race' and ethnicity in schools, in particular, questions concerning the pace of change and teachers' fear of the accusation 'racist!' These issues are examined in detail in the next chapter.

Conclusions

In this chapter I have begun to explore the processes of antiracist change in secondary schools. The analysis reflects a micro-political concern with the daily realities of school policy-making and practice. In particular, it is acknowledged that schools are frequently experienced as 'arenas of struggle' (Ball 1987: 19) where conflict and a diversity of expectations and goals is a normal state of affairs.

Building on the experiences of three schools, with very different histories and student populations, I have noted that certain common features are visible. All three schools, for example, began work on antiracism as a result of changes in the student population. Most important, however, in all three schools antiracist change has been led by a small and committed 'core' group. These have adopted a range of working styles; Seacole built up slowly, while Morgan attempted systematically to involve subject departments from an early stage. All three core groups benefited from the clear support of the headteacher and senior management team. This is a continuing theme in the following chapter, where I examine moves to involve the whole school in antiracist change, and consider the continuing struggle to sustain antiracism as a genuine part of educational practice in the schools.

six

Antiracism and the whole school

> It has become ever more evident to us that anti-racism in symbolic gestures is meaningless and can clearly reinforce racism. If the school does not involve the total community, teachers, ancillary staff, students and parents, both black and white, in the efforts to tackle racism in school, the whole exercise will end in failure.
>
> The Burnage report (Macdonald et al. 1989: 347)

The inquiry into the murder of an Asian schoolboy in Burnage High School in Manchester highlighted the many practical problems of enacting genuine antiracist change; change that challenges commonsense racism in schools, without being tied to dogma that reify the views of certain groups while rejecting the involvement of others (see Chapter 4). One of the most important messages to come from the Burnage report is that ways must be found actively to engage the whole school community in the development of antiracist practice. The inquiry team also highlight the need for careful reflection on practice and consideration of others' viewpoints:

> we have been unable to find any theoretical ready-made model for success. Schools and local authorities need to proceed by an element of trial and error and by listening and talking.
>
> (Macdonald et al. 1989: 403)

In this chapter I consider teachers' experiences as they attempted to build whole-school commitment to antiracism. This includes a discussion of the uncertainty, even fear, that some experience when facing calls for antiracist change. Among the issues I address are the consequences of the pace of change and the style of challenge in Seacole. Of critical importance are a range of strategies by which the core group worked to help colleagues deal with the threat of being accused of racism by students.

The second part of the chapter describes some of the ways that Seacole and Morgan have attempted to routinize antiracism as an essential part of educational practice. This includes a discussion of policy-making and micropolitics in Seacole, and examines the moves that the core groups are taking to sustain and protect antiracism from wider changes in education policy.

Addressing the whole school

Beyond confrontation: the pace of change/the style of challenge

> Sometimes, when you are passionate about something, you can be
> very hard on any 'mistake' that somebody might make, and use your
> antagonism to what they are saying or what they are doing in a way
> that can be very hurtful and may, even, drive them into the other way
> of thinking.
>
> (Headteacher at Mary Seacole Comprehensive)

I have noted how the head at Seacole played a less direct role during the
early development of the core group. By settling a long-running dispute
about Muslim young women and school uniform requirements, the head
signalled her support for change that took account of the school's ethnic
diversity. This made space for the core group to develop its work. A
deputy headteacher played a central role in the group, while the head
stood outside their deliberations. As the group's confidence became greater,
so they began to take their views to a wider audience within the school;
organizing inservice education and training (INSET) events, making explicit statements about school policy and challenging colleagues whose
work failed to meet their expectations. It is at this point that the head
identifies her next key involvement in the developments at Seacole, moving
with other senior colleagues to try to temper what they saw as a potentially damaging development:

> In the early days there was a little bit of that sort of *harder* attitude;
> raised by people who were very committed and very keen but, because
> of this deep-seated belief that was within them, were a little bit un-
> willing to allow other people to make a mistake and think through
> what the mistake was (. . .) it was almost that the pendulum had
> gone rather a long way the other way, and now it has come back
> to . . . <she pauses> Not a more *comfortable* level, that is the wrong
> word, but a more *positive* level in knowing what we are about.

INSET events provided some of the clearest signs of the conflict generated
by approaches that stressed confrontation as a primary means of achieving
change. This approach was frequently modelled by outsiders to the school
(whether from other sections of the educational world or from various
community groups) and taken up by members of the core group – as one
of them recalls:

> In the inservice programmes we used to have people from community,
> we used to have, you know, this philosophy or this approach was to

be confrontational. And people, I think, felt uncomfortable with that approach; 'You are a racist', 'You are this'. And it tends to draw people apart. The people who were doing the inservice courses had this attitude, including us – I think that was the thing in those days, when they were a newly-discovered antiracist approach.

It is important to recognize that the 'newly-discovered antiracist approach' was (and still is) developing and changing all the time. The teachers in Seacole, like colleagues elsewhere in the UK (see Mirza 1992: 66–9) were caught up in debates that repeatedly emphasized the limitations of multiculturalism. In contrast, antiracism was defined in language that was explicitly oppositional (see Brandt 1986: 121; Gillborn 1990: 157). In such circumstances, many teachers who were centrally involved in the debates felt required to demonstrate their dedication to the issue by openly attacking anything that might be construed as racism among their colleagues. Sometimes this could extend to a position that interpreted any form of '*compromise*' as a '*sell out*', a negation of their real duty as antiracists. In this context 'compromise' becomes a dangerous term. It can suggest sacrificing one's ideals for the sake of expediency (a 'soft' or halfhearted approach); and yet, as the Burnage report emphasizes, it is essential that antiracism recognize and work within the 'complex reality of human relations' (Macdonald et al. 1989: 347). Working through this dilemma in practice is not easy.

In Seacole there seems to have been a gradual shift among the core group that reflected several factors – some managed, others more haphazard. The headteacher became more directly involved for a time, stressing the need to keep other staff involved in the debates and to avoid polarizing opinion. As the core group became more confident of their own positions and their understanding of the issues, so they were able to make greater inroads into local groups and community organizations. This acted as a basis for wider discussions and the presentation of a broader range of views within the school. At the same time, a key early member of the core group secured advancement to an LEA post in another part of the country. While the group still acknowledges her major contribution to the developments in Seacole, there is a sense in which her departure allowed them to reconsider 'tactics' without being accused of going soft on racism.

Two other factors seem also to have been important; the work of a teacher of minority ethnic background, and a growing sense of uncertainty, even fear, among the wider staff group.

One of the most influential members of the Seacole teaching staff is a woman whom many colleagues originally identified simply in terms of her 'Asian' background. She was seen as a minority teacher, employed on a Section 11 contract, with special expertise in 'race' issues – a position that is forced on many black and Asian teachers (Ranger 1988). In dealing with racist views among some colleagues, this teacher argues that simple confrontation is unlikely to succeed. She adopts an approach that challenges stereotypes and racialized assumptions, but within a relationship where she first builds links as a fellow teacher; 'you make the person secure and comfortable':

> My own personal views are that you don't change people by criticizing them in the beginning. You need to make them think otherwise. And then they come back to you and say, 'Oh right, this is how we do it. Oh gosh, when I first came how naive I was'. For example, I have read about them – in many many magazines as well – but I never realised these things would happen in real life: for example, they say, 'I would dread to think of going to [an Asian student's] home, but I wouldn't mind coming into yours.' They would say that this person is unhygienic and I am different. Because the more you are Western the more acceptable you are. And in one way it is an insult, but at that moment I wouldn't say anything. And I would work with that member of staff individually and make her realise (. . .) I used to support her in lessons and then say things like, 'What does Seacole represent?' 'What are your views about the Asian pupils in Seacole School?' 'Do you think everybody's the same?' 'Do you think we all belong to the same groups?' And she didn't know. She just thought '*Asian*' meant everything is the same – and everyone knows it isn't.

This is a time-consuming and extremely demanding strategy. It would be unrealistic to expect this approach to work in all cases; worse still it would be racist to lay the responsibility for antiracism at the feet of ethnic minority teachers – such a position would absolve white teachers of responsibility while further marginalizing minority teachers and channelling them towards narrowly (and racially) defined careers. Although the strategy sometimes worked (for this individual), of most importance in Seacole was the fact that one of the few black or Asian teachers on the staff was arguing for (and modelling) approaches that did not require open warfare all the time and dealt with non-essentialized notions of ethnic identity.

In retrospect this seems to have been an important factor in helping the core group, and others in the school, to find a balance that maintains the pressure to be reflective about current assumptions and practices – a critical approach – without shading into hostilities that merely reproduce (and even amplify) existing conflicts: a perspective that, in the head's words, is '*positive*' without being '*comfortable*'. This has not been achieved without pain. A significant factor was the core group's recognition that their work with colleagues ought to enable, rather than paralyse, them.

'Racist!': dealing with a shift in power

[Symbolic, moral and doctrinaire antiracism] has reinforced the guilt of many well meaning whites and paralysed them when any issue of race arises . . . It has taught others to bury their racism without in any way changing their attitude. It has created resentment and anger and topped free discussion.

(Macdonald et al. 1989: 348)

I have noted several factors that worked towards a shift of emphasis within Seacole Comprehensive; from an approach that sometimes stressed aggressive and essentialist opposition to a more reflective and enabling form of dialogue. A final influence in this area was the recognition, among the core group, that some colleagues seemed to have hit a stage where they had little or no confidence in their ability to behave in ways that were not, by some definition, racist. Undoubtedly this partly reflected the commitment and eloquence of the core group: elsewhere I have examined how the 'converted' in any educational initiative can (often unwittingly) intimidate colleagues who are not so versed in the new discourses (Gillborn 1994). However, the teachers' uncertainty also reflected genuine doubt about what did and did not constitute fair and non-racialized views and behaviour. A deputy headteacher recalls:

When we began to become more aware I think people felt threatened. I think people possibly felt that they had to think about everything that they said and did, and that it would be misinterpreted or written down and that they would be accused of being racist. But I think we have moved a long way since then.

In making sense of this period in the school's history it is necessary to recognize the importance of several interrelated issues – some of which surface in this quotation.

First, there is the uncertainty caused by a new set of perspectives that challenge the legitimacy of previous assumptions and practices – *'they had to think about everything that they said and did'*. Second, there are clear consequences here for power and authority within the school. The quotation only hints at these issues (the problem of misinterpretation; the threat of accusation) but they are central to the effects of antiracist developments. In this context a key issue is that there is a change in the existing power structure – *'people felt threatened'*. This concern frequently surfaces as 'jokes' or staffroom 'banter', for example, in comments such as 'Watch out, your name'll be taken down' whenever someone *mentions* 'race', or tells a sexist joke. Members of the core group usually interpret such comments as a form of opposition – ridiculing the point of their work and presenting them as overzealous beginners whose concerns are not worth taking seriously. Undoubtedly, this is the point of some staffroom 'humour' (cf. Hargreaves 1981), but there is also the possibility of humour operating in more complex ways (cf. Dubberley 1988; Fox 1990; Goffman 1959). Where senior management has made its support for antiracism public, for example, such 'jokes' may be one of the few ways in which some teachers can seek public reassurance that they are not the only ones who feel uncertain or threatened. Comments about surveillance ('Look out, that'll go in the book') seem particularly common, and highlight the threat that many teachers experience when they are held accountable for assumptions and actions that they may never have questioned previously.

It is understandable that white teachers feel threatened by these changes; not only are their existing assumptions and practices being challenged by colleagues, but a new 'weapon' is handed to the students. Once Seacole began to signal that it was prepared to take racism seriously, the students recognized that this offered those of minority background a new strategy in relations with both peers and teachers. A teacher who has worked in the school for twenty years reflects on the change:

> You will get the odd [student] now, because I feel we have come some way, who will try it; 'You are picking on me because I am black' (. . .) I don't think that ever happened before. I think that is one of the things that has come out of being far more aware. Now I might be wrong but I think so. I think in the old days they maybe resented it and there was probably a lot more of it [racism], but I think now, because we have taught them to question and because we have said 'You don't have to accept it and you shouldn't accept it', some will use it.[1]

There was, therefore, a genuine shift in power relations: students could now use the term 'racist' as a powerful accusation – one that the school was committing itself to opposing, and that many white teachers were unsure of. In these circumstances it is easy, in the words of the Burnage inquiry, for 'many well meaning whites' to become 'paralysed'.

Faced with such accusations some teachers (and even whole schools) adopt short-term responses that simply dismiss the students' viewpoint as either mistaken, or malicious[2] (for an example see the school described in Gillborn 1990: 42–3). That kind of response makes a mockery of attempts to take racism seriously; it argues that teachers cannot be implicated in racism simply because of who/what they are. It is a hypocritical position that students recognize immediately. A basic requirement of successful staff–student relationships is acceptance that the school's expectations of students should be reflected in its expectations of staff (see Gillborn et al. 1993). Any genuine attempt to challenge racism in schools must, therefore, involve the views and actions of staff as well as students.

In Seacole the key to overcoming staff fears and uncertainty lay in several areas, not least the use of INSET to support all teachers' growing awareness of 'race' and ethnicity. This instilled greater confidence among staff and continues to play an important role in the school's antiracist work (more on this below). At one level, however, the teachers' response had less to do with 'race', than with questions of reflective teaching (Schön 1983) – a principle of any good teacher's practice – the ability to stand back and question what one is doing. A teacher in Seacole notes:

> [You] begin to challenge yourself and say, 'Look. Hey, come on a minute. This is a behavioural problem with this child. This isn't because she is black, or because she is Asian, or because she is white, or because she is Vietnamese, or whatever. This is a girl being naughty – deal with her.'

The vital corollary to this is that the teacher must not only have the confidence to reassure her/himself that this or that action is fair, they must also be able to recognize actions that cannot be justified. For example, when a teacher is controlling a student because of their perceived 'attitude', or singling out a 'ringleader', they must be able to question the evidence upon which such judgements are made; are they merely reflecting wider stereotypes? In Seacole, the extensive and planned use of inservice training helps to build the confidence and knowledge necessary to help teachers make such decisions.

Staff development and training

Inservice education and training played an important role in the development of the core group in Mary Seacole Comprehensive. Therefore, once they began to address staff more widely within the school, the core assigned INSET a central role. The support of the headteacher and senior management team has been critical in establishing a programme of activities that, over a sustained period, established antiracism as a key part of the school's agenda – without ever presenting it as something that could or should be adopted in a piecemeal or unthinking way. In Seacole the INSET simultaneously works on two main focuses: at once looking *outside* the school, engaging with local communities, while also examining practical concerns and issues *within* the school, especially at the classroom level.

The core group's own experience of using outside speakers persuaded them of the need for care in organizing early INSET for the whole school. In starting to break down their colleagues' ignorance and suspicion of some local communities, the core wanted to avoid the sense of disappointment they had felt when outside speakers 'gave them flack' without engaging with the work they were doing (see the previous chapter). The Section 11 staff, who routinely work with different sections of local minority communities, proved especially valuable in helping to identify people who could constructively address issues of which the whole staff needed to be aware. As one member of the core group recalls, the Section 11 teachers were able to 'sus out who would be a useful person, who would understand where we are coming from'.

In Garret Morgan School also, the core group gave a central role to INSET that included members of local minority communities. Here too, the emphasis was on breaking down preconceptions; helping the staff to confront their assumptions in a situation that was challenging but not destructively so. For example, I asked the leading member of the Morgan core group whether there had been any particular moments when things really seemed to be changing in the school? In reply he singled out an INSET event that, in his eyes, began to break down many teachers' racist assumptions and set a positive tone for future work:

> We had a conference organized by a number of staff who felt, like me, that we should do something as a whole staff body. And we had a whole day actually, one of these INSET [training] days, looking at the issues. It raised lots of things because obviously it confronted some staff with their own prejudices – but I felt that had to be done at sometime, we couldn't pussyfoot around all the time – to get things done you have to, you know. So it worked at that level, but it also *informed*; it also cleared up misconceptions. And also, I think very valuable, it allowed many teachers who had no experience of meeting, or working with, or talking to Bangladeshi adults – Asian adults – to talk to them on a one-to-one in informal sessions, which I felt was quite vital.

In this way the core groups, in both Seacole and Morgan, brought members of local minority communities inside the schools. This work challenged essentialist views, gave minority communities a voice they had not previously enjoyed and began to break down the fears that some teachers felt.

Where minority groups are seen largely in terms of *difference* (different language, different religion, different dress, etc.) it is easy for teachers to assume a position that is at best patronizing, at worst disparaging and crudely racist; many simply do not know what to expect. By bringing a community perspective into the school, and challenging staff perspectives based on difference, the core groups began a process which first, actively involved minority groups, and second, helped teachers to realize some powerful common ground between themselves and people of minority ethnic background.

At the same time staff were encouraged to apply new perspectives to their routine work; linking the wider issues of ethnic diversity in society to their specific experiences and concerns as classroom teachers. This work included sessions on a range of curriculum materials that could be used to address antiracist issues, also sessions that sought to challenge teacher stereotypes about certain groups of students; such as 'boisterous' African Caribbean students or 'shy'/unambitious Asian young women (cf. Brah 1992b).

Antiracist INSET is now an established part of life in Seacole, where a rolling programme takes in all members of staff. Originally this programme focused on teachers with special pastoral responsibilities. Subsequently sessions for non-pastoral staff, including departmental heads and senior management, followed a similar pattern. Current inservice work retains the early dual focus; looking beyond the school (to research literature, local communities, etc.) as well as highlighting immediate and practical concerns and strategies:

> [We do] all kinds of things. Looking at literature; looking at examples; talking things through; talking about how to handle situations; talking about questions that might come up from the pupils; talking about how to deal with any racism that arises within [teaching] groups. One of the things that we have stated categorically is that it must be challenged, it should *never* be ignored because it is then condoned. It must be challenged but not necessarily challenged aggressively, but challenged so that they recognize what it is they have done and also so that the victim knows that it has been dealt with.

As a teacher who recently joined the school notes, a particular concern is to induct new members of staff into Seacole's antiracist assumptions and practices:

> We have an INSET on antiracism for the new staff coming in, so they know how to handle situations as they occur. If people are calling each other names; how to cope and what to do about it, what the school procedure is really. Because you can have your own individual views but whatever they are you have got to stick to the school policy about these things. I think that is important.

In fact, new members of staff have played a key role in the developments at Seacole. As the antiracist changes were being pioneered in the school, newcomers added fresh perspectives and drive to the core group. Now they offer a way of consolidating developments; ensuring that antiracism continues to draw widespread support.

It has been argued, from a managerialist/business school perspective, that as successive reforms increase headteachers' responsibilities, they should give up certain traditional parts of their job, such as the appointment of 'junior staff' (Torrington and Weightman 1989: 144). Such a move fails to appreciate the micro-political significance of staff appointments. In maintaining a school's commitment to antiracism, new appointments are critical; offering new sources of support and extending the range of experience within the staff body. This is clearly reflected in Seacole where, besides the antiracist induction programme for all new staff, all communications with prospective teachers emphasize antiracism as an integral part of the school's philosophy and practice. A newly adopted 'Antiracist Multicultural Policy' states the school's position as follows:

Appointments and Promotions

Seacole School will:

Ensure that applicants for posts in the school are informed of the school's antiracist policy and that those appointed support it.

Encourage a policy which encourages the appointment of both teaching and non-teaching staff from a range of cultural backgrounds at all levels in the school.

Encourage the view that the appointment and promotion of staff should take into consideration a teacher's commitment to antiracism as well as their technical expertise.

Develop a policy which encourages the promotion to positions of responsibility within the school of staff from a range of cultural backgrounds.

Commitments such as these are both a reflection of the progress made to date, and part of the attempt to sustain and extend antiracism in the school. Indeed, the development of Seacole's formal antiracist policy adds a further dimension to our understanding of the dynamics of change in the school.

Sustaining progress

Policies and practice

For some teachers the 1980s were a decade dominated by policy. They were involved in the creation, implementation and/or the subversion of a whole range of policy initiatives – some were generated at the school level, others originated outside the school, from national Government, local authorities, business and training interests. As the decade progressed, schools were increasingly required to have written policies in a range of fields, especially once national reforms got underway. As both national and local government took greater interest in the daily running of schools, teachers could find themselves working (usually in what passed as their 'free time') on policies for anything from lunchtime supervision through to the entire curricular structure of the school.

The link between policy and reality is often patchy, sometimes non-existent. Some school policies serve a primarily cosmetic function; existing only because they are required (by central and/or local government) or as a politically expedient symbol of the school's awareness of particular issues. It is in this respect that many local authorities developed 'multicultural' and/or 'antiracist' policies during the 1980s (see Troyna 1993a: ch. 1; Troyna and Williams 1986).

The gap between LEA rhetoric and school practice can be considerable. Even when the local authority provides a lead, and a committed group of teachers take responsibility for drafting a school policy, further progress can be frustrated by the larger body of teachers. Barry Troyna has described one such case ('Outskirts' Community College) where a modest three-point antiracist policy met with widespread suspicion and opposition which threatened to deny even the most basic statement of principles. A minimal statement was eventually adopted, but only after a member of the senior management took a strong lead because of a series of violent incidents between students (Troyna 1988b).

In this context it is especially useful to examine the development of an antiracist policy at Seacole Comprehensive. The account shows that the means by which a policy is created can play a crucial role in its acceptance by staff and students. Indeed, the formulation of the school's policy on antiracist education was a critical part of the overall process of antiracist change in Seacole. Hence, policy formation can be an integral part of the process of change, not merely an empty exercise by which yet another document is produced to be debated, adopted and ultimately forgotten by the majority of teachers.

Creating a meaningful antiracist policy

[The group working on the policy] has been running for three years. It has been taking that long. But so be it, if that is how long it takes to get something done properly then that is what you do.
(Head of Year in Seacole Comprehensive)

In Seacole the core group had already begun antiracist INSET activities across the school when they decided to work on the creation of a formal policy. Indeed, the impetus for this decision arose from their feeling that staff wanted more concrete guidance about how the antiracist work they were doing fitted together across the school. In particular, certain flashpoints, such as accusations of staff racism and name-calling among students, operated to heighten teachers' awareness that they would benefit from clear statements of principle and practice. One of the core group states:

> The whole staff felt the need that there should be a written policy. At inservice events it had been raised quite often and I think certain crises, like name-calling, had all started to happen and we thought it was time now that every staff member should know what exactly is our stand on different issues. It was as a result of that need that we brought it forward.

The policy began life, therefore, in response to a general recognition that an explicit framework on antiracism was needed. Even those staff who were not directly involved in promoting antiracist initiatives in Seacole recognized the virtue of some form of whole-school policy; unlike the case at 'Outskirts' College (Troyna 1988b), the policy could not be seen simply as the imposition of a minority of 'do-gooders' or 'loony lefties' (Klein 1993: 104).

The first moves towards creating a formal policy were taken by a group that included the original core, plus the entire Section 11 staff, all senior management and other teacher volunteers. This group met to decide certain ground rules, such as what kind of areas the policy should cover and how basic questions of terminology might be solved. The official title of the document, for example, became the 'Antiracist Multicultural Policy'; this was chosen to signify that while aspects of *cultural* diversity are essential, the need to combat *racism* is the most pressing goal – one that cannot be sidestepped despite scare stories in the national media. As the headteacher explains:

> That word can be an emotive word, *'racism'*. But I think to back off it doesn't say what we are about, that is being dishonest. And at the end of the day that is what you have got to stand by. We are *anti*-racist. (. . .) 'Anti' sounds a rather cold word in some ways [but this] is a positive 'anti' – it is *pro* antiracism.

Once the scope of the document had been decided, the headteacher again withdrew from personal involvement in the group, leaving the Section 11 staff to take the lead. Specific writing tasks were delegated to small groups, ensuring that each department was asked to contribute in some way: 'we broke off into groups where two people would work on one area, like home and community. One group would work on discipline, things like that.' A social science teacher who worked on successive drafts of the policy describes the experience as 'very positive'. She continues, 'I think everyone who was involved got involved because they had a belief in the policy. They all had a variety of experiences and perceptions to put in, so it was very positive'.

A first draft was presented to the whole staff (again using statutory INSET time) and, from that, new members were recruited to the working party, to help refine the document. Subject departments were kept informed of progress and fed back any observations or queries. In this way all staff knew how the document was shaping up and they had a chance to argue specific points as the various drafts were being refined.

In Seacole, therefore, consultation between the policy working group and the wider staff took many forms; it was not limited to fairly formal presentations of an entire document. Although the majority of Seacole teachers did not feel closely involved in the production of the policy document, they each knew of its development and recognized its major features. When a second full draft was presented to the whole staff, given the changes that were already taking place in the school and the long process of discussion, the document was seen as an important, but unspectacular, piece in the wider jigsaw puzzle. This can be judged from the view of a science teacher who joined the school as the document was being written:

> I really can't remember too much about it, so it can't have been a tremendous event. But I think the staff here, on the whole, are fairly positive (...) I can't imagine there being any antagonism. It would have been taken on board fairly positively and probably not a lot of questioning really. And I think a lot of the practice was already there.

As a special needs teacher in Seacole notes, the full extent of the changes in the school is not always appreciated by the staff, whose capacity to challenge their own, and others', racist assumptions has grown with the antiracist developments:

> I think you become quite blasé about it within your own school and it is only when you go out of that environment that you realize perhaps how far you have come – or how stale you have become. You tend to think this is what it is like everywhere, and you think everyone is moving forward. Then you realize that no, that is not the case at all. Even within your own friends you realize. I feel that racism is becoming less but I think that is because I am cocooned in this environment. And it is only when friends come out with racist comments that I can't believe it and I think we haven't come forward, we haven't made any progress, there are still these prejudices.

Seacole's formal antiracist policy runs to nine (A4 sized) sides of text. The policy is a thorough and wide-ranging document. It commits the school to practices and philosophical positions that clearly reflect a determination to recognize and oppose racism, while addressing cultural diversity in as positive and rigorous a way as possible. In addition to the section on appointments and promotions (already quoted above), for example, the document reviews the need for increased awareness and training across the school (especially for promoted staff); lays down guidelines for the pastoral and academic curricula; includes sections on student and community consultation; and commits the school to continual monitoring of examinations, assessments and testing for any indication of bias – premised on the view that, as the policy states, selection procedures 'can be discriminatory in practice, whatever their intention'.

Student and community involvement

The teachers involved in writing the draft policy feel that their colleagues' acceptance of the final document is a testament to the success of INSET and the continual review of antiracist issues among staff. These factors were crucial, but there is an additional element that core group members do not always give full credit. That element is the students. Although the core group are proud of their efforts to 'consult' the students, teachers who were not directly involved in the policy-writing, when asked to describe the changes in Seacole, tend to assign greater importance to the students. They saw and heard the students' enthusiasm and recognized that the school was *already* changing in line with the spirit of the policy.

The teachers working on the draft policy used some of their time in the classroom to sound students out about their views and expectations regarding key issues. This included work with their form groups and occasionally in lesson time. This rather *ad hoc* process confirmed that students were interested in the issues and had things to say. As one teacher recalls:

> They weren't just dismissive of it, they weren't saying, 'Oh, what do we want to know that for?' It was all, 'That's good. That's interesting. We should have that.' And they also had their own ideas.

Seacole runs a student council to facilitate student involvement on certain issues. Generally the students take a rather jaundiced view of this body; 'I'm on that, right. We talk about things but it's still up to [the headteacher] in the end.' In relation to the antiracist policy, however, the student council did play a significant role by encouraging wider distribution of the draft document.

Building on the *ad hoc* student involvement, and following the meeting of all staff to discuss the first version, a copy of the draft document was presented to the student council for their views. The council requested that a copy be posted in every form room. The head agreed and more formalized means of student feedback were organized. First, the form tutor and/or a member of the core group held a discussion with each form, talking them through the document and relating responses to the working party that was redrafting the policy. Second, any student (individually or as part of a group) could send written comments to the head of Section 11 (a friendly and well-liked teacher) who was co-ordinating the policy working group. The comments were overwhelmingly constructive, indicated strong support for antiracism among students, and frequently highlighted the complexity of defining racism in certain school contexts: Figure 6.1 presents a representative sample of the student responses.[3]

Many teachers were impressed by the students' enthusiasm for the draft policy and the seriousness with which they approached it.[4] It was noticeable that while several students gave strong support to the policy, and even called for harsher penalties against racism, they also sought to modify parts which they felt applied blanket condemnation to issues that had to be seen within their particular context. A concern with the pronunciation of names and the composition of friendship groups was particularly strong. In view of these points the wording of particular sections of the draft was reconsidered. Perhaps more important, however, the students' responses (both in writing and in their conversations with teachers and friends) raised the profile of antiracism within the school still further and helped to convince all teachers that the document was something the school needed and could respond to positively. The very fact of the students' enthusiasm made it difficult for teachers to argue that the policy might simply 'stir up trouble' – a common suspicion when antiracist change is proposed.

The students' enthusiasm for the policy did not stop at the school gate. Many told their parents about the debates and, in the case of some South Asian and African Caribbean students, quizzed peers and youth workers in community organizations about what (if anything) was happening elsewhere in the city. This provided an informal means by which groups outside Seacole came to hear of the school's work. More formally, several ethnic minority community groups played an *indirect* role in the development of the antiracist policy; most notably through their contributions to inservice events for both core members and the wider staff group. Such contributions varied in length, style and content but they undoubtedly had a key influence on the way the policy developed.

The *direct* influence of community groups was less marked. Copies of the draft were sent to several local organizations, including those that had been involved in INSET provision. No formal responses were received, suggesting perhaps that the groups did not have the mechanisms by which school-based developments could be subject to full scrutiny. However, informal follow up, often using personal contacts, suggested that no one reading the document identified any significant omissions or other problems.

Copies of the draft were also made available at open evenings and other school events for parents of students (and prospective students) to take away and read: with a covering note encouraging them to contact the school if they wished to discuss any points about the policy. A statement

We thought of how we felt the school should respond to racist behaviour. All our ideas are included in the policy's list of procedures. We feel that sometimes parents do not always take such matters seriously enough, even when they are informed by letter.

We were a little concerned about the procedure on 'exclusive groupings'. We do not feel that friendship groups should be manipulated to produce an ethnic 'balance'; friends should be left to sort things out for themselves. However in a work situation, we are happy to mix freely and work with students from all backgrounds. Basically we didn't like the idea of someone telling us who our friends should be.

Teachers should be having discussions with pupils and how they feel, because pupils have been experienced about racism.

We agree with all that is said.

---

1 Victim support group.
2 Recording of racism more than 3 times out of school.
3 Monitors.
4 Parents meeting about racism.
5 Everybody should be informed more clearly about the A-R policy.

Just because we sit in groups does not mean we do not mix especially mix in PE + Drama.

Increase teachers' awareness - Student contribution to teachers' inset.
Who will counsel the students? - Perhaps other victims could be used.
Exclusive groupings would depend on attitudes and reasons for groupings. If disruptive then change. If threatening then change.
General - will the school carry out the policy?

If a group do not wish another to join them they should be told in front of everyone that they are being racist. The group should be split up and the 'unwanted' girl allowed to choose where she wishes to go.

The mispronunciation of names still occurs but it shouldn't be taken that seriously as it is a matter of learning how to say the names correctly.
Friendly jokes between friends in a group maybe taken as a joke within the group, but to outsiders it seems a serious offence.
Serious racist attacks should be dealt with a lot more severely by the teachers.

In the library there are loads of books written in English well I think there should be more written in Urdu or Punjabi...

Although we understand the reasoning of the anti-racist policy in Seacole, we feel that it is not being carried out to its full potential. (...) it states that Seacole School will not accept any form of racist behaviour. We feel that this is not true. Many girls every day in Seacole suffer racism in some form. We ourselves have been victims of racism in the five years of our educative lives at Seacole. (...) Although we are not contradicting the brochure, we are stating our feelings towards its contents. We also feel that the brochure will give people a 'chip on their shoulder' that everyone is being racist towards them.

Catalogue every racist incident. If perpetrator is same three times, automatic suspension.

---

1 Taking off [mimicking] other people's accents is a form of racism.
2 Mispronunciation of names only when deliberate or can't be bothered to try and learn the name.

Figure 6.1 Student responses to a draft antiracist policy

in the school brochure (circulated to all parents) does not go into the detail possible in the full document but retains the emphasis on antiracism and highlights the importance of this as a central aspect in the life of the school.

Parents have been generally supportive of the developments in Seacole, which is known throughout the city as a multi-ethnic school. Members of the core group explain the parents' support with reference to the general atmosphere of the school, as a place where reality lives up to the rhetoric of equality of esteem and treatment for all people. They highlight the fact that because antiracism is given such a high profile, crudely racist parents are unlikely to send their children to the school. Other parents are more open to persuasion and the students' commitment to the school and its stance on antiracism may be powerful factors. Occasionally there are problems. During the Gulf War, for example, two white families removed their children from the school, one for openly racist motives. Generally, however, the staff are skilled at explaining the school's work in ways that break down stereotypes about 'loony left' campaigns (cf. Troyna and Carrington 1990).

In both Seacole and Garret Morgan schools, white parents have shown support for the antiracist developments. In a research project of this size it was impossible for me to gather data from a suitable sample of parents. Consequently, I can only hypothesize about further reasons why these schools have managed to take white parents along with them, rather than alienate them. A clue may lie in the way that the schools' antiracism is part of a wider commitment to justice and to the need to value and respect all the people (students, teachers, and others) who make up the school community. Antiracism in these schools has not been 'tagged on' separately as an afterthought or as a doctrinaire position. Antiracism in the schools has developed as a way of being critical and self-critical while retaining a basic commitment to care for, and work with, each other. In the following chapter I explore this in more detail. Before leaving policy development behind, however, it is necessary to note the steps that members of the core groups are taking to protect antiracism and retain its critical edge in their schools.

Protecting the gains: staying critical

Having created a policy, and made real progress towards changing the whole school, it is essential that teachers monitor the implementation of the policy and look for ways in which changing circumstances may produce new demands and problems. This is especially important in the current climate of rapid externally driven change. Even in schools like Seacole and Morgan, where antiracist developments have been prominent, it is easy for teachers to switch their attention to a new aspect of the school's development or to become obsessed with short-term pressures and deadlines, not recognizing the consequences for antiracism and equality. As a teacher in Seacole notes:

> I think at this school we tend to go in cycles. We have a push and everybody seems to be aware and then they think that is that, we have done that. And then you realize that instead of going forward you have suddenly gone backwards and you are not tackling some of the problems.

In this context it is vital that members of the core group retain an active concern with antiracism. One important way in which both Seacole and Morgan have begun to routinize their concern for antiracism is through self-monitoring exercises.

The antiracist policy in Seacole requires a member of the senior management team to produce an annual report that gives a statistical picture (by students' ethnic origin) of option choices, composition of classes that have been set by ability, and performance in both internal and external examinations. The policy states:

> We recognise that procedures such as examinations, assessments and grouping of students can be discriminatory in practice, whatever their intention. (. . .) Any imbalance should be carefully investigated to look for and to try and eliminate under-achievement.

The monitoring report in Seacole draws attention to any significant discrepancies between students' representation in the figures and the predicted level based on their numbers in the school population. Any causes for concern are discussed with staff in the relevant departments or pastoral sections. These issues are then given particular attention in the following academic year. Monitoring in Garret Morgan is not as advanced as Seacole, but the core group have begun work on the school's test results and are pushing for further measures. Monitoring patterns of selection and achievement is a valuable development that reflects current best practice in this field; the Commission for Racial Equality, for example, has advocated self-monitoring to help identify injustices in school admissions and academic selection practices (CRE 1992b and c).

Members of the core groups, in both Seacole and Morgan schools, are proud of their achievements but fearful for the future. It is useful to note that in both schools the core groups continue to act as the antiracist conscience of the school – examining each new development from the perspective of cultural diversity and 'racial' inequalities. A member of the Morgan core states:

I think the danger is being satisfied; 'Yes, we've got a policy, good that's it'. And I think the important thing, the real concern is where do we move on to? How do we develop and grow? I haven't got the answers to that. I think that is what we need to do. (. . .) Unless it has a high profile, unless you've got a group of people who are actually going to say, 'Right. It *is* important. It's got to be. It's cross-curricular. It's *life*: and we have got to keep it in focus, in everybody's attention'. It can so easily be pushed in a cupboard and forgotten. And that's what I am *very* concerned about.

In Seacole added weight has been given to the core group deliberations by the headteacher's decision to ensure that procedures for monitoring the effects of the antiracist policy are written into the role of the senior management. Despite significant strides towards an antiracist future in these schools, however, the core groups retain a crucial role in sustaining progress and resisting the 'logic' of external changes that are often contrary to the schools' stated commitments. A core member at Morgan notes:

I think the equal opportunities committee will still continue to thrive. And as long as it does, and we meet regularly, then it will continue to challenge and say that 'this is not on' and 'this is not on'. If that were to stop working then I think everything else would. Because there is just so much going on. So I feel that it is absolutely paramount. That committee gives us *space* to think about, and look at, and report back to staff meetings about anything that we are not happy about. (. . .) That committee is essential to us continuing to change and continuing to adjust to new situations and to spot anything that is happening.

Conclusions

Antiracism is essentially a democratic concept; on a theoretical level we can see that in order for antiracism to become internalized into our schools there needs to be maximum commitment and maximum participation.

(Allcott 1992: 181)

The literature on antiracism is full of statements about the need for democratic approaches and whole-school/whole-community participation. The literature is less forthcoming about how these principles might be put into practice – especially in schools that serve diverse local populations (differentiated by class as well as ethnicity), and where many of the, overwhelmingly white, teaching force hold ambivalent or oppositional attitudes towards ethnic diversity. Add to this the consequences of a massive state-sponsored campaign of education reform, which explicitly sets itself against concerns such as 'equality', and the gulf between theory and practice can sometimes seem impossible to bridge.

In this, and the previous, chapter I have described key events in the recent history of schools that have genuinely begun to explore antiracism in practice. The schools serve different communities and face a range of demands. Yet certain similarities suggest the outline of processes that may be relevant to other schools which share their aspirations. The case study schools do not provide a straightforward blueprint for success; they are still struggling to change for the better while sustaining the progress they have made. The experiences of teachers in Seacole and Morgan, however, do shed empirical light on questions concerning the nature of antiracist school change.

The case studies highlight the key role played by a relatively small and committed group of teachers who are willing to recognize and oppose racism: in their own school; in society; and in their own assumptions and perspectives. These core groups gained considerably from the support of their senior management teams – especially the headteachers – who conferred status on their work and made available basic resources, which, for example, enabled them to organize relevant inservice events.

The significance of the core groups (which continue as part of the attempts to sustain and extend antiracism in the schools) might seem at odds with democratic principles. And yet, given the very real differences that exist within every staff group, an attempt to involve all staff at all stages, may be a recipe for inaction rather than antiracism. Nevertheless, bringing others into the process *is* essential: whole-school change can be more than a slogan, but involves difficult and changing relationships between a variety of actors and groups. This chapter illustrates how the involvement of students, parents and members of local communities varied over time. The students were especially important; in Seacole, for example, they were active in creating the conditions under which a fairly radical set of antiracist commitments could be adopted by the whole staff.[5]

The history of the schools' antiracist policies highlights the important balance that the core groups had to strike; at once leading the changes while simultaneously maintaining a basic level of wider staff involvement. Indeed, by the time that draft policy documents were presented to staff there was nothing of substance that they did not recognize. In this way, the core groups succeeded in helping their colleagues feel a sense of involvement and investment in the policy developments – what some would term shared 'ownership' of the changes.[6] This is necessary, not simply for reasons of 'democracy', but for reasons of power and politics.

Without first being worked *on* (through INSET) and worked *in* (through a range of consultation mechanisms), subject departments may oppose even the most basic moves towards antiracism; seeing them as a threat to their professionalism and integrity (cf. Troyna 1988b). If antiracism is to be anything more than rhetoric, the involvement of subject departments is crucial. The way that antiracist frameworks and policies translate into practice is inextricably tied to what happens in the classroom. As the next chapter shows, however, the classroom (like the staffroom) is a site of ideological and political struggle where antiracist progress is rarely simple.

Antiracism in the classroom ____

pedagogy assumed such marginal significance in nascent antiracist
policies that even those researchers who scrutinize their content failed
to recognize the absence of clear-cut recommendations for classroom
practice.

(Troyna 1993a: 131)

Analyses of 'race' and racism in society have become increasingly sophisticated. Although post-structuralism and postmodernism are becoming increasingly influential, there is no single theory of 'race' relations that could
be said to dominate current approaches in the social sciences (cf. Rex and
Mason 1986). Writers concerned with 'race' and ethnicity have adopted a
range of research strategies and theoretical models. As new projects seek
to build on the strengths and weaknesses of previous work, it can become
increasingly difficult to make connections back to the routines of classroom life. One of the strengths of qualitative research is its engagement
with the day-to-day realities of teaching and learning; such work, however,
is usually concerned with identifying problems, rather than seeking solutions. In this context the lack of attention paid to antiracist pedagogy is
perhaps not so surprising, especially given the highly complex nature of
the problems with which antiracists are dealing. The best recent work
highlights the multifaceted nature of racism and warns against simplistic
approaches (see Chapter 4). Nevertheless, there is an urgent need for research that suggests ways in which we might move forward – albeit firmly
rooted in a clear recognition of the complexity and size of the task facing
us. It is in this spirit that I now turn from school micro-politics and policy-
making, to life in the classroom.

The chapter begins by reviewing some of the strengths and weaknesses
of attempts to establish antiracism across the curriculum. This includes a
critique of citizenship education as a vehicle for antiracist teaching. The
analysis then switches from antiracism *across* the curriculum to antiracism
on the curriculum. I examine the case for additional, discrete programmes
of social education, which complement and extend antiracism in subject

departments. By focusing on a programme of work (called 'people's education') in Mary Seacole School, I look at how teachers and students in the school presently explore the ways that 'race' and ethnicity influence their lives. The programme suggests that successful antiracist teaching can be built on a range of pedagogies, but always faces new challenges and uncertainties – some raised by students; some the consequences of wider reforms.

Antiracism *across* the curriculum

> To avoid the topic of race . . . is to falsify the relationship of our subject to real life outside the school.
>
> (Stenhouse 1982: 3)

In previous chapters I have examined the strategies used to involve subject specialists in antiracist developments in secondary schools. The most committed antiracist teachers found that colleagues in certain subject areas tended to see their specialisms as somehow removed from the school's growing concern with antiracism. This is often the case. Mathematics and science specialists, for example, have made important contributions to the development of multicultural/antiracist materials and analyses (cf. Gill and Levidow 1987) yet classroom teachers in these subjects frequently fail to see a connection between their subject and wider moves to address 'race' and other inequalities:

> maths staff insisted that the [draft antiracist] policy had little relevance to their work and they would resent the intrusion of other staff from different faculty areas into their deliberations and curriculum planning. Amongst other points raised in their meeting, maths staff claimed that they had 'checked through syllabus and textbooks, etc. for problems with course content but these are not really applicable to Maths'.
>
> (Troyna 1988b: 169)

In fact mathematics and the natural sciences are especially important areas for antiracist work. These subjects enjoy high popular status; they are thought to deal in 'hard facts' and are frequently seen as essential for all students (reflected in their core status in the National Curriculum). As they are currently taught, however, mathematics and the natural sciences often present very particular notions of 'rationality' and 'progress'. Black, Asian and other 'non-Western' influences and achievements are typically swamped amid Eurocentric representations that unthinkingly reproduce familiar stereotypes, such as Western (white) technology coming to the aid of impoverished and underdeveloped non-Western (black/Asian/other) nations.[1] Critical work on antiracist science and mathematics now offers an alternative to such presentations (see Mears 1986; Shan and Bailey 1991).[2]

The growth of antiracist work in science and mathematics is echoed in other subject areas across the curriculum. Although the materials and ideas tend to be of variable quality, and all require care and sensitivity in their use, there is now the beginning of a useful literature on antiracism across the curriculum: whatever a teacher's specialism there is a source somewhere to get them started on antiracist work. Some teacher unions and subject associations have published both broad-based and subject-specific guidelines (e.g. NUT 1992) while academics and other practitioners have also contributed, sometimes trying to make implementation easier by tying their recommendations closely to the requirements of the National Curriculum (e.g. Runnymede Trust 1993c).

If antiracist approaches are to be fully effective across a school it is necessary for *all* subject areas to acknowledge their responsibilities and take advantage of available opportunities. To do otherwise threatens to marginalize antiracism. All subjects *can* make a contribution; if subject specialists decide *not* to reflect antiracism in their classroom work (as well as in their other dealings with colleagues, students and parents) this can send a powerful message to students: the school's wider commitment to antiracism may be undermined where students perceive some subjects to be 'neutral' or exempt from the need to challenge racism. These messages can be especially dangerous if sent by high-status subjects (like mathematics and science) which often carry greater credibility with students (Ball 1981; Gillborn 1987).

It is crucial, therefore, that antiracist developments extend into each area of the curriculum. In isolation, however, even this may not be enough. Quite apart from the need to co-ordinate these developments, ensuring that consistent positions are taken with regard to the school's antiracist policy, for example, there may be a case for *additional* explicit treatment of racism (and other forms of exclusion and oppression) within a discrete part of the curriculum. In this sense antiracism may need to be *on* the curriculum, as well as extending *across* it.

Antiracism *on* the curriculum

If antiracist education aspires to 'permeating' each subject area, the question then arises, is there any need for further work, beyond the individual departments? There is considerable debate about this issue and, at present, no single answer commands widespread support (see, for example, Klein 1993: 139). There are, however, several good reasons why teachers may decide that such additional work is necessary.[3]

The problems of permeation: antiracism and subject pedagogy

Even in schools where all subject departments take seriously their duty to address antiracist issues it may be necessary to supplement this with additional work. Certain issues, sometimes including the most difficult and potentially inflammatory of concerns, cannot be fully explored within the limited time and material resources available to core and other foundation subjects in the National Curriculum. While all subject specialists have the potential to critique racism within their own field, for example, none may feel that an explicit and thoroughgoing focus on racism itself falls within their expertise or subject remit.

Additionally, working within core and foundation subjects there is a tendency for antiracist materials and ideas to be used only if the opportunity arises via more familiar subject-specific concerns or materials. In this way, without proper co-ordination between and within subjects, antiracism may appear to be incidental to the 'real' work of the group and occur in haphazard ways – again, threatening its credibility in the eyes of students.

The status of cross-curricular work

Recent research on the teaching of cross-curricular themes in England and Wales suggests further pedagogic and micro-political reasons why additional separate work on antiracism may be a necessary part of successful whole-school approaches. Until recently there was no reliable information on how (if at all) cross-curricular aspects of the National Curriculum are being taught in schools. A project combining survey, interview and observational approaches (conducted by colleagues at the Institute of Education, University of London) focuses on the fate of the five cross-curricular themes: economic and industrial understanding; careers education and guidance; health education; citizenship; and environmental education (NCC 1990a). The project's findings have a direct bearing on attempts to promote antiracist education in secondary schools.

First, as was widely suspected, although some schools claim that the cross-curricular themes 'permeate' all or most subjects, often their presence is difficult to identify in practice. Indeed, even where subject teachers are aware of the opportunity to make explicit connections with the cross-curricular themes, they frequently choose to emphasize only subject-specific issues, judging that direct reference to the themes would interfere with 'the message of the subject' (Whitty et al. 1994). Whitty and his colleagues discovered that students are most aware of the themes which are *least* permeated: careers education and guidance (CEG) and health education. These themes appear in the fewest subjects, but are more likely than the others to enjoy their own curriculum slot or to be part of a personal and social education (PSE) programme (Rowe and Whitty 1993). Having 'their own space' allows teachers to deal with these themes outside the conventions of particular academic subjects;[4] they can look at different material, in new and challenging ways that make direct connections with the students' everyday lives and concerns (Whitty et al. 1994). This is, of course, an essential requirement of work that seeks to challenge racism.

Citizenship education: some practical concerns

The project on cross-curricular work in secondary schools has produced a second important finding for those concerned with antiracist education; it draws attention to the generally weak position of citizenship as a cross-curricular theme. This is significant because of the emphasis some observers have placed on citizenship as a potentially useful device in antiracist and antisexist developments. Despite being part of the 'conservative restoration' (Apple 1992), many practitioners have seen 'Education for Citizenship' (NCC 1990b) as a means of placing antiracism on schools' agendas.

> One cross-curricular theme most explicitly related to MC/ARE [multicultural/antiracist education] is 'citizenship' . . . the NCC's guidance on *Education for Citizenship* (1990b) has offered a framework for schools covering eight components of study and three levels of practical experience over the four key stages of schooling . . . In addition to one component entitled 'A Pluralist Society', several other components explicitly refer to multicultural, antiracist and equal opportunities issues. In response to these national directives, it is not surprising that much of current curriculum development and interest in relation to MC/ARE has coalesced around citizenship.
>
> (Taylor 1992: 2–3)

If Monica Taylor is right about citizenship being used as a focus for 'much of current curriculum development and interest' in this field, then it is a dangerous trend.

The research by Geoff Whitty and his colleagues indicates that citizenship has little or no track record in most secondary schools: less than 10 per cent of respondents claimed to have been engaged in any work on citizenship before the 1988 ERA.[5] Furthermore, despite citizenship's new found status as a cross-curricular theme, by 1992 only 25 per cent of schools surveyed claimed to have a written policy on it. This compares badly with information technology (77 per cent), personal and social education (76 per cent) and special educational needs (75 per cent). Indeed, 'equal opportunities' and 'multicultural perspectives' have a firmer foothold in their own right (with written policies in 66 per cent and 43 per cent of schools respectively) (Whitty et al. 1992: 2). Under these conditions, and given the current invisibility of the most permeated themes, trying to tie antiracist teaching to citizenship education may actually *reduce* the possibilities for genuinely critical work. Indeed, the NCC document itself reveals a narrow and assimilationist approach that would require considerable local initiative before citizenship education could really offer a significant way forward. It is worth looking at the document in a little more detail as a means of sensitizing oneself to some of the pitfalls and complexities of this field.

Citizenship education: some conceptual problems

The official guidance on citizenship education grew out of a period of reform and debate that was frequently characterized by what Sally Tomlinson has called 'educational nationalism': that is, an ideology that asserts the existence of a single (white) British culture and heritage threatened by the presence of ethnic minorities with 'alien' cultures (Tomlinson 1990: 36–41). The Honeyford affair and more recent controversies over 'standards' of education in ethnically diverse settings are clear examples of this form of discourse (see Demaine 1993; Foster-Carter 1987; Halstead 1992; Vincent 1992). Such views are central to 'the new racism' (Barker 1981) of New Right politics – a view that stresses *cultural difference* (rather than 'racial inferiority'), and uses this as the basis for denying any 'racial' intent while simultaneously promoting policies with racist consequences (see Chapter 2). The NCC's formula for citizenship education does not, of course, simply reproduce new racist ideas; as the quotation from Monica Taylor (above) demonstrates, superficially at least the guidance looks promising. The lesson of the new racism, however, is to look closely at what is *not* said; to read *between* the lines.

As Wilfred Carr notes, although the NCC 'clearly made strenuous efforts to depoliticize the concept of citizenship . . . any suggestion that it is a politically neutral document should not be taken too seriously' (Carr 1991: 374). The NCC guidance presents Britain according to a pluralist model that assumes equality before the law and equal access to political decision-making processes. There is no reference here to immigration rules that systematically discriminate against black and Asian people (Dickinson 1982; Lal and Wilson 1985; Troyna 1988c) nor to a system of criminal justice that, at each stage, treats black people more severely than their white counterparts (Hood 1993; NACRO 1988; 1991).

According to the pluralist model presented in *Education for Citizenship* justice and fair-play are the norm, while 'racial prejudice' and 'discrimination' reflect 'the tensions and conflicts that occur between groups which perceive each other to be socially, racially, ethnically or culturally different'

(NCC 1990b: 6). Therefore, 'prejudice' and 'discrimination' are defined in terms of a reaction to *difference* while racism, as a persistent feature that reflects and recreates the unequal distribution of *power* in society, is conspicuously absent. Despite its liberal façade, therefore, the guidance on citizenship is at best weak and superficial, at worst, a recipe for new racist analyses of cultural difference, that place the 'blame' for racism upon the alien 'newcomers'.

There is an important lesson here concerning the kinds of issue and analysis that must be addressed in any discrete additional antiracist work beyond the usual school subjects. While some forms of antiracism have been rightly criticized for devoting almost exclusive attention to what Tariq Modood calls 'colour racism' (see Chapter 4) there is a danger that the left revisionist critiques might be interpreted as supporting the dominant rightist discourse of fixed and essential cultural differences (new racism). Work on difference and diversity is important, but it is not an end in itself. Unless teachers retain a concern with 'race' and racism, as distinctive factors (that connect directly with issues of power and oppression), antiracist work might revert to the worst kind of multiculturalism (typified by a fascination with difference and exotica): what is sometimes disparagingly referred to as 'the three Ss' – saris, samosas and steel bands. One of the advisers/inspectors surveyed by Taylor, for example, predicted that 'racism and its effects will be replaced in focus by responses to ethnic diversity' (Taylor 1992: 26).

There is, therefore, a strong case for separate additional provision that complements and extends antiracist work in subject departments. Occasionally it may be politic to use the cross-curricular elements of the National Curriculum as a policy lever in the face of strong opposition, say from governors who might associate talk of antiracism with images of 'loony left' politics. Government sponsored moves on 'education for citizenship', however, do not offer a model of good practice.[6]

Multiple inequalities and antiracist teaching

Having set out the case for additional work on antiracism, as a discrete part of the curriculum, it is now time to think about the forms that work might take. Before looking at the experiences of teachers and students in one such programme, however, it is necessary to emphasize that while my analysis focuses on 'race' and ethnicity, these do not exhaust the kinds of issue such programmes should address.

When considering 'race' and ethnicity in society, it is important that other areas of inequality are also dealt with sensitively. Social class, gender, disability and sexual orientation, for example, all operate to label and exclude certain groups. These issues often cut across racism, but do so in complex and sometimes ambivalent ways (Gibson 1991; Gibson and Bhachu 1988; McCarthy 1990; McCarthy and Apple 1988; Phizacklea 1983; Westwood and Bhachu 1988). 'Race', gender and class, for example, do not simply 'add up' to triple oppression in all cases – black young women of working-class backgrounds tend to achieve more highly than their male counterparts (Drew and Gray 1990) and, in some ways, experience school differently.[7] Research by Mary Fuller (1980) and Máirtín Mac an Ghaill (1988; 1989a), for example, suggests that different peer and teacher pressures may amplify male resistance in ways that lead to more serious school responses (such as exclusion from school). Similarly, the harassment of Asian young women embodies a range of complex, sometimes contradictory, racist and sexist stereotypes (as at once demure yet licentious, alluring yet ugly):

> If I'm with a white boy, say just on the way home from college, they shout in the street, 'What's it like to fuck a Paki?', or if I'm on my own with other girls it's, 'Here comes the Paki whore, come and fuck us Paki whores, we've heard you're really horny'. Or maybe they'll put it the other way round, saying that I am dirty, that no one could possibly want to go to bed with a Paki...
>
> (quoted in Brah 1992b: 73)

As the Burnage inquiry team emphasize (Macdonald et al. 1989), students' first-hand knowledge of class and gender can help white peers make direct links between some of their own experiences and those of their black and Asian peers. While the remainder of this chapter focuses on issues of 'race' and ethnicity, therefore, it should not be assumed that classroom work should adopt an exclusive focus on these issues. Indeed, because racism operates in contexts that are also fundamentally shaped by the dynamics of class, gender and sexuality, so these themes will continually surface in discussions of 'race' (and *vice versa*).

People's education: an antiracist programme

> Education 'which serves the people as a whole, which liberates, which puts people in command of their lives and which is determined by and accountable to the people'.
>
> (Sisulu 1986)

> Education 'which prepares people for total human liberation and for full participation in all social, political or cultural spheres of society, helps people to be creative, to develop a critical mind and to analyse'.
>
> (Mkatshwa 1985)

These statements refer to an idealized version of 'people's education' as it was originally formulated as part of the struggle against Apartheid education in South Africa. As Harold Wolpe and Elaine Unterhalter document, a variety of forces have acted to limit the effectiveness of people's education, threatening to co-opt it into reformist programmes that limit its 'transformative' power (Wolpe and Unterhalter 1991). Nevertheless, the original aims of 'people's education' describe well the kinds of transformations that teachers in Seacole hope to begin through a programme of teaching which directly addresses issues of power and exclusion in society.[8] Like its namesake, the programme emphasizes process as much as content:

> people's education is seen as an ongoing process, the development of a new practice, rather than a given, defined entity.
>
> (Levin 1991: 118)

In this section I examine the development and use of a 'people's education' programme of antiracist teaching in Mary Seacole Girls' School. The programme has undergone several changes, often in response to students' comments. Indeed, the increasing awareness and sophistication of the students has become a constant impetus for change in the programme. As one of the teachers most involved notes:

> It changes every year because every year the pupils seem to be far ahead.

Before considering the programme in more detail it is necessary to note that the teachers involved are conscious of some of the problems that have hindered previous attempts to develop systematic teaching on 'race' and other forms of oppression. Despite the aims of many committed and well-meaning teachers, for example, the 'black studies' movement, of the 1970s, was heavily criticized for removing black students from the mainstream curriculum and acting as a form of social control (see Mullard 1982; Nixon 1985; Stone 1981). Learning from such experiences, the teachers in Seacole try to gear their programme towards all students (whatever their ethnicity, social class background, and 'ability'): 'people's education' in the school forms a component of the personal and social education (PSE) of all students.

The origins of the programme

> If racism isn't going to go away, the pupils have to learn to cope with it.

This is how a Section 11 teacher, centrally concerned with designing and teaching people's education in Seacole, remembers the rationale for beginning separate, additional work on antiracism.[9]

It was like an *urgent* need of coping and surviving; how do you handle it? And at the same time it was to broaden the horizon of the pupils and to get at their different points of view.

The first people's education course paralleled the staff training, which the core group organize for teachers, and focused on students in year 9 (their third year at the school: aged 13–14). The teachers soon realized, however, that 'the third year is too late. We should start from year 7, when they first come in'.

The course now builds up throughout the students' secondary schooling. When they enter the school (year 7) antiracist work is built into the tutorial programme of all form groups, delivered by form tutors (after relevant INSET) and members of the core group. This continues in year 8 but is extended by specialist seminars as part of the PSE programme. In year 9 the specialist sessions become more lengthy and completely replace the work in tutor groups. Once established, this pattern continues through years 10 and 11.

The course starts with general issues about difference and 'prejudice', without any explicit emphasis on 'race'. The work is structured to try to engage the students' own interests and experiences, to give them confidence in expressing their own perspectives and to relate things that have happened to them. This does not, however, mean putting the black, Asian and other minority students on the spot – presenting them as some kind of 'exhibit' that represents their entire community. Such approaches, no matter how well-intentioned, can embarrass and alienate minority students, serving to reinforce (rather than deconstruct) existing racial stereotypes and conflicts (see Wright 1992b: 40–1). The school benefits enormously from the central involvement of a teacher of minority ethnic background. As someone who experiences daily the kinds of conflict that the course aims to address, she is well aware of the need to avoid turning her minority students into 'objects' of enquiry:

If you introduce it coldly – 'You are going to do a course on race awareness' – you obviously are not going to start on pleasant ground, because nobody wants to feel uncomfortable. Both sides, if anybody stopped and said, 'Okay, we are going to be looking at race', then everybody starts looking at you [the minority student]. And you think, 'Oh, God. Please let this not happen'.

Towards antiracist pedagogies

There is a lot of emotion in it, but at the same time you have to see the reason.

(Teacher at Mary Seacole Comprehensive)

A present controversy in antiracist education concerns the 'rationalist pedagogy' that some critics identify as a weakness of existing antiracist approaches. The accusation is that too much antiracism (like multiculturalism) assumes racism to be illogical, and simply tries to undermine its basis with reasoned argument. Such an approach fails, therefore, to engage with the reality of students' lives in and outside school, where many plausible and apparently reasonable arguments might be adduced to support racism – concern about competition for jobs and sexual partners are just two of many possible examples (cf. Centre for Multicultural Education 1993; Mac an Ghaill 1994; Phizacklea and Miles 1979). Hence, a straightforwardly 'rationalist pedagogy' is unlikely to influence many students:

> Like the multiculturalists, antiracists have often failed to confront the limitations of a rationalist approach to education. The *rationalism* of their educational project is contingent on the supposed *irrationalism* of the racist subject – often conceptualized as a collective, class subject. In the context of schooling one significant issue that is paradoxically neglected is the 'rationality' of the working-class students' resistance to antiracist curricula and classroom discussions in so far as this resistance is bound up with a more generalized opposition to the degrees of surveillance, discipline, authoritarianism and class domination involved in conventional forms of schooling... Like the multiculturalist project of reducing prejudice by teaching about other cultures, the antiracist project of providing superior explanations for unemployment, housing shortages, and so forth, has so far, and for similar reasons, produced only patchy success. The point is not simply to abandon this type of teaching but to acknowledge and analyse its limitations in the light of a more complex understanding of the nature of racism and to develop forms of educational engagement more likely to open up racist subjectivities and common sense to alternative discourses.
>
> (Rattansi 1992: 33 original emphasis)

Barry Troyna (1993a: 133–6) questions the foundations on which Ali Rattansi claims antiracism to have achieved 'only patchy success'. Troyna also points out that analyses of the 'logic' of racism are not new (cf. Cashmore 1987) and rejects Rattansi's characterization of antiracism as a 'rationalist' project:

> Antiracist education projects are not designed to engage with the irrationalism of (young working-class) people – they are concerned with providing them with alternative explanatory frameworks... providing pupils with the opportunity of perceiving things through an

alternative and more plausible lens is likely to provoke changes in their racist construction of the way things are.

(Troyna 1993a: 136)

Despite Troyna's response, and his note that antiracist teachers frequently adopt 'democratic and collaborative pedagogies' (ibid.), to date the literature on secondary schools contains few concrete examples of such work. Ali Rattansi offers a useful note of caution, therefore, into a literature that – as in the case of much school-based innovation and change – often relies on practitioner-based accounts that can simplify the processes and exaggerate the gains (Hargreaves 1982). The people's education programme in Seacole, therefore, may offer some useful insights into the demands, strengths and weaknesses of practical antiracist pedagogies.[10]

People's education in Seacole begins by examining various forms of difference and prejudice. This includes looking at the kinds of group that the students might be predisposed to view sympathetically. By looking at 'disability', for example, a group might begin to make explicit the kinds of emotional and other responses that they experience. This can become a means of questioning whether the pity that most feel is actually of any help to people so labelled, or whether it is part of a system of labelling and response that contributes to the exclusion of people who are affected by society's attitudes towards disability (cf. Barton and Oliver 1992; Rieser and Mason 1990).

The teaching of people's education relies on building a strong relationship of trust between the students and the staff who are involved. Throughout the work, students are encouraged to reflect on their feelings and personal experiences. This means that the teachers have to be prepared to share *their* feelings, doubts and experiences. One of the teachers involved notes:

It depends very much on the personal relationship you develop between you and your pupils. If you do it in a manner that you are *aloof*, then you are not going to bring everything out.

When students share their views in these sessions, they do so as volunteers – participants in a joint exploration of the feelings and actions that relate to the particular topic under discussion. Because the sessions are not part of a subject-centred presentation, the teachers have a freedom that is not available to subject teachers (Rowe and Whitty 1993; Whitty et al. 1994). This allows work in people's education to move beyond the traditional boundaries of student and teacher roles, and to make more immediate connections with the students' lives (in the school, on the street and in the community). In relation to name-calling, for example:

We are open. We actually say, 'Look, this is it. We are going to be very open about it and it doesn't matter if swearing is going to be used. We are going to write everything on the board. What sort of names have you been called?' And they use four-letter words and they use 'bitch' and so on. And this is a very common one – I even say it – a fourth-year girl first introduced it, and she said, 'It was ever so hard for me when somebody called me a "black bitch" (. . .) Not the "bitch", the "black". I can say to myself I am not a bitch but I can't say to myself I am not black. That is something I can't do anything about. And I know in what context it is used, it is used as an insult.'

Examples such as this generate heat and conflict. But the teachers have learnt to try to use this positively. For example, when year 7 students argue about the severity of name-calling, with white students exclaiming 'We don't mind if they call us "Whitey"'. The teachers try to help the students get beyond the surface features of the insults (as simple 'name calling') to expose how some insults carry more weight than others – where 'Paki' is experienced as a highly contentious and hurtful term because in reality it operates as a generalized, racially derogative signifier, not as a neutral shorthand for people of Pakistani background (cf. Gillborn 1993; Troyna and Hatcher 1992).

The sessions can get highly charged. The students are talking about very personal issues, frequently having views challenged that they have heard their parents and other adults endorse time and time again.

Moira (white: year 10):

If you have got somebody in your family who is racist, or you have got a friend at home who is something like that, you can talk about it. And if you have been in the past, if you have been racist and stuff, you can *talk* about it in the lesson.

The lessons offer a voice to all the students, allowing them to explore racism from different perspectives.

Melanie (mixed race: year 9):

Telling you what kind of experience, people that *do* get racism, you know what I mean? And it just tells you what they go through and how they are feeling and everything. And in people's education you can really express yourself, if you *have* been called.

Jodie (white: year 9):

You have the freedom to say what you want to say, as long as you don't butt in when other people are saying what they want to say.

Not surprisingly these discussions frequently become the arena for arguments. Far from seeing this as a negative aspect of the programme, however, the students tend to see the anger as indicative of the issues' importance. The students equate the anger and emotion of the sessions with the experience of 'race' and racism in 'the real world':

> *Sarujit (South Asian, Sikh: year 10):*
> It is better the way that we argue, because if we agreed with everything it is not *real* and it is not right at all. It is better because it is the kind of arguments that we have to face as we get out in the real world.
> *Robina (South Asian, Muslim: year 10):*
> Sometimes bad feelings can be brought up. If you go too far sometimes, from experience ... The last lesson we had, not long ago – Bad feelings can be brought up <to the other students in the room> can't they.
> *Keri (African Caribbean: year 10):*
> Yes. We had a lot of arguments.
> *DG:*
> What happens when, in your words, it goes 'too far'? How do the teachers react?
> *Robina:*
> They want it to happen. They want to see how we deal with it.
> *Moira (white: year 10):*
> That might be the whole point of the lesson; to see how we take things. That's reality isn't it?

The conflict, emotion and anger that surface during the programme, therefore, are seen by some students as a legitimate, indeed as a *necessary* part of the discussions: they form a genuine link with 'the real world' and set the programme apart from traditional subject-based teaching. One of the architects of the programme agrees that emotion is a central part of the process of people's education in Seacole. She also notes, however, that this places an additional responsibility on the teachers – to ensure that the emotions are used positively and do not simply translate into a heightened sense of conflict that reinforces previously held positions:

> You *have* to have conflicts, I feel, and you *have* to explore these delicately. Sometimes it does end up in [students shouting] 'Oh this is not racist.' 'We don't agree.' 'What about if this was an Asian company, they won't employ a white person.' But all these things are important and the only thing you have to remember is when you close the session they don't take away this anger and hatred.

The teachers use a range of debriefing strategies to help the students deal productively with the issues and emotions raised by the programme.

Sometimes this can be done in small groups, or even with the entire teaching group. Occasionally, especially when the students are young and/or new to the programme, the debriefing has to be done through one-to-one counselling:

> If they are 11 year olds they are going to get very personal about it (. . .) But then you have to break it up and talk to the people individually. And then come back and say, 'Okay, both of you sit together'. And 'Do you realize how this person felt?' And luckily, just because I am Asian myself, I could use my example . . .[11]

This kind of approach is, of course, expensive in terms of staff time and effort. In addition to the demands this places on the individual teachers who are involved, the system also requires material, professional and social support from colleagues in the rest of the school. This is a feature that reoccurs when teachers discuss the programme; they draw attention not only to their own preparations, but also to the essential school-wide support that makes such an approach possible:

> You have to be so confident and you have to be prepared. You have to be *prepared* for outbursts. You have to be prepared for everything. But luckily we have the support of the staff and we have the support of the head to back us up. And if there is anger, then you just try and deal with it.

Students' ability to handle this kind of experience increases as they move through the programme and grow older. A measure of the programme's success is that older students accept as routine the fact that feelings and experiences aired during the sessions have a special kind of significance – they do not usually create lasting resentments:

> DG:
>   If you've had an argument in one of those lessons, does it help you afterwards being able to talk about it or does it just make the situation worse?
> Keri (African Caribbean: year 10):
>   Makes it better.
> Moira (white: year 10):
>   You tend to forget about it afterwards.
> Robina (South Asian, Muslim: year 10):
>   One minute, you don't sort of like go, 'Oh, she's the girl who said *that*'. We just apologize and say sorry for saying this, and that is it.

DG:
It doesn't set up long-standing conflicts?
Robina:
No, not really.

This view was repeated in almost all my conversations with Seacole students. Most found it difficult to express precisely *why* or *how* it was that views expressed in the lessons came to enjoy a special status – as at once being extremely personal and yet not acting to label the individual in any lasting way. For example:

With these lessons it is good because whatever you say in that lesson, it is not like your opinion. When it is break you don't split up and say, 'You said this in the lesson and I am going to punch you up' or something like that. There is nothing like that. Whatever you say, your opinion is accepted. They respect your opinion, although they don't *agree* with it.

This description, from Sarujit (a 15 year-old South Asian student), begins by saying that views expressed in the lesson are 'not like your opinion' – referring to the fact that (within the programme) teachers encourage them to say whatever they have heard or think about an issue without being too guarded for fear of others' interpretations. Sarujit finishes, however, by saying that while others may disagree with 'your opinion' they do not deny your right to express it. The students come to appreciate – although they have difficulty putting it into words – that the people's education programme relies on them being free to express a view or idea without being committed to retaining and defending it throughout the lesson. It is in this way that the programme uses students' views constructively without simply reinforcing conflict and suspicion.

Not all students are convinced that the people's education programme makes a significant impact. Some students (though their peers think the number is fairly small and decreasing) continue to hold racist views. Additionally, in talking to a range of young people within Seacole, I discovered some, especially younger ones, who feel that racism is simply a matter of 'some people's nature'. Even here, though, they are clear that the school is setting itself against the kinds of racism they often experience elsewhere.

Le (Vietnamese: year 8):
[I met this boy at a party] He was being racist to me and I goes, 'If you're racist to me once more I'm going to knock you across the room'. And he just goes, 'Oh, yeah. What you gonna do you Chinky?' I went – *slap* <Mimics striking him across the face>.

DG:
  Does the school talk much about racism?
Shahida (South Asian, Muslim: year 8):
  Yes. They did in the second year [year 8 – when separate people's education sessions begin].
Le:
  It talks about racism and [a teacher] says, 'Right, let's try and get it out of this school'. But you can't actually stop people from being racist. It might be in some people's nature to be racist and it might not be.
Shahida:
  You can't change the way people feel about other people. You can't change the way the teachers feel about us, and we can't change the way another girl thinks about me, or a group of girls that feel about another group of girls.

It is impossible to predict whether these students will change their views, about the fixed nature of racism, as they move through the school and experience more of the people's education programme. My interviews with students clearly indicate, however, that few older students in Seacole hold such views; for them, racism is a more complex phenomenon:

Sarujit (South Asian, Sikh: year 10):
  Because when you are younger you think, 'Oh, somebody white has been racist to me, that is really wrong'. But as you get older and as you mature you find –
Koli (South Asian, Muslim: year 10):
  <interrupting> Everybody is not like that. Some people are prepared to be friends with the people, and not just their own race.
Sarujit:
  And you see their point of view, and why they have actually done something like that, and how they feel. And you see things like how they have been brought up and things like that. And you look at it from their point of view. (. . .) Especially with older girls, it is not like <in a dull preaching tone> 'racism is wrong'. Racism *is* wrong but we see it from the people who are actually racist to someone and how *they* feel.

Danger: work in progress/progress in work

The views of teachers and students in Seacole clearly illustrate important issues thrown up by teaching that seeks to tackle racism through a separate curricular slot – additional to antiracist teaching in subject departments.

The first thing that emerges from this analysis is the need to draw on a range of teaching strategies. There is no single 'antiracist pedagogy' that can be taken off the shelf and always used successfully. The Seacole programme relies on the skill, patience and confidence of teachers who vary their approaches according to the lesson and the students' responses. People's education in Seacole is delivered, therefore, through a variety of antiracist pedago*gies* – sometimes didactic; often democratic and collaborative; occasionally highly personal and making use of counselling techniques.

Second, both teachers and students value the *emotional* content and character of the work. In some ways the descriptions of people's education break with students' conventional notions of good/bad lessons. Most students, even those who are typically described as 'anti-school', expect lessons to be fairly orderly, and are damning of any teachers whom they feel cannot exercise adequate control (Beynon 1984; Gannaway 1976; Woods 1983; 1990). Similarly, where the content and form of lessons are fluid – where the pedagogy and subject matter are loosely framed and classified (Bernstein 1977) – students tend to see the lessons as lacking rigour; they are not 'proper' (high status) subjects (Burgess 1983; Whitty et al. 1994). In people's education the lessons cover a huge variety of issues, take many different forms and are sometimes noisy and conflict-riven. Yet in this case the students see these as *positive* features; the conflict and emotional content are interpreted as evidence of the programme's ability to tap into issues of importance in 'the real world'.

Third, my conversations with students in Seacole clearly indicate the ability of working-class young people (from different ethnic backgrounds) to engage critically with complex and sensitive issues such as racism.[12] Despite the very real difficulties of opening these issues up to public discussion, almost all the older students I spoke with were positive about the programme and the way it helped them to rethink their assumptions about 'race', racism and racists. In this sense 'working-class students' resistance to antiracist curricula and classroom discussions' (Rattansi 1992: 33) may not be as simple and fixed as some have feared. Ali Rattansi's comments on the current state of antiracist theory and practice, however, are a timely warning against the excesses of some previous analyses of antiracist practice. The people's education programme is still changing, the teachers and the students are, in a very real sense, learning together. Before leaving this discussion of the programme, therefore, it is necessary to identify some remaining loose ends and other issues arising from the experience to date.

Continuing issues and concerns

The first cautionary finding has already been stated, but bears repetition; it is that the particular structure, content and style of the people's education programme, like the school's general approach to antiracism, have

changed over time and continue to alter as new demands are made and
new issues arise. There is no 'one right way', racism takes too many forms
and is too complex for such a solution (see Chapter 4). It is a measure of
the staff's sophistication that they realize this and continue to challenge
themselves, their colleagues and their students. A special needs teacher
notes:

> Some people think 'Oh, I have been on a race awareness course. I am
> okay. I've done it.' But I am concerned that people see it as a continu-
> ous journey (. . .) You have to recognize the changes that are happen-
> ing in communities and with young people.

A second issue for Seacole concerns the antiracist work across the curriculum. Although many educationists and policy-makers continue to champion the case of antiracist work that 'permeates' the entire curriculum, the
reality is often rather bleak. Unlike many schools, Seacole has made genuine efforts to make antiracism a visible element in all subject areas.
Students are aware of antiracist elements in many subjects and argue that
it *is* relevant. At present, however, the students seem to recognize its
presence only by rather crude markers – most often the presence of black
and Asian people in subject materials:

> *Jodie (white: year 9):*
> In history we have just done about the slaves.
> *Melanie (mixed race: year 9):*
> Yes. How the slaves were treated and everything. And even the little
> tiny ones, they were chained with these things round their necks.
> And how they were treated and everything.
> *Jodie:*
> It sometimes crops up in other lessons, even though that is not what
> we're talking about. But it is always connected to the actual thing
> that we are doing, it is not just said for the sake of it.

Without a more detailed observational study of cross-curricular work in
Seacole, it is impossible to say whether more subtle forms of antiracist
work were absent from subject teaching, or were simply not 'recognized'
as such by students. It was the case, however, that some African Caribbean
students specifically highlighted the lack of a 'cultural' representation of
black people in the curriculum:

> *Mary (African Caribbean: year 8):*
> We learn about Islam and civilization in the Middle Ages and that,
> but we don't learn about black history or anything like that. In RE
> we learn about Islam and all that, Miss never looks at like what the

black people are doing (. . .) Some people say that you do it later, right, in the fourth year, but the fourth year's too late.

This issue is recognized by the core group and materials are being produced that address a wider range of issues through black experiences and achievements; for example, describing prominent black figures in science and the humanities. This kind of work looks promising. Materials on Davidson Nicol, Mary Seacole, Charles Drew and Garret Morgan, for example, highlight the variety of black people's work and achievement and their contribution to the world we all inhabit. Each of their stories also points to the experience of racism – as a very real part of their lives (and death in the case of Drew). Yet their biographies are not 'about' racism as such – they celebrate important achievements, often overcoming class-based structures, and do not fall into the trap of reducing all black life to a response to white racism (cf. Gilroy 1990; Rattansi 1992). The quotation from Mary (above) illustrates the need for this kind of work from the moment the students enter the school.

A further issue that Seacole, and many similar schools, must face concerns changes to the structure and funding of Section 11 provision. I have already noted some of the changes' damaging effects (see Chapter 1); in the context of the people's education programme, further problems now arise. As Section 11 resources become more scarce fewer staff will be employed in this way – restricting one of the main routes through which teachers of minority background currently enter the profession. Additionally, the tighter definition of the duties of Section 11 teachers (including named caseloads) will make involvement in wider ranging work – like the people's education programme – more difficult to sustain.[13] The programme relies on a variety of teacher skills and experiences and the involvement of minority teachers has proved invaluable. While these changes present many problems, paradoxically, they may spur some schools to more positive changes. Senior management in Seacole, for example, now recognize the urgent need for staff recruitment to live up to the school's antiracist policy in giving special weight to applicants' potential contribution to antiracist work. This kind of response is essential if the school is to safeguard the advances it has made. Other schools will need to respond in equally constructive ways if they are to limit the damage caused by the reform of Section 11.

A final question, which can only be answered through an analysis of work in more schools, concerns the importance of the single-sex nature of Seacole Comprehensive. Undoubtedly, the single-sex intake has consequences for the character of life in the school; whether these differences are crucial to the form of the people's education programme, however, cannot be asserted. The Macdonald inquiry into racism and racial violence in

Manchester (Macdonald et al. 1989), for example, drew attention to the part played by the aggressive 'macho' atmosphere that developed in Burnage High School – a single sex boys' school. Violence, however, is not exclusive to boys' schools or male encounters (cf. Drouet 1993; Keise 1992). Similarly, the sessions in Seacole frequently become extremely heated and cover issues such as physical violence, in addition to sustained and bitter name-calling. Undoubtedly the students' experiences of harassment outside the school offer another means of deconstructing racism in the programme.

Shazia (South Asian, Muslim: year 9):
 Some people call this 'The Paki School' because loads of –
Jaswinder (South Asian, Sikh: year 9):
 <interrupting> And lesbians.
DG:
 Who calls it that?
Sally (white: year 9):
 Boys.
Jaswinder:
 And other girls.
Shazia:
 Pupils from other schools.

Parallels between the oppressive use of gender, sexuality and 'race' clearly offer a strong basis for critical discussions in Seacole. Social class is also a crucial category for the students, especially in their dealings with other – 'posher', 'stuck up' – schools in the city. These parallels are used constructively in the people's education course and it seems likely that similar dynamics could emerge in mixed and all male settings.

These factors notwithstanding it is almost certainly true that gender issues play a crucial role in the way that people's education is experienced in Seacole. The concern with expressing feelings and emotion, for example, might have to be reworked somewhat in mixed or all male contexts where such things are typically seen as signifying weakness (Mac an Ghaill 1994).

At this point in the analysis it is also worth reflecting on the fact that, in each of the case study schools, the headteachers (and their predecessors) are women. The sample is, of course, too small to add much to the debate about whether male and female heads tend to adopt different styles of leadership (see Ouston 1993; Ozga 1992). British data on this issue is, in any case, rather sketchy (Hall 1993). As sociologists we should not, perhaps, be surprised if women managers *tend* to adopt rather different styles, since the social construction of gender is likely to have influenced their life and career experiences. Such a constructivist position also makes space for good headship styles whatever a teacher's gender (it does not embrace an essentialist argument about women's innate abilities). The really important issue here is the kind of headship styles adopted, not the heads' sex or whether their styles are typical of one gender or another. It is interesting to note, however, that whereas antiracism is frequently portrayed in aggressive 'macho' terms (see Brandt 1986; Macdonald et al. 1989), the styles of headship that have supported antiracism in my case study schools tended to be relatively 'collegial, open, consultative and team oriented' approaches that, to date, 'are more evident in women's management styles' (Hall 1993: 41, after Bolam et al. 1993; see also Shakeshaft 1987; 1993).

Conclusions

In this chapter I have described an example of the kind of separate additional provision that secondary schools may need to develop if they are to realize antiracism as a genuine and thorough element of the whole school. The relationship between antiracism *across* the curriculum (as a part of subject teaching) and antiracism *on* the curriculum (as part of a separate programme) can be one of mutual benefit. The involvement of subject departments demonstrates the importance of antiracism as a legitimate strand in any good education – whatever the subject; the additional programme allows teachers and students to stand outside subject boundaries and explore issues in ways that are not possible in more rigidly defined subject areas.

The people's education programme in Mary Seacole Comprehensive provides an important example of how PSE time can be used to address a range of controversial issues in ways that students recognize as important and valid – in terms of their experiences and concerns in 'the real world'. The programme uses a variety of pedagogies and succeeds in helping many working-class students (of diverse ethnic backgrounds) begin critically to deconstruct taken-for-granted assumptions about 'race', racism and racists. The programme is, however, still changing and developing. While other schools and practitioners may learn a good deal from Seacole's experience, the chapter does not offer a blueprint that can be adopted unthinkingly elsewhere. The programme gains strength from the particular skills and concerns of the participants and makes use of local issues that are important to the students. These are significant factors in the success of the programme and require others to think carefully about how similar approaches might work in different contexts, especially where the construction of masculinity in class might present additional barriers in mixed and boys-only schools.

In analysing how the people's education programme works in Seacole, I have consciously drawn on the perspectives of students from a range of ethnic backgrounds. The students play a vital role in determining how these sessions develop and it is only by talking with students that we can gauge the true success of such programmes. The following chapter continues this theme by focusing more explicitly on student perspectives and experiences.

eight _____

Student perspectives _____

> You can't put yourself in their skin. You can empathize as much as you like, but at the end of the day, you can walk away from it because you're white.

This is how a white teacher in Mary Seacole Comprehensive explains her professional commitment to dialogue with students; giving them a voice in lessons, engaging with the world as they see and experience it. She is especially keen to connect with students of minority ethnic background. This is a vital part of antiracist change, yet – as this chapter demonstrates – *white* students must also be recognized as a crucial part of the equation.

In this chapter I focus explicitly on the perspectives of students in Mary Seacole and Garret Morgan schools. My general aim is to explore how students (from a range of social class and ethnic backgrounds) make sense of their schools' antiracist pronouncements and practice.

In the first section I use interview data to examine students' views on ethnic diversity and their attitudes to racism and racist harassment among peers. The students' appreciation of the complex and dangerous nature of racism extends to their interpretation of teachers' actions; sometimes highlighting actions or issues that the adults should reappraise.

The chapter also includes an account of students' role in the creation and adoption of a 'respect for all' policy, as part of anti-oppressive moves in Morgan. The school's experiences illustrate the importance of student perspectives in supporting antiracist change.

In the final section I look at the experiences and perspectives of white students – a group who are rarely given the attention they deserve when antiracist programmes are initiated. Their views throw up several crucial issues, including the need for consistent responses to accusations of racism; the problem of just *who* can be defined as a racist in school; and the inadequacy of current conceptions of white ethnicity.

Antiracism in young people's lives

Ethnic diversity and opposition to racist harassment

Students in both Mary Seacole and Garret Morgan frequently express positive views about ethnic diversity. When discussing the range of ethnic backgrounds represented in their schools, for example, they tend to single out the benefits of knowing a variety of people (sometimes as close friends) and the greater appreciation that they gain for other cultures and religions.

In Mary Seacole Comprehensive

> *Nigath (South Asian, Muslim: year 7):*
> I think it is good because otherwise you would just know your own culture and you wouldn't know anything about the others.
> *Hayley (white: year 7):*
> Yes. Rather than you just going and talking with your own colour you should go and talk to some other people and make some more friends.

In Garret Morgan Comprehensive

> *Stacey (white: year 9):*
> It makes you more aware of where people are from and how they live and that. It makes you more aware. So like not to say something to put your foot in it, make yourself look a bit stupid.
> *Ajaz (South Asian, Muslim: year 9):*
> Just makes people work together, *understand* each other.

It is interesting that in schools which have taken a high profile stance against racism, many students first highlight their concern for what might be called the 'multicultural' elements of their experience – including white young people's desire to avoid inadvertently offending ('putting your foot in it') through lack of information. The comments hint at, but do not fully reveal, the opposition to racism that is a strong feature of student relations in the schools. This antiracist blend of concerns and perspectives frequently goes beyond an interest in 'culture' and 'difference', and involves an active challenge to negative assumptions and inequitable treatment (whether by peers or teachers).

In Seacole, for example, racism between students is seen somewhat differently to other forms of bullying, and brings about a range of informal sanctions from peers. Before examining this further, I should perhaps emphasize that the students fully appreciate the serious physical and emotional hurt caused by other forms of bullying:

Karen (white: year 10):
> It's like one minute I was all great and they all liked me and every-
> thing like that, and they used to talk to me; and then the next
> minute they were *calling* me and everything like that. What got me
> mad was that they didn't admit to themselves what they were doing
> to me – because they *were* bullying me. And it is *worse* than being
> beat up and things like that because they just take your confidence
> away from you, you know. It really destroys you. You don't want
> to come to school and then you are upset at night and in the
> morning. And I used to *dread* lessons because they used to pick on
> me in lessons . . .

Karen was supported by other students who helped her cope with the
situation. Despite their moral support, however, these students did not
openly challenge the aggressors. Rather, they supplied an alternative
(friendly) peer network that helped Karen deal with the attacks until she
finally decided to report the situation to teachers. In contrast, incidents
that students read as 'racist', are often dealt with more directly:

Sally (white: year 9):
> There is some racism still (. . .) that's why we beat her up <she
> laughs>. Well, we didn't beat her up, we just mouthed off at her
> because of what she was doing. We didn't talk to her for *so* long.
> She was being racist and everything.

Robina (South Asian, Muslim: year 10):
> We find if people are racist, for example, to an Asian girl, or a
> white person racist to a black girl or something. We find that that
> person is isolated. You know, even their *own* friends will isolate
> that person. Like if I'm racist to Karen [a white peer] or something,
> everyone will go against me. We will isolate that person, that's the
> way we are. (. . .)

Nina (South Asian, Sikh: year 10):
> It is just immediate isolation. Within that minute, that is it. Every-
> one is against that person; whether they are new, whether they are
> the most popular person, headgirl, deputy, *anything* – that is it.

Moira (white: year 10):
> If they've been racist.

Nina:
> It is taken seriously.

Karen (white: year 10):
> Even if you aren't *that* bothered about racism and that – but most
> people *are* in this school – but you say, 'You are racist' and that is
> it (. . .).

Moira:
> There is a white group in our class, and this girl called another girl 'Paki'. And this girl in the group said, 'Shut up, you're being stupid'.

Nina:
> Pupils can stop the racism themselves.

Robina:
> Like if a black girl calls another black girl racist names, they won't take it seriously because they find it funny. It is like, if Nina called me a 'Paki' I wouldn't really be bothered. I have got to admit, I do it myself to my other friends and we enjoy it, you know, calling each other 'Pakis' and everything. <she laughs>

Moira:
> But if *I* said that, then it would be totally different wouldn't it.

The students' action against peer racism, therefore, tends to be swift and forthright. Additionally, as the final sentences illustrate, the students are well aware that racist labels carry different meanings in different settings. Although Robina seems almost confessional, in admitting to enjoying swopping 'fake' racist insults with friends who are also of minority background, Moira (a white friend) sees no contradiction in this and (to make sure that I have understood the point) emphasizes that – as a white student – these kinds of 'game' are not available to her.

Karen's comment highlights the degree to which opposition to racism has become an accepted part of student culture in Seacole: even those for whom racism is not a major concern – who 'aren't *that* bothered about racism' – often react to comments and actions they see as racist. The 'people's education' course (described in the previous chapter) has clearly encouraged these students to begin thinking through the issues raised by racist violence and harassment. They are convinced that racism is a more serious offence than, say, harassment about the failure to wear fashionable brands of clothes.[1] According to these students, verbal attacks about poverty, although painful, do not reflect upon you as a *'person'*, or upon others who are associated with you. This is not the case with racist harassment:

Moira (white: year 10):
> Because if somebody says something like, 'You are not wearing the right trainers', then we tend to be more sorry for the girl who isn't wearing the trainers (. . .) It doesn't matter what trainers you wear it is what you *are*. But if you are racist then you are insulting the *person* –

Robina (South Asian, Muslim: year 10):
> <interrupting> And their *community*.

Moira:
> Yeah, you are insulting *more* than one person, aren't you. So all the people who don't wear 'Nike' trainers don't feel all offended do they? But [racism] is much more strong though isn't it – it is *a way of life* and you're insulting *them* . . .

It is clear, therefore, that in Seacole some students (possibly a majority) – including working-class whites – have come to view racism as a serious matter that should not be tolerated. Compared to other forms of bullying, racist harassment in the school causes a more immediate and substantial response. In my other case study school (Garret Morgan) the students also appreciate the serious nature of racist harassment. However, Morgan has focused a good deal of attention on a wide range of student rights and anti-bullying measures. Here the opposition to racism generally takes a less dramatic form than in Seacole and is matched by the opposition to other forms of bullying (the background to these developments in Morgan is discussed later).

My conversations with students in the schools, therefore, illustrate the potential influence of antiracist teaching and whole-school change. In these schools much student culture has come to reflect a genuine opposition to racism which translates into direct action against racist peers. As the students have developed a greater awareness of 'race' and racism, so they have also become increasingly critical of teachers who fail to live up to their antiracist expectations.

Student perspectives: seeing beyond the rhetoric

In the previous chapter I described how the students in Seacole came to adopt a more sophisticated view of racism and racists; realizing, for example, that racist comments may spring from a variety of causes and can be open to change. Students in both Seacole and Morgan are also skilled at identifying actions that may have racist consequences, despite benign intentions. The schools' work on antiracism has made the students both more perceptive and more confident about questioning actions with which they do not agree. In Morgan, for example, many students disagree with elements of the dress code; some are aware that it particularly clashes with styles favoured by African Caribbean young men:

Deep (South Asian, Hindu: year 9):
> I would change the rule about haircuts because sometimes you are suspended for your hair.

DG:
> What kind of haircut would get you in trouble?

Deep:

Some people have designs [shaved] on their neck.

Tom (white: year 9):

Tramlines and stuff. (...)

Deep:

A boy had his hair all shaved except the front and he got told to shave off the front (...)

Liam (white: year 9):

Your haircut's not going to make any difference to how you work. It's stupid.

Deep:

It's up to the individual I think. They [teachers] say it looks untidy.

Liam:

Not *respectable*. (...)

Deep:

It is kind of being racist because some people like, they can't do much with their hair and that's the way they can really change it.

Here an Asian student recognizes something of the importance to black peers of shaved patterns in their hair (at the time of our conversation a popular style among African Caribbean young men). This suggests that the school has failed to demonstrate to its students that any real consideration has been given to the 'racial' consequences of the dress code. This is an issue some teachers might see as non-racial, but which (as Deep notes) potentially disadvantages people of African Caribbean background.

Young people's ability to perceive racism in others' actions and assumptions can sometimes come as a shock to teachers – even in schools that have an actively antiracist ethos. When discussing the already controversial issue of terrorism, for example, a Seacole teacher upset some students by suggesting that Saddam Hussein and Muammar Qaddafi might be popular assassination targets:

Robina (South Asian, Muslim: year 10):

It makes you feel funny because they are both Muslim. And it makes you feel like she has got something against Muslims.

Students in both Seacole and Morgan are angered by actions that they feel betray a lack of understanding on the part of some teachers. *This is especially the case where teachers seem to adopt what, to the students, is a simplistic view of minority communities as homogeneous groups, neither changing nor internally differentiated.* For example, when a teacher assumes that all Muslim students, in view of arranged marriages, will be against casual relationships with members of the opposite sex, they reveal a well-meaning but simplistic perspective on their South Asian students.

In the previous chapter I noted some students' feelings of embarrassment and/or anger when they are 'put on the spot' and expected to speak for their entire community, for example, when discussing racism or cultural diversity. Seacole's antiracist programme of 'people's education' avoids this by relying on the strength of its content to draw students into sharing their experiences and feelings – as individuals, rather than 'representatives' of any wider group. Students in both Seacole and Morgan, however, note that, in some subject lessons, teachers continue to fall into this trap. Teaching strategies that are meant as a positive means of valuing and using ethnic diversity in a class, can be experienced as demeaning by minority students:

Nina (South Asian, Sikh: year 10):
There is this girl, Jaswinder, she is a Sikh, and they were doing about Sikhism and [a teacher] asked *her* questions straight away (. . .) And she goes, 'How am I meant to know, even if I am a Sikh? How have I got to know? (. . .)

Robina (South Asian, Muslim: year 10):
He assumed all – like, 'How many prophets have you got?' *It's like if you don't name them all you are not a Muslim!*

In this case the students object to being 'tested' on their religious knowledge in ways that single them out and seem to presume a depth of learning the teacher does not expect of Christian students: they are rejecting teachers' essentialist and reductionist perspectives. The students' anger echoes that of Le (Vietnamese: year 8) who resents the possibly genuine, but ultimately patronizing, interest that white peers show in her language abilities:

What really gets me is when you are in school, and it is parents evening and you talk to your mum, and then your friends see you and they just come up to you and they say, 'Oh, say "Hello" in Chinese. Say "Hello" in Chinese' or something. It really bugs me, because I am not ashamed of my nationality or race but it just bugs me the way that they want you to speak Cantonese for them, so they can get amused and so they can mock you.

It is important that Le interprets the actions of teachers and peers as a form of self-serving amusement. This argues the need to consider how students experience and interpret actions by teachers and others, regardless of the intent behind them.

All of this points to the need always to question taken-for-granted assumptions about ethnic minority students and their communities; especially essentialist and reductionist perspectives that gloss over important internal differences. An occasion that showed the significance of such differences occurred in Seacole when the headteacher agreed to an Asian student's request that a room be set aside for prayer during Ramadan. The incident is a reminder of the complex and diverse nature of student perspectives, even among groups that many assume (mistakenly) to be relatively homogeneous:

> *Robina (South Asian, Muslim: year 10)*:
> It was the Holy Month and I said – 'cause we pray five times a day – I said, 'Are we allowed to pray in school Miss?' And Miss said that was a good idea. So we have booked a room, me and another girl, and we invited girls. We got a good response first, about twenty people. It's not *very* good, but that is a *good* response. And then after that it broke down and now nobody comes at all <she laughs>.
>
> *Nina (South Asian, Sikh: year 10)*:
> And there was this Muslim girl and she just *laughed* at Robina and said, 'Gosh, you're *stupid* doing this'. And it is her *own* religion as well.
>
> *Robina*:
> We had a few Muslim girls coming and saying <angrily> '*What do you think you're doing?*' Because to them religion is left at home, they don't want to bring it to school. For them school is a *social* occasion. (. . .) For *them* school is a time of letting go of home life . . .

In this section I have examined the significance and complexity of student perspectives on 'race' and ethnicity. Even in schools that are consciously adopting antiracist policies and practice, students frequently perceive remaining areas of doubt and concern. If these perspectives go untapped they could undermine a school's efforts to confront racism. At the very least they represent an important source of information that warns against essentialist viewpoints and may point to improved practice in the future.

Students and school policy-making

Students often play a key role in bringing about antiracist change. At the most basic level, the mere presence of minority students can spur teachers into reconsidering taken-for-granted assumptions and facing up to the need for change (see Chapter 5). The schools at the centre of this research went further: both attempted to involve students directly in the policy-making process.

In Mary Seacole Girls' School students were consulted over a draft antiracist policy. Their comments were overwhelmingly constructive and helped the policy writers to identify areas of continued doubt or confusion. In addition, the students' enthusiasm for the policy helped persuade other teachers that antiracist change was possible and even necessary (see Chapter

6). In Garret Morgan Comprehensive students are credited with having actually *written* the school's policy statement on the rejection of labelling and oppression: known within the school as the 'respect for all' policy. In this section I examine how the policy was created and consider the limits that shaped student participation. Despite these limits, however, the policy gains weight from the students' involvement and from the daily actions of teachers, most of whom hold themselves – as well as their students – accountable to the policy.

Students and policy writing in Morgan: a con trick?

When I first contacted Morgan, I discovered that teachers had clearly set limits to the students' involvement, never losing their position of final veto. I was conscious of many teachers' fear of losing traditional areas of power and control (see Gillborn et al. 1993: ch. 5) and worried that the student involvement might be little more than a confidence trick, trying to manipulate students' compliance by claiming to have let *them* write a document which could be slotted into a wider behaviour policy. In contrast, an informant advised me that the school was worth a visit and pointed out that a recent HMI report had praised the developments in Morgan; describing the 'respect for all' policy as 'a unique document'.

On a preliminary visit to the school I spoke with the head, several teachers and students (and was allowed to wander around the corridors and drop in on a couple of lessons). This convinced me that the school is genuinely addressing antiracism, and developing work that challenges other forms of stereotyping, including disability. I decided that further visits would be worthwhile. Nevertheless, I remained cautious about the 'respect for all' policy; my tour of the school confirmed its prominence – displayed in many classrooms and hallways – but I still felt uneasy. When I began the main period of fieldwork in Morgan, however, I was surprised at how frequently students spontaneously raised the policy with me. Clearly something significant has been achieved.

The origins of the policy

it was like bits and pieces of what we said and bits and pieces of what they [teachers] said.

This is how Teresa (a white sixth form student in Morgan) recalls the creation of the 'respect for all' policy. Teresa was in year 9 when the policy was drafted, using student ideas as the basic material. To date the policy has not been changed. The headteacher (appointed after the policy was in place) relates the following account:

I think they all began by writing lists of things which they had experienced and suffered from. And so each tutor group of [year 9] children thought about the things that they had been either bullied over, been made to feel uncomfortable over, unhappy over, had been insulted by or whatever. And then I know that all these lists were funnelled to our school council and the creation of the policy was the work of the students' council, but working on inputs from *all* classes. And I know that they wrote this themselves and the staff were very clever – I think they were very clever – because they have left it quite imperfect, which is what is good about it. One could have polished the English, but if you had you would have taken it from the language and the context of the children's writing.

The final version begins by stating the school's opposition to all forms of harassment and abuse. The body of the policy takes the form of a list of characteristics that may form the basis for harassment, which the school rejects:

> *We particularly reject the way that some people abuse others*
> *because they are richer or poorer, older or younger,*
> *because they are small or tall, thin or fat,*
> *because of the colour of their skin,*
> *because ...*
> *because ...*

The list continues with a series of statements committing students and teachers to rejecting abuse of others because of gender, appearance, disability, ethnicity, religion and so on. At the end of the policy statement there is advice about who to see/where to go if you feel it is not being respected.

The head's comment about the 'imperfect' construction of the policy is interesting. The repetitious structure – beginning each new line, 'because' – is read by many adults as a direct signal of the students' hand in writing the policy. To the students who were originally involved, however, the document itself was something of an anti-climax:

> *Bev (white: year 12):*
> I thought they had gone into too much detail. I thought, people *know* this; that you shouldn't be treating people this way. I always thought it was too long (...) I assumed at the time that it was common sense that you shouldn't treat people like this.

The students were aware that their participation was within well-defined limits. Nevertheless, they remember the excitement of the period and the fact that issues of diversity and inequality achieved a high profile around the school:

Alison (white: year 12):
  I think it was just a combination of what everybody thought. From our point of view, they [teachers] just came round and said, 'Do you want to write this?'
Bev:
  It was really what they felt should happen in school. That people – minorities – shouldn't be treated differently to everyone else. Because at the time we had a handicapped girl in the school and I think we had a wider range of people at that time, who had disabilities and everything.
Teresa:
  We had to write down what we thought, our ideas. (...) But it was like bits and pieces of what we said and bits and pieces of what they said.
Bev:
  That's usually what happens actually. We have our say and then the teachers have their say and then [the headteacher] will sort it out from that.

It appears, therefore, that in Morgan (as in Seacole) involving students in the process of policy debate and formation had the immediate effect of raising the profile of key issues. In the longer term, however, it is necessary to ask how subsequent cohorts of students perceive the policy? Indeed, is the policy anything more than a short-lived anti-bullying exercise?

The policy in practice

Given that the policy is now several years old, there is the possibility that its importance has diminished as successive groups of students enter the school and simply 'inherit' others' work. The policy might lose all meaning, becoming just another piece of rhetoric adorning classroom walls and the school prospectus. This has not happened. In fact, current students are keen to highlight the policy when describing the school and their experiences. Conversations with younger students reveal that the policy is kept very much in their minds; for example, through specific sessions (in tutor groups and in PSE) that discuss the policy, its creation and consequences. Some students complain about having it 'drummed into us' and hearing teachers 'go on about' how 'different' the school is. Despite these reservations, most seem to view the policy as something that really *is* important in their school. The following interview extract shows how a student chooses to highlight the policy (in answer to a very general question):

DG:

I'm trying to build up a picture of the school. Do you think there's anything else that's important, for me to understand how the school is from your point of view?

Deep (South Asian, Hindu: year 9):

There's the 'respect for all' policy, I think that's very good.

DG:

Can you tell me something about that? Why do you think it's good?

Deep:

Because it was set up by pupils in the school. It was not the teachers' ideas, it was the pupils' ideas. (. . .)

DG:

What do you think about it?

Liam (white: year 9):

<positively> I think it's all right.

Tom (white: year 9):

Yeah.

Deep:

It says it all.

A group of younger students also raised the policy with me. Again they drew particular attention to how the document had been created:

Andy (white: year 8):

It is a thing that was written by the pupils. They helped write things in it, and it was all put together, and it is published in the school prospectus for new pupils. It is things like, 'people of different race, colours, will not be discriminated against. Different sexes . . .' (. . .)

Karl (African Caribbean: year 8):

When we first came to this school, we had an information booklet on it. And you had to write stuff about it. (. . .)

Andy:

Yes, because I think it is better because it has been written by the *kids*. Sometimes it is written by the teachers and the kids won't take any notice of it.

DG:

So do you think the teachers and the kids take notice of it?

Andy:

Yes.

The head and teachers in Morgan are conscious that mechanisms must be found to keep the policy alive in the students' eyes. They have judged it unnecessary to repeat the entire process with any successive year groups; rather they try to give all students some small sense of ownership by taking them through related issues and discussing how the policy was created. The students quoted above suggest that this process is successful. However, it must also be noted that many students fully expect a chance to rewrite the policy in the future; they will be disappointed if some means are not found to keep them engaged with the ideals of the policy, throughout their career in the school.

A key aspect of the policy's success to date appears to be teachers' willingness to apply it to their own behaviour and assumptions around the school. I noted previously that some staff were slow to become involved in the antiracist work in Morgan; indeed, staff racism was a factor in sparking the first core group meetings (see Chapter 5). As the 'respect for all' policy has become an established part of school life, however, it has added to the weight of antiracist (and other anti-oppressive) developments in the school. Despite their reservations about the format and style of the policy, the students who contributed to its creation now look back over their careers in Morgan and feel that important changes have occurred – some of which they attribute directly to the policy:

Catherine (white: year 12):
   I think it's been significant, because there's not much bullying around.
Bev:
   I think it's helped most of us to develop as people really. I think our attitudes have changed over the years – I know mine has. And I think the way that was drummed into us really made me think about my beliefs.
Alison:
   When we were in the first-year, you tended to see so much more bullying around.
Bev:
   Yes. I don't know if it's because we don't mix with the lower school anymore (. . .) But there always seemed to be a lot more.

Conversations with younger students reveal that some forms of harassment still survive in Morgan, though they are mostly seen as relatively trivial. Importantly, however, racial violence and harassment are considered especially rare. The most common reports concern disputes between boys, especially where some young men are identified as targets because of perceived arrogance about their ability ('boffins') or because they adopt macho ('hard') personas which others decide to test. Also there is some petty harassment of younger students by older peers, such as jostling in corridors and staring at them as they pass by. Overall, however, students are extremely positive about relations with peers and teachers in Morgan. A group of year 7 students note how classmates rally around in case of problems (such as family illness or bereavement) and describe the school as 'a bit like a big family'. When she joined the school, for example, one female student was surprised by the atmosphere: 'I wasn't expecting them [teachers] to be as caring as they are.' This seems to be a common view:

DG:
How do you get on with the teachers? What are they like?
Deborah (white: year 9):
Some good, some bad.
Stacey (white: year 9):
Most of them are very good to you.
Deborah:
You get the odd one or two [who aren't].
DG:
So what makes a teacher a 'good' one?
Stacey:
Enthusiastic. Friendly.
Deborah:
Yeah, and relationships between –
Stacey:
<interrupting> You can talk to them. They don't just teach. They are not like a robot just teaching you. It has got to be a normal person.
Deborah:
And they have got to give you some respect too.
Stacey:
Yeah, like the 'respect for all' – they actually do think about it. It's not just there for decoration.

As these transcripts indicate, the 'respect for all' policy is something many students spontaneously raise when describing life in Morgan. They feel that most teachers accept the consequences of the policy in their dealings with students. My conversations with teachers confirmed that it is given a high profile in staff discussions. A head of department, who has worked in the school for three years, notes:

[The 'respect for all' policy] is the ethos of the school in my eyes. I really feel very strongly about it and so I make a big thing of it. And I know I am not the only one who does that. And we hope the children will take it on board and it will be important for them. It is obviously the case that it is not important for *all* the children, but I think they should see that as a big thing. (. . .) You may think this is a PR [public relations] exercise but I know *I* feel that this school . . . (. . .) I just feel that we *do*, as a whole staff, try to ensure that the children are happy here. That feeling is obvious to parents because the number of parents who actually said to me last night [at a parents' evening] – and that is new parents coming to the school – who just had this *feeling* (that I have had all the way through) about this school. There is this feeling of caring and concern.

This teacher is right to qualify her praise: the policy 'is not important for *all* the children'. As I have already noted, some bullying does still occur in Morgan; additionally, the antiracist developments do not receive total staff support – some of the core group identify their most immediate task as defending the gains they have already made. However, my data suggest that (contrary to my original fears) the 'respect for all' policy does play an important part in the antiracist developments in the school – it is not simply 'a PR exercise'.

The students who took part in the policy-making process were fully aware of the limited role staff would allow them and felt a little disappointed by the final product. Nevertheless, through the use of the policy (in student and staff relations) some simple ideas have assumed real power within the school. New cohorts of students welcome the fact that policy was 'written' by peers; this, and the content of the policy, sets up a series of expectations about staff behaviour. As in Seacole (where students' comments helped prepare the micro-political ground for the school's antiracist policy), so the teachers in Morgan have used student ideas to highlight antiracism and produce a document to which all – staff and students – can be held accountable. The gains are not total, but they are significant.

'No one asks about us': white students and antiracism

In the realm of categories, black is always marked as a colour (as the term 'coloured' egregiously acknowledges), and is always particularizing; whereas white is not anything really, not an identity, not a particularizing quality, because it is everything – white is no colour because it is all colours.

(Dyer 1988: 142)

When set in the midst of ethnic particularity, this dully monolithic and asocial character works to enhance the mythical connotations of superiority and purity that have so often surrounded notions of 'whiteness'. 'White' appears as the Other of ethnicity; a natural, transcendental state untainted by the swarming, thoroughly earth bound, histories and geographies that are so important to the categorisation of 'non-whites'.

(Bonnett 1993: 175–6)

These quotations are taken from the small amount of work that has begun to deconstruct notions of 'whiteness'; they are useful in pointing to the

discursive power of 'white' as a category. There is a need for more research in this area, especially work that takes seriously the power and
importance of white ethnic identities.

Analytically, white students occupy a somewhat ill-defined space in most
of the literature on 'race' and ethnicity in education. Research, whether in
'all-white' schools or more ethnically diverse contexts, tends to cast white
students in the role of potential antagonist/racist rather than fellow antiracist
(let alone 'victim'). This is hardly surprising since racism in schools (as
elsewhere) is mostly supported and extended by the actions of white people (students and teachers). At the same time, however, it has always been
clear that widespread progress depends on the involvement of white people. Indeed, as antiracist analyses and pedagogies become more sophisticated, it is increasingly obvious that white students occupy a *pivotal* role:
any genuine attempt to challenge racism in education must engage with
their perspectives and experiences. This is as true in multi-ethnic schools
(cf. Macdonald et al. 1989) as it is in all/mainly white contexts (Troyna
and Hatcher 1992).

An example of what can happen where schools fail to take seriously the
views and experiences of white students is provided by Máirtín Mac an
Ghaill (1994). In his ethnographic research on the social construction of
masculinity, Mac an Ghaill discusses a group of white young men, of
middle-class background, who view the simplistic and dogmatic antiracism
of their parents and school as deeply hypocritical:

Ben:
> The teachers and our parents when they talk about racism always
> say white people mustn't be racist to blacks. That's fine. But they
> won't say anything when Asians and black kids are racist to each
> other.

Adam:
> And how come they keep on saying that racialism is really bad but
> we've had a load of hassle from black and Asian kids (. . .) But no
> one asks about us. The older generation don't ask what it's like for
> us who have to live with a lot of black kids who don't like us. No
> one says to the black kids, you have to like the whites. They'll tell
> them to fuck off.

> (quoted in Mac an Ghaill 1994: 85)

Unless the views and experiences of minority *and* white students are taken
seriously, attempts at antiracism will lurch towards the kind of doctrinaire
'moral' approach that operated so disastrously in Burnage High School:

> Since the assumption is that black students are the victims of the
> immoral behaviour of white students, white students almost inevitably

become the 'baddies'. The operation of the [doctrinaire 'moral'] anti-racist policies almost inevitably results in white students (and their parents) feeling 'attacked' and all being seen as 'racist', whether they are ferret-eyed fascists or committed anti-racists or simply children with a great store of human feeling and warmth who are ready to listen and learn and to explore their feelings towards one another.

(Macdonald et al. 1989: 347)

I have discussed the development of antiracism in two schools and noted how they have attempted to move beyond the limits of 'moral' or 'symbolic' antiracism. Of importance has been the attempt, in both schools, to incorporate student perspectives into the antiracist programmes. The programme of 'people's education' in Seacole (Chapter 7), for example, seems to have been especially successful; providing a forum for students to discuss how they feel about controversial issues, in ways that connect with 'the real world' as they experience it. The programme has genuinely helped many students (of minority and white backgrounds) critically to reconsider 'race', racism and racists. In a similar but less dramatic fashion, teachers at Morgan have used the 'respect for all' policy as a cornerstone for anti-oppressive education strategies that seek to avoid the problems of essentialism and reductionism identified in the Burnage report. Despite these advances, however, areas of doubt remain. In particular, it is worth examining the position of white students in a little more detail, for clues to future developments and lessons the schools may hold for others contemplating similar work.

White students and the accusation of racism

Teachers in Seacole and Morgan report unease among white students when the schools began to focus attention on issues of 'race' and racism. In Morgan, initial reactions from white students indicated a sense of bias against them. In relation to racial harassment procedures, for example, a member of the core group recalls:

The feedback we had, as we put together the policy, was that it was all biased towards the Bangladeshi/black students, rather than the white students (. . .) And this was the feedback we got very strongly from the white kids; this system wasn't for them. And why were we doing this?

In Morgan the core group worked with students (often using PSE time) to take them through the various antiracist procedures – always emphasizing that white students could take advantage of the system if the need arose:

It enabled us to explain, go through the forms, and make them realize,
in fact, it wasn't biased; it was actually a system for *any* group.

Despite these lessons, and the use of the 'respect for all' policy, the core
teachers at Morgan feel it took three years fully to establish antiracism as
a legitimate feature of the lives of white students.

The additional work the Morgan core group had to undertake, with
white students, shows the need for schools to stay responsive to student
perspectives. Rather than backing away from the changes, or simply as-
serting their 'moral' value, here the teachers worked to involve students in
the changes and get beyond any initial sense of injustice on the part of
white students. This is a crucial part of the antiracist changes in both case
study schools and directly parallels the challenge that many white *teachers*
feel when faced with antiracist change.

I have already discussed how the core group of teachers at Seacole
worked to give their colleagues confidence when dealing with accusations
of racism in the school. In accusations against teachers, the crucial point
was to encourage them to deal properly with any accusation (neither
paralysed with fear; nor simply rejecting accusations out of hand).[2] Similarly, when dealing with accusations against students, teachers have to
demonstrate (to both the alleged victim and aggressor) that they are interested in the facts of the case; take seriously the students' feelings; and work
through agreed school procedures in as fair a way as possible. This may
sound relatively straightforward but is demanding in practice. Where schools
introduce high profile policies against racist harassment, for example, initially they may witness a sharp rise in the number of reported incidents.
Some teachers (and governors) are likely to interpret this as a sign that the
policy has simply 'stirred up trouble'. Paradoxically, however, such a rise
may be a sign of progress. If the newly established policy is properly
enforced (thereby winning students' trust), an increase in *reported* incidents can reflect a decrease in the number of *unreported* cases. The *true*
number of incidents may not have changed, or could even have begun to
fall (Gillborn 1993). In this context teachers have to work within the
procedures to ensure that each case is treated fairly; neither brushing incidents aside (which weakens action against racist harassment) nor automatically assuming every white student to be guilty of racism (which
undermines antiracism in the eyes of white students).

When antiracist changes were first introduced in Morgan and Seacole,
this was a particularly pressing problem. Now the changes are well-
established, white complaints about bias are less common. Nevertheless,
conflict can emerge quickly, sometimes followed by accusation and counter-
accusation. A head of department at Seacole notes:

There was a big fight when I first came, about a black girl pushing
another one and then the girls say, 'There is nothing we can do or say

to defend ourselves, because they know here that if it involves Asians and us . . . they won't listen to us.' Sometimes it is very strong in the classroom.

Although this issue did surface in my conversations with teachers and students, few volunteered much detail. Possibly such cases are now rare; maybe they did not want to exaggerate the problem; maybe they felt that complaining threw a shadow across their own commitment to antiracism. Overall, it was a teacher of minority background who spoke out most strongly. She notes the danger that such cases can present:

> [Following an attack on her son by an Asian youth and his friends, the teacher contacted the aggressors' school]
> The one that actually did it confessed and said, 'Yes, I did it but I did it because the boy made a racist remark.' I said to the deputy [headteacher], 'I am sorry, I am tired of that (. . .) This boy mustn't have noticed that Stephen is just as brown or black as he is. And not only that, you don't make a racist remark when there are nine of them behind you.' (. . .) It is not fair that people start shouting 'racism'. And I take it seriously because we are a mixed family, so if I hear people abusing it, that means that when you *really* need it nothing will happen.

It would be surprising if such cases never happened. Students are very resourceful and quick to spot issues they can exploit. This teacher's anger at the misuse of accusations of racism – as a defence for wrongdoing rather than a weapon against it – indicates the importance of the issue and perhaps offers a clue to the frequency of such cases. Students in Seacole and Morgan take racism seriously – most probably share this teacher's view that, in this context, 'crying wolf' is a dangerous strategy.

Although such events may be rare, however, they are extremely important. It is crucial that teachers retain the ability to discriminate between genuine cases of racist harassment and those where an accusation is used after the event to excuse one's behaviour.[3] An encouraging finding is that in Seacole and Morgan most students (of all ethnic backgrounds) seem generous in their readiness to find positive motives in teachers' actions. The teachers do not always get it right, but the students seem to recognize that the effort is usually genuine and always worthwhile.

White perspectives and conceptual issues in antiracism

Before leaving this section, it is useful to note a couple of conceptual issues that are thrown into relief by the perspectives and experiences of white students. The first concerns the definition of racism in school contexts and how this can be reconciled to wider analyses of 'race' and racism in society. Second, the issue of white ethnicities has to be addressed.

First, both Seacole and Morgan have adopted a clear position (through their practice) on the complex and controversial issue of just *who* can be said to be racist. A long-established debate in antiracism concerns the question of whether it is only white people who can be said to act in 'racist' ways. During the 1980s a convenient and oft-quoted means of coping with this issue was to adopt the slogan that Racism = Prejudice + Power. In an extreme form this definition holds that generally only white people have power, therefore only white people can be racist. More subtly, some writers recognize that power means different things in different situations. Hence, while black and Asian people – as a group – can be said to be *relatively* powerless in Britain, in certain situations black and Asian individuals clearly exercise power; therefore, they have the potential to act in ways that are racist. This would apply to the school situation where black and Asian students may enjoy power through peer relations – making 'black racism a very real thing' (AMMA 1987: 14). This approach, however, is also open to critique.

Although 'Racism = Prejudice + Power' is a striking phrase, it dangerously oversimplifies the nature of labelling and social interaction in schools – many teachers who are not 'prejudiced' in any conventional sense, nevertheless act in ways that have racist consequences (Gillborn 1990). As Barry Troyna (1993a) argues, antiracist analyses of power and racism have developed in an attempt to understand the complex and changing nature of racism in society. The formulaic approach to racism, and the use of 'institutional racism' as an ill-defined catchall concept, have been criticized (Carter and Williams 1987; Troyna 1988b; Troyna and Williams 1986; Williams 1985) long before more recent contributions (e.g. Cohen 1992; Rattansi 1992).

Despite these developments, however, some prominent antiracist authors maintain a theoretical position that privileges white racism. In explaining their approach to the analysis of racist harassment, for example, Barry Troyna and Richard Hatcher stress the fundamental significance of 'the asymmetrical power relations between black and white citizens in Britain' (1992: 16). They continue:

At its basic common denominator, then, a racist incident is about the misuse of power: the collective power enjoyed by White people in a society characterised by racist ideologies and discriminatory practices. It is on these grounds that we reject the all-embracing nomenclatures of 'racial incidents' and 'inter-racial conflict' which the CRE, Home Office and others endorse. We are committed to ensuring a clear distinction between attacks *of whatever form*, by Whites on Blacks and those perpetrated by Blacks on white people. So, it is not simply a matter of semantics. This distinction goes straight to the heart of our theoretical positioning of this phenomenon and the way we seek to interpret and deal with its occurrence.

(Troyna and Hatcher 1992: 16, emphasis added)

In their treatment of racist incidents in mainly white primary schools, Troyna and Hatcher focus largely on name-calling. They note that while some white students recognize the special damage done by racist insults, many feel that teachers unfairly single it out for attention. Some interpret this as a sign of bias against them as white people (Troyna and Hatcher 1992: 168–71). Troyna and Hatcher recognize the difficulty that this can cause and argue for increased work on 'race' in the curriculum, possibly as a means of helping white students conceptualize the incidents in a wider context (ibid.: 200).

In both Seacole and Morgan antiracist work is incorporated into the mainstream curriculum (though by no means as well as the core groups would like) and supported by discrete work, such as the 'people's education' programme. Here, work on racist name-calling consistently emphasizes the difference between racist insults and other forms of abuse: a distinction that most white students seem to accept in these schools. In comparison to other forms of bullying, for example, racist harassment triggers a more immediate and severe response from many students. Nevertheless, the schools have adopted a rather different position on the wider principle of racism *per se*. As I have noted above, during the first stages of antiracist work, white students frequently raised issues of equality and argued that the moves were 'biased' against them. The school's response, that the procedures *could* work just as well for white students, seems to have been significant. Similarly, it is important that they continue to deal consistently with accusations of racism – taking seriously white students' perspectives. In practice the procedures on racist harassment continue to be used almost exclusively against white aggression/racism: yet the schools' acceptance of the wider principle (that *'racism and ethnocentrism are not necessarily confined to white groups'* – Rattansi 1992: 36, original emphasis) has avoided 'moralizing' about white power in ways that do not make sense to many white students – especially those from working-class backgrounds, for whom talk of their being in a position of power might seem absurd. Clearly this is a complex issue, but we should be careful about rejecting out of hand the schools' decision that a consistent approach could not afford to deny the possibility of white victims of racism. Although the case study schools have adopted this position mostly out of pragmatism, it echoes important advances in theorizing racism and difference.[4]

The second issue, to arise from a consideration of white students' perspectives, concerns the status of white ethnicities. Presently much teaching has consequences for the presentation of white people in history and for white students' sense of ethnicity; unfortunately, most of it is either dangerously slanted (such as ethnocentric presentations of the 'civilizing' process of colonization and global capitalism) or experienced as negative (caricaturing white perspectives as deeply flawed and implicitly racist). Multicultural and antiracist materials challenge the former, but can lapse into essentialist and reductionist attacks on white people:

> Multicultural education, according to Gus John, a member of the [Burnage] inquiry, implies that white working-class children 'have to pay due deference to the culture of others even before anybody checked out with them what their perception of their own culture actually was' (John, 1990, p. 70). The children in our schools also seemed to be left high and dry on such matters.
>
> (Troyna and Hatcher 1992: 200–1)

This is a pressing problem. The political right have successfully appropriated many symbols of British (and especially English) ethnicity to their own ends. In the creative renegotiation and reconstruction of ethnic identities among the young, white students are as active as their peers of minority backgrounds, sometimes adapting minority symbols and 'styles' to new ends (see Back 1993; CME 1993; Hewitt 1986). Yet the right have begun to 'hijack' the very notion of 'Englishness'. As Stuart Hall notes, although capitalism and the market increasingly operate on a *global* scale, new and different forms of the *local* are developing. The latter include a renewed emphasis on ethnicity as a basis for group and individual identity that is at once political and cultural (cf. Hall 1992b and c). Clearly antiracist teachers and schools have a crucial role to play in the search for positive elements of a white ethnicity – elements that challenge the right's 're-vamped', 'aggressive' and absolutist 'little Englandism' (Hall 1992b: 308).

This is an area where both Seacole and Morgan need to do further work. Their present emphasis on antiracism, as opposed to an isolated focus on culture and diversity, has not thrown this issue into relief, but it is clearly important. Recent policy developments, while adopting a deracialized discourse, carry strong messages about the superiority and dominance of a particular post-colonial imperialist white history and sense of ethnicity (see Chapter 2). This poses a crucial question for future antiracist programmes:

> whether we can begin to construct modern forms of progressive English national identity to counter the New Right's appropriation of the discourse of nationality with its projected atavistic representations of the strong British state.
>
> (Mac an Ghaill 1994: 85)

There is an immense wealth of anti-oppressive struggle in British history, for example, concerning popular movements against the exploitation of wage-labour. These highlight the complex and multifaceted nature of conflict and exploitation (especially via the operation of social class). A pressing task for practitioners and theorists is to create ways of using this positively in the deconstruction of current fictions about a homogeneous white ethnicity, culture and nation.

Conclusions

Writing on education frequently emphasizes the huge differences (in power, experience, goals and interests) between teachers and students. In the field of 'race' and ethnicity, an image is sometimes projected of black and other minority students as mere 'victims', with white students cast as proto-racists. In this chapter I have questioned some of these images.

First, while conscious of the limits placed on their participation, I have shown that students can play an active role in antiracist policy formation; not only questioning staff and school assumptions, but becoming antiracist in their own interactions (with peers and teachers). This strengthens the antiracist ethos of schools, making it increasingly difficult for individual subject departments or teachers to maintain that such issues are of no relevance to them.

Second, I have examined the position of white students in antiracism. The data from my case study schools show that white students (irrespective of class background) can play an important role in antiracist change. It is vital, however, that schools resist the temptation to adopt attitudes that patronize or essentialize them. Adopting the doctrinaire approach of 'moral' antiracism – singling out white students as the only ones capable of racism – undermines the legitimacy of antiracism in their eyes. Similarly, teachers must ensure that their commitment to equality translates into a genuine concern for the rights of all students, visible in their daily actions in the classroom and playground. This means taking racism seriously, without being terrified by the idea and simply deciding that any 'incident' is automatically the 'fault' of white students or an 'invention' of their minority peers.

Like other actors in the school, students will display a range of characteristics and responses. The school's attempts to engage students actively in the process of change is both an indicator of progress and a means of greater progression.

nine

Rethinking racism and antiracism

> The rewards are gained by struggle rather than any kind of
> inspirational ploy.
> (A headteacher on the experience of antiracist change)

> [Racism] is inside the schools and outside the schools, but we must
> struggle where we are.
> (Stuart Hall on racism and antiracist education, ACER 1985)

Racism is a fact of life in contemporary Britain. It takes many forms,
changes between contexts and over time, but nevertheless acts to shape
people's experiences and opportunities. Education alone cannot remove
racism from society; but as one of the major agencies through which we
learn our place – and sometimes stake a claim to a different one – those
of us working in education have both an opportunity and a responsibility
to 'struggle where we are'.

In this book I have examined some of the ways in which racism works
through and *on* the education system. Throughout I have sought to link
the insights offered by a range of theoretical positions and the practical
experiences of teachers and students in real schools. I begin this final
chapter by drawing together the most important conclusions arising from
the study. One of the book's distinctive features is the attempt to move
beyond rhetoric and get to grips with antiracism as a micro-political (as
well as curricular and pedagogic) issue. By focusing on two schools with
a strong recent history of facing up to racism, I have been able to show
that genuine progress is possible. Nevertheless, the schools' experiences
also highlight the painful, slow and uncertain nature of antiracist change.
Neither school would claim to have 'solved' all the problems nor answered
all the possible criticisms. Indeed, in the second part of this chapter I point
to the continuing need to question assumptions and remain critical. The
chapter ends by considering the prospects for antiracism in the future. All
of this must be read within the context of a critical rethinking of the
meaning and significance of 'race', racism and antiracism.

'Race', research and policy

In Part One I examined how ideas about 'race', ethnicity and racism figure in debates about contemporary policy, social research and the theorizing of difference. The debates are complex and changing. Since the late 1980s, for example, the avalanche of reforms (in Britain and elsewhere) has prompted developments in theory that raise important questions about the nature of education policy analysis (see Ball and Shilling 1994; Deem 1994; Grace 1991; Raab 1994; Whitty et al. 1993). In all of this, however, 'race' is rarely accorded centre-stage (Troyna 1994). This perhaps reflects the deracialized form of current policy developments, where 'race' and ethnicity are effectively removed from the vocabulary of policy makers, substituted with coded or proxy concepts such as nation, heritage and culture.

In Chapter 2 I focused particularly on the spurious deracialization of education policy – spurious because the discourse asserts that 'race' is not centrally implicated in the reforms. Although current policy discourse makes almost no direct reference to 'race', it embodies a familiar line in Conservative political ideology, which supports and extends a racist conception of the 'essential' England and the 'true' British people. Within deracialized policy discourse, three interrelated themes can be identified.

First, there is 'the new racism' that presents minority ethnic groups as *cultural* outsiders who pose a threat to both the national identity and interest. Second, the discourse subsumes 'race' within more general concepts that symbolize the country's supposed moral and educational decline. Hence, notions of 'disadvantage' and 'inner city problems' come to deny any special importance for 'race' and ethnicity. This, of course, does away with the need specifically to address racial inequalities. Simultaneously, individuals and groups who use racialized discourse in an attempt to highlight such issues are represented as dangerous political extremists and/or self-serving bureaucrats.

Finally, the deracialization of policy discourse defines racism in the most minimal and individualistic way. The problem is seen to lie with a few 'rotten apples'; wider structures and assumptions are left unchallenged. Indeed, the deracialized discourse threatens to create ideal conditions for the further development of racial inequalities beneath a supposedly 'colour-blind' façade, where notions of 'Britishness', commonsense and 'tradition' frequently express racialized assumptions.

Problems of definition and the need to challenge taken-for-granted assumptions are especially pressing in sociological research. In Chapter 3 I examined some of the issues facing researchers who seek to examine the complex and sometimes hidden processes through which 'race' and racism operate in schools. Quantitative research often carries great status, particularly where it draws on large samples and presents apparently 'hard' statistical data. Such work has an invaluable role to play, notably helping to chart broad patterns of attainment and progress. Unfortunately, survey approaches are not well suited to piercing the superficial characteristics of schools, and rarely illuminate the diverse and changing social processes which underlie the more easily measured outcomes.

On the other hand, qualitative research – for all its contextual sensitivity and attention to detail – is frequently criticized as 'soft', 'subjective' and 'speculative' (Burgess 1985). These criticisms have been developed further by a small group of writers (some of whom have a track record of qualitative research) who systematically critique qualitative research on 'race' and racism in schools. The ensuing controversy focuses attention on several crucial questions: *Can we ever 'prove' unintended racism? Is apolitical research possible? What status should we accord qualitative material?* The questions are deceptively simple. They address key problems in the way that 'race', racism and antiracism are conceived both in research and in practice. The questions are relevant to quantitative and qualitative research. In Chapter 3 I reviewed these issues and concluded that the methodological critique of most qualitative work on school racism has gone beyond the bounds of useful criticism. The critique has reached a point where simplistic binary oppositions (research versus politics; proven versus unproven; for teachers or against teachers) threaten to obscure the highly complex nature of 'race' and racism, and return sociology to its conservative past.

In Chapter 4 I turned to recent theoretical critiques that expose dangerous assumptions in some previous forms of antiracist theory and practice. Of particular interest are the views of writers who draw on analyses of the changing nature of politics and identities in postmodernity.

An understanding of the fluid and complex dynamics of identity politics underlies an emerging left critique of antiracism. These critics tend to focus on only a limited number of high profile cases, especially the work of the now abolished Greater London Council (a case study in local authority 'municipal' antiracism) and Burnage High School (a well-documented case of 'moral' antiracism). Nevertheless, they force a radical reappraisal of antiracist thinking which reflects the fractured and rapidly changing nature of contemporary identities – where traditional divisions between class, gender and 'race' intersect in new and unpredictable ways. In this context, a perspective of 'racial dualism' (viewing the world as only black and white) is no longer tenable.

The Rushdie affair, where many Muslims from across the class spectrum (and across the world) mobilized around their religious identity, finally established the legitimate and necessary place of *culture* on the antiracist agenda (Modood 1992). But this should be a careful and questioning approach; one that recognizes the power of cultural identities (and cultural racisms) but does not fall into the trap of ethnicism – treating culture as fixed and essentializing diverse groups around a single cultural trait such as religion. Paul Gilroy (1990) argues for greater awareness of the constant negotiation and remaking of culture – an aspect of young people's lives that is still rarely explored in academic research. This approach embraces the new cultural politics of difference and does away with the well-intentioned but ultimately dangerous idea that all whites are racist and all blacks are victims. This critical position does not negate antiracism (though it destroys the more narrowly conceived and essentialist versions), rather it suggests a more sensitive and sophisticated basis upon which antiracist theory and practice might be built.

Within all of this it is crucially important that antiracism remains critical. An awareness of difference, complexity and change should not blind us to the wider operation of power and oppression. The left critique of antiracism establishes the need for more diverse and flexible approaches – approaches that may work in one context at one time, but will never be totally successful or automatically transferable to new contexts. Hence antiracist theory and practice will be stronger for rejecting simple closed analyses and becoming less self-assured. A self-critical, reflexive approach is perhaps the best protection against the kind of essentialism and reductionism that has characterized some attempts at antiracism in the past. It is in view of this analysis that, in Part Two, I focused on antiracism at the micro-level: examining the processes of antiracist change in schools that were prepared to move beyond rhetorical stances and question deeply held assumptions about their role, the nature of their students and their relationship to the world beyond the school gates.

Antiracism and change at the school level

Two schools – Mary Seacole Girls' and Garret Morgan Comprehensive – provide the bulk of data for Part Two. Both are LEA schools that were recommended to me as having made genuine progress with antiracism, facing up to difficult but necessary questions about 'race' and racism in the school and beyond.[1] The schools serve very different populations (in terms of social class, gender and ethnic origin). Nevertheless, certain common issues arose and, by analysing how these were experienced by teachers and students, important findings emerge about the nature of antiracist change in secondary schools.

My analysis is built on a micro-political perspective which views schools as 'arenas of struggle' (Ball 1987: 19) where individuals and groups use a variety of ploys to pursue their (often conflicting) interests. Change – whether internally generated or imposed from outside – brings great uncertainty where the previous status quo is disturbed and new claims are staked for a role in defining the ethos and direction of the school. This perspective recognizes the importance of *conflict* as a 'normal' feature of school organization, piercing the calm, orderly and rational façade that often cloaks talk of the management of change.

In Chapter 5 I noted that the schools each began work on 'race' and ethnicity in response to the changing composition of the student intake. Of special importance was the role of the headteacher – signalling support for antiracism and encouraging a 'core' group to take on the task of unpacking what antiracism might mean for teaching and learning in the school. Although the core groups adopted somewhat different strategies there were clear similarities, not least in their determination to involve the wider staff body. The aim of achieving *whole-school* change, however, did not easily translate into practice. Initially the majority of teachers were ambivalent about antiracism; some were opposed. The core groups saw whole-school change as a goal, but worked towards it through a variety of approaches, most stressing work with small groups of staff (building especially on shared departmental or pastoral roles).

In Chapter 6 I examined the problems that arose as the core groups sought to establish antiracism across the school. Staff development and training was especially important, particularly where essentialist assumptions were broken down through work with members of local minority communities. The core groups worked *on* their colleagues (through a variety of inservice activities) and tried to work them *in* (through consultation mechanisms) by building familiarity with and support for antiracism.

The core teachers had to strike a difficult balance between first, challenging racism and pushing for change, while second, trying not to paralyse colleagues through dogmatic and insensitive approaches. A good deal of the schools' success can be traced to sensitive management styles, with the core groups encouraged and supported by headteachers and senior management teams who were prepared to let them take a lead, but also ready to intervene strategically when necessary. The process was, nevertheless, fraught with uncertainty and, in no small part, success was also due to contingent factors such as changes in the staff body (not all of which can be planned) and the dynamics of personal interaction between colleagues and between teachers and students.

One of the most important stages in the schools' work with antiracism seems to have involved dealing with accusations of racism by minority students. Rather than adopting an essentialist (and moralistic) tone, the core groups tried to help colleagues work through their uncertainties: dealing with the issues seriously, without abdicating responsibility and capitulating simply because the accusation has been made. This is a most difficult task which teachers are still confronting. However, the situation was eased somewhat by the recognition that students hold a variety of diverse and often highly perceptive views on 'race' and racism. In both case study schools, for example, the students themselves have played an important part in the development of antiracist policies. In Seacole, the students' enthusiastic and serious treatment of a draft policy document played a key role in changing the micro-political context – demonstrating to the staff in general that antiracist change was not only possible, it was expected.

The core groups continue to play a central role in sustaining and developing antiracism in the schools. A vital task is to work against the apparent 'logic' of national education reforms, many of which are antagonistic to antiracist theory and practice (more on this below). Core members are also active in helping translate antiracism into work at the classroom level. They do this both directly (through their own teaching) and more indirectly (supporting subject specialists in developing new materials or trying different pedagogic approaches). In Chapter 7 I examined these issues in detail.

In Seacole there has been a conscious push to make antiracism a key part of the curriculum. Like many schools, Seacole attempts to 'permeate' all subjects with an awareness of antiracist issues. In Chapter 7 I noted the problems facing such a strategy, where subject teachers' practical concerns and philosophical assumptions can define non-specialist issues as something of an unnecessary distraction. National data confirm the generally low priority given to cross-curricular matters and warn against some practitioners' belief that citizenship education might hold the key to future antiracist developments. Quite apart from the weak position of citizenship education in most schools, there are also serious conceptual and practical problems with such an approach.

It is in view of these kinds of problem that Seacole began a separate and additional programme of 'people's education'. This has developed into a rolling programme of anti-oppressive work where antiracism is an important, but not exclusive, focus. The programme asks a great deal of both staff and students; sessions are often highly charged, with emotions running high. I examined the development and structure of the programme, paying particular attention to students' interpretations of the lessons as important and directly relevant to their experiences in 'the real world'. The programme does not offer an easy blueprint for replication elsewhere, but it does demonstrate students' ability (whatever their ethnic origin and social class background) to deal with complex and controversial issues such as considering the operation of 'race' and racism in their lives.

Part Two ends with a more detailed exploration of student perspectives. In Chapter 8 I review their feelings about ethnic diversity, noting in particular their generally positive views and sensitivity to racial injustice. Antiracist commitment has become an important part of student culture in

Seacole and Morgan. Peer interactions that seem racist, for example, often bring about a prompt and forthright response from peers. The students are extremely perceptive and, in both schools, they continue to highlight areas where teachers should reappraise their assumptions.

Students in Morgan were encouraged to play a central role in the creation of the school's 'respect for all' policy. Although their participation was within limits set by teachers, the policy has taken on real importance within the school – becoming an ideal to which most staff, as well as students, are committed. As in Seacole (Chapter 6), the students' involvement in policy making seems to have been especially valuable. This is not to say, however, that some problems do not remain. Chapter 8 concludes by focusing on white students – a group that is pivotal to successful antiracism but rarely given much consideration in antiracist theorizing. My data confirm that white students (regardless of social class background) can play a crucial role in antiracist developments. It is vital that schools do not fall into the trap of 'moral' antiracism by demonizing white students and presenting antiracism as something that will simply control them and support black and Asian students at their expense. Teachers in Seacole and Morgan have begun working through some of these issues, most notably by making it clear that no one (whatever their ethnic background) is automatically guilty of, or free from, racism. This echoes recent theoretical developments by adopting non-essentialist and non-reductionist perspectives: it is also a solid and pragmatic strategy, making space for white participation in antiracism on an equal footing with their peers.

The struggle continues

Before considering the future for antiracist education more generally, it is useful to reflect briefly on the limits exposed by my research in Mary Seacole Girls' and Garret Morgan Comprehensive schools. Both schools have begun to change fundamentally the way that teachers and students think about 'race' and racism. Nevertheless, areas of doubt and uncertainty remain.

Throughout Part Two of this book, while documenting the genuine and important advances that have been made, I have also sought to represent the continuing struggle within the case study schools. In both schools, for example, the core groups are convinced of the need for vigilance in the face of new policy developments (see Chapter 6); some subject departments remain relatively inactive in terms of opposing racism (Chapter 7); and students still identify ways in which some teachers must rethink racialized assumptions and actions (Chapter 8). Beyond these specific points it is worth noting two broader areas which highlight the scale of the task facing antiracist schools.

Deconstructing the myth of a black challenge to authority

The first area of concern relates to disciplinary conflict between white teachers and African Caribbean students. In a previous case study I tried to analyse the complex processes that lay at the heart of such conflicts (Gillborn 1990): I drew particular attention to teachers' expectations of African Caribbean students as a more frequent and severe disciplinary challenge. This 'myth' prompted teachers to greater control and criticism of African Caribbeans, creating the potential for escalating conflict and worsening relations between teachers and students (see Chapter 3). The teachers' expectations reflected beliefs, about black physicality and violence, that can be traced back for centuries in white racist ideologies and take new forms reflecting the immediate influence of stereotyping in the media and the staffroom culture.

My research in Seacole and Morgan was not, of course, of the scale and depth of a full ethnography – I cannot, therefore, say how far the myth of a black challenge is replicated in either. However, in Seacole (where black students make up a significant proportion of the population) my interviews with teachers and students confirm that some African Caribbean young people are frequently in disciplinary conflict with teachers. Of particular concern is the way that a small minority of teachers express generalized views that depict African Caribbean students (as a group) as a greater threat to their authority:

> I think there is a problem with Afro-Caribbean girls in this school (. . .) I am not sure how to handle them, how to cope. You try not to sound racist but some of them are very lively. They have got a lot to offer. I have one in my tutor group with whom a lot of the time I don't get on very well . . .

What is worrying here is the way the teacher moves between the general and the specific. Disciplinary problems with some students of African Caribbean ethnic origin are to be expected – as is conflict with individuals of all other ethnic backgrounds. Of concern is the way this teacher switches between an individual ('I have one in my tutor group') and a general view of African Caribbean students *as a group* ('there is a problem with Afro-Caribbean girls').

Realistically, we should not be surprised that some teachers still hold negative and essentialist views despite the wealth of antiracist work in Seacole. The school has achieved a great deal but it is utopian to expect *total* success, especially in the face of such deeply rooted stereotypes. This testifies to the need consistently to address such views on a school-wide basis, for example, as part of inservice and policy review work. More encouragingly, the quotation also suggests that the teacher (who has worked in Seacole for just over a year) is sensitive to the possibility that their generalizations are inappropriate (even racist). The latter reflects the high profile given to antiracism in the school but reminds us of the resilience of racist stereotypes, particularly concerning images of African Caribbean students as a disciplinary threat. Given the greater proportion of South Asian students in the school, Seacole has been especially active in addressing the diverse needs, experiences and perspectives of Asian young people and their communities. Even here, though, the school is still coming to terms with the changing perspectives and demands of its students.

Working with Asian mobilization

Just under half of all Seacole students are of South Asian ethnic origin, mostly with family backgrounds in Pakistan and northern India. Islam is one of the principal religions in the school and, like colleagues in multiethnic schools across Britain, Seacole has recently faced controversial issues which threw into relief wider stereotypes about Muslims in particular, and South Asian communities more generally.

I have already noted the racialized political reactions to the furore surrounding Salman Rushdie's novel, *The Satanic Verses*, and the Gulf War of 1990/91 (see Chapter 2). In both cases, politicians and the media frequently constructed an image of Muslims in particular (and all South Asians by implication) as acting contrary to 'British' traditions and/or representing a potential threat to 'British' interests. Both episodes led to increased racist attacks on South Asian people in the UK. As the headteacher at Seacole recalls, many Asian students were themselves victims or personally knew people who had been targeted:

> some of the Asian families were on the receiving end of some dreadful behaviour in the early days of the Gulf War – simply because they were Asian.

Yunas Samad has noted the importance of white racist attacks as a spur to the political mobilization of Asian youth (Samad 1992). Similarly, Seacole serves a city with a significant Asian and African Caribbean population, where the former have become increasingly vocal and white racist action has strengthened their belief and determination to have a voice. Young people have played a prominent role locally, for example, in campaigns about Rushdie's novel. This political mobilization raises many difficult questions for schools, who can now find themselves simultaneously presented with issues of an overtly political and 'racial' nature. The Gulf War provides possibly the most extreme case to date; with most white students seeing the allied forces as heroic liberators, while some Muslim peers argued the Iraqi case (for example, by pointing to the West's material – as opposed to simply humanitarian – interest in the region).[2]

In Seacole, teachers prepared for the Gulf conflict by deciding on a common strategy. As the likelihood of armed conflict in the Gulf increased, the school prepared students for the fact that friendships would be strained and emotions would run high. The headteacher recalls:

a war situation makes people *afraid*. And in those early days they were. There were [students] who could almost envisage that any minute now something awful was going to happen to *them*. We talked about the way that friendships could be destroyed because of different attitudes (. . .) firm friends could suddenly find themselves falling out because they had a different attitude or point of view.

The senior management stressed to teachers that students should be allowed to discuss issues that worried them, but always within a supportive atmosphere which privileged students' right to their own view – within strict limits set by the school's commitment to antiracism:

We took racism as an example, that this applied within [the Gulf War] situation as well. That just as you never ever downed a person because of their race, or because of a handicap, you never ever rubbished a person or downed them because of their point of view in a situation like that.

It is a mark of the strength of antiracist sentiment in Seacole (among teachers and students) that a case was made for political tolerance on the basis of antiracist principles. Seacole's treatment of the Gulf War provided a clear framework for students to talk about their concerns while also containing potential flashpoints. Teachers in the school look back on the episode with pride, as a time when they faced a severe challenge but came through with their commitment to antiracism enhanced. In contrast, the Rushdie affair – although apparently less dramatic in terms of the scale of events – proved to be a somewhat greater test of the teachers' ability to adapt to changing circumstances. The headteacher notes:

There was a march in the city one weekend and one of the girls said could she call together the Muslim girls to tell them about this march? So what do you do? Do you say 'no' or do you say 'yes'? Well, I said 'yes'. She called them together in the community room. I also went along and once she had given the message about this – the information was what she asked for – then I stepped in and said, 'Right, you have got your information, go off and have the rest of your break.' In other words it didn't develop then into discussion and into factions arguing about things. And we ended up with three of our fifth-year girls photographed on the march actually [they were featured on the front page of the local newspaper]. And they were very proud of that, even though some of the things that they were saying were really indoctrinated comments rather than anything else.

The response to the Rushdie affair, therefore, seems to have been less confident than the school's subsequent treatment of the Gulf War. In relation to *The Satanic Verses*, for example, discussion was not encouraged. A sense of the headteacher's indecision is clear from her recollection of the events ('So what do you do? Do you say "no" or do you say "yes"?'). Furthermore, she describes the young women's views on the book in terms of '*indoctrination*', suggesting that (like many antiracists and liberals alike) Seacole teachers were uncertain how best to interpret the religious anger generated by the episode (see Modood 1992).

Even Seacole, with its recent history of whole-school antiracist change, therefore, was challenged by elements of the Rushdie affair and had no 'automatic' responses. Most important, however, is the way that the school maintained its commitment to taking seriously the views of students and minority communities. Seacole's attempts to understand and work with the political mobilization of its Asian students epitomizes some of the key lessons to arise from this study; there is no blueprint, no 'one right way'. Rather, teachers, students and schools' communities have to work through new issues; respecting the diversity of experience and perspective, and resisting the temptation to resort to 'quick fixes' which assert (overtly or implicitly) the political or moral supremacy of any one group.

Reform/deform: the future for antiracist education

The second part of this book has shown that progress can be made developing antiracism at the school level. When considering the likely future for antiracist education, however, it is vital to retain a sense of the interplay between individual schools and external constraints (most obvious in the effects of national policy, but also including various local factors). Empty speculation about the future serves no useful purpose, but a critical awareness of the unfolding patterns of constraint and opportunity is especially relevant.

Changes in Section 11 funding

In many schools, changes in the nature and scale of funding for Section 11 work represent the most immediate threat to antiracist developments. I have noted how the Morgan core group were keen quickly to establish antiracism as a distinct aspect of the school's work; Section 11 staff are involved, but are not dominant. In Seacole, however, Section 11 teachers have remained pivotal to antiracist developments (see Chapter 5). There is now widespread uncertainty about how antiracist work will be affected by a probable reduction in the number of posts and changes in the nature of Section 11 work (for example, increasingly making teachers responsible for a named case load of students). In Seacole the headteacher recognizes that the role of Section 11 teachers will change, although she hopes they will continue to feed into school-wide debates and initiatives:

> I think officially it is going to become less of a role, the antiracist work and all the other side. Although the same people will be around and so I suspect in effect – in *this* school – obviously they will still be part of it.

In Seacole the greatest fear, at present, is that all students whose language needs warrant extra support cannot be catered for within the Section 11 budget. Even students with relatively severe language problems cannot all be included. According to the head of Section 11, 'it is really playing God' – a situation that is denying students basic opportunities and draining teachers' morale. In Morgan the situation is a little better, but here too Section 11 staff realize that their future work will be exclusively with the weakest students. For some teachers this is a severe blow: in the past, by supporting students across the ability range, they have helped individuals achieve higher examination grades, sometimes reaching the all-important grade C at GCSE. Such work is not possible within the new limits on Section 11. The head of Section 11 in Morgan notes:

> We are more strongly directed now (...) I am being directed to the beginners [those with the most severe language problems]. And I think that means that we are not going to have achievement because of me. We might have achievement because the child has been in the country for ten years but I am not going to see achievement caused by my effort. Because in a way I am not going to be allowed to go and support the children who perhaps could be pushed into a higher GCSE grade.

In some schools the reform of Section 11 is already having even more serious effects. One of the schools I visited in the early stages of the project, for example, had used Section 11 staff and resources as the engine for its antiracist work. After losing half a dozen teachers because of Section 11 cuts, antiracist work in the school has been severely weakened. Talk now is of survival rather than progress.

The National Curriculum

A frequent complaint among subject teachers in Seacole and Morgan is that the National Curriculum is too restrictive. In some subjects the weight of prescribed material means that teachers have little flexibility about introducing new topics or materials which challenge Eurocentric perspectives. Additionally, separate work on antiracist issues (for example, as part of PSE provision) is often squeezed by timetable pressures. Therefore, Sir Ron Dearing's recommendation that the statutory content for most National Curriculum subjects be 'slimmed-down' might, at first, appear to offer some hope of improvement (Dearing 1994). On closer inspection, however, it is unclear how far schools will be able to use these changes towards anti-oppressive ends.

The School Curriculum and Assessment Authority (SCAA) has emphasized that the 'reduction in curriculum content' should be 'concentrated outside the core subjects' (SCAA 1994: 1). In English, mathematics and science, therefore, the levels of prescription seem unlikely to change significantly. Furthermore, Dearing stressed that the 20 per cent 'discretionary time' (which the curriculum streamlining was expected to produce) should be used:

> to support work in the basics of literacy, oracy and numeracy. Beyond this, the bulk of the time released should be used for work in those National Curriculum subjects which the school chooses to explore in more depth.
>
> (Dearing 1994: 7)

As the *Times Educational Supplement* noted, when Dearing published his interim report (Dearing 1993), in view of 'the blood spilt in the battles to give every subject due prominence on the timetable . . . subject specialists will not readily relinquish hard-won territory' (6 August 1993: 6). The transitional period may, therefore, see increased micro-political battles between discrete subject departments. In the short term at least, it seems unlikely that teachers will find promoting anti-oppressive education significantly easier than it was pre-Dearing.

More generally, there is also cause for concern in the philosophy implied by Dearing's analysis and recommendations. His reforms further enshrine the traditional élite status of the 'core' subjects (English, mathematics and science) and raise the spectre of increased curricular differentiation and selection between the ages of 14 and 16. Especially worrying is his idea that secondary schools develop different *'pathways'* ('academic', 'vocational' and 'occupational') so as 'to respond to the *particular aptitudes and inclinations* of their students' (Dearing 1994: 46, emphasis added). This echoes the assumptions that underlay the tripartite system of selective state education.[3] It remains to be seen whether distinctive 'pathways' emerge. It is vital that such developments are monitored for any systematic ethnic bias. Experience suggests that minority students may find themselves facing additional hurdles: for example, because of teachers' perceptions of their linguistic ability (in the case of South Asian students and others for whom English is a second language) or their past disciplinary records (in the case of African Caribbean young people).

Accountability and standards: selection and control

Among the teaching profession there was a generally warm welcome for Sir Ron Dearing's recommendation that, following the implementation of his proposals, no further changes should be made to the National Curriculum for five years. This does not, however, signal a respite from all education reforms. During the late 1980s and into the 1990s education has become a key ideological battleground; an arena where each new Government initiative or strategy is assumed to have a natural consequence requiring further reform. Most of these changes are bad news for those of us concerned with equality in education. I have noted, for example, how changes in initial teacher education (with an emphasis on practical craft knowledge over 'theory') threaten to create the conditions for more unintended and institutionalized racism (see Chapter 2). Changes in the nature of GCSE examination courses provide another piece in the jigsaw puzzle of recent reforms – each threatening the opportunities of ethnic minority students. Restrictions on the amount of coursework permitted (generally not more than 20 per cent) threaten especially damaging consequences for students whose first language is not English. In some subjects, for example, teachers in Seacole have managed to delay decisions about the specific level which students study; they use the modular format of certain courses to maximize flexibility while satisfying coursework requirements. For example, the head of science notes:

> a lot of the pupils that had English problems [early in] year 9 have got over much of that by year 10. And so rather than penalize them for poor *English* we are now actually managing to look, largely, at what their *science* is like.

By encouraging earlier selection onto separate courses, which mostly will be assessed by written examination papers, changes in the GCSE threaten to have racialized effects – disproportionately restricting the opportunities available to those for whom English is a second language.

More generally, moves towards antiracist education are also threatened by changes that many practitioners feel are pushing schools to maximize academic attainment at the expense of less easily quantified aspects of the education they provide. In the rush to satisfy a narrow range of performance indicators, certain groups might find their interests sacrificed to the demands of the educational market.[4] The annual publication of crude quantitative material is particularly important in this respect.

The most important document parents will ever need to read

The official report reveals which schools are best

At a glance, facts about your children's schools

These headlines are taken from the special 'Exam Report' supplement in *The Sun* (17 November 1993: the UK's biggest selling national newspaper) and capture the popular image of the DFE's 'performance tables for schools and colleges'. First published in 1992, the figures form part of the 'information revolution in education' promised as part of the Government's *Citizen's Charter* (DFE 1994). In only the second year of this practice the 'league tables' (as they have come to be known) were reproduced in *every* national daily newspaper. The DFE provided information by school, listed alphabetically within each local authority. However, many newspapers (national and local) reworked the DFE's data into new formats, including ranking schools in every area by the proportion of students gaining five or more GCSE passes at grade C and above (*The Independent* and *The Daily Mail*, 17 November 1993). The inclusion of figures on non-attendance made front-page headlines in *The Daily Mail*, which (like several other papers) also listed separately the 'best' and 'worst' areas and schools. The scale of sensationalist and inaccurate reporting exceeded many people's worst fears.[5]

Even where the figures are reproduced accurately, the 'league tables' present an extremely simple and one-dimensional picture. For example, they have been widely criticized for failing to reflect differences in the composition of school populations, taking no account of relevant contextual factors. The latter would include the proportion of students for whom English is a second language, the numbers with special educational needs and those from disadvantaged social and economic backgrounds (including those in poverty and/or living in overcrowded households).[6]

Despite their many limitations, the 'league tables' have attained a position where for many non-educationists they provide an easily accessible and high profile account of apparent 'success'/'failure'. They hold schools publicly 'accountable' on a selected range of issues that reflect the Government's chosen agenda; an agenda where crude measures of achievement are equated with 'standards', while a concern for equality of opportunity and social justice is dismissed as 'left-wing' politicking (see Chapter 2). In both Mary Seacole and Garret Morgan schools, many teachers view the publication of such data as a powerful threat to the schools' philosophical commitment to *all* students regardless of ability or background. A member of the Morgan core group notes:

> to be a successful school [in the published tables] you need to be full of academically bright children – they are the priority. There is the

sense of, 'if they are going to publish the results, what are we going to do in that situation?' You find little things creeping in at the moment, quite a lot of little things creeping in which I see as threats to the equal opportunities policy (...) like suggestions being made that we now begin to put down positions in class for exam results and this sort of thing.

Where raw examination results become the single most important measure of a school's performance, calls for increased use of academic selection can gain considerable force. In particular, the use of hierarchically organized teaching groups ('set' by ability) may be increasing (NCC 1991). Certainly such a development was predicted in my case study schools. Even before the first 'league tables' were published many teachers felt that the tenor of national reforms clearly supported a return to more selective, authoritarian and hierarchical structures. It is a theme that most teachers in Seacole and Morgan see as deeply distressing, but (because of the sheer weight of changes) one they are not confident of completely resisting. The following, from a head of department, is typical:

> I think setting is going to become more paramount, simply because of the implementation of the National Curriculum and SATs [Standard Assessment Tasks] and league tables and all the other things. I am afraid we are going back. I think it is against our policies and our philosophy, but we are being *forced* into this because of Government legislation (...) I think we are in a dilemma because I think it is anti everything that we stand for. And yet we are being forced into it.

Previous research suggests that among the first to suffer will be students of ethnic minority and/or working-class background: groups that frequently have to contend with stereotypes of low ability and poor motivation (see, for example, Bates and Riseborough 1993; Eggleston et al. 1986; Gillborn 1990; Gillborn et al. 1993; Mac an Ghaill 1988; 1989a).

Exploiting opportunities

Current reforms of state educational provision, therefore, offer little en-couragement for those engaged in antiracist practice. Although a 'slimmed down' National Curriculum may allow some teachers more freedom to explore new approaches and materials, other aspects of the Dearing re-forms cast a threatening shadow of institutionalized racism via increased selection and differentiation. Nevertheless, there are opportunities to be exploited if educationists have both the vision and determination to pursue them. One of the most encouraging aspects of my research in Seacole and Morgan was the level of commitment displayed by many teachers. Despite setbacks, and in the face of continued state intervention against egalitarian developments, teachers retained a belief in the potential for antiracist change:

> If you really believe in it, it doesn't stop.

> If you believe that what you were teaching was good then as a teacher I don't think you could get rid of it. It would go against the grain.

In isolation these quotations might look simplistic and naive. But a textual presentation loses the genuine sense of determination that renders such positions important. An indication of the depth of commitment displayed among teachers is that, for some, antiracism has become an acid test of their preparedness to stay within the system: it is an *essential* part of their professional practice. A head of department at Seacole states:

> I am in teaching because I have a belief: it is not just a job (. . .) I will continue to [work on antiracism] and we, as a department, will continue to do that as long as we are able. Now if the time ever does come that the constraints become so tight that we have got to be careful about multicultural activities, then I don't know what I am going to do. That is the dilemma I don't wish to face at the moment. I have got enough worries . . . I might take the coward's way out and jump out of education.

Successive Conservative governments have shown themselves willing to attempt dramatic and far-reaching changes in the provision of state education. Nevertheless, the trail of reform after reform signals how difficult such manipulation can be. Each new attempt to shape education from the centre creates new and unexpected spaces which can be exploited to resist the push of central policies. To take a single example, changes in the structure and powers of school governing bodies were undoubtedly intended, in part, to help counter 'progressive' developments: school governors (like other 'volunteers') have an unrepresentatively high social class profile (Brehony 1992: 209). And yet, with supportive governors, these changes actually create the potential for thoroughgoing antiracist change, even in the face of a hostile LEA. In this context it is perhaps not surprising that a survey of local authority inspectors and advisers suggests:

> that the lines of development adduced were often . . . promising or ad hoc – rather than carefully coordinated and thoroughly institutionalised. Whereas 'concerns' and 'constraints', were often perceived as structural and closely related to national developments in policy, curriculum and funding, 'promising lines of development', were local, often ingenious attempts to keep MC/ARE [multicultural/antiracist education] on the agenda.
>
> (Taylor 1992: 34)

It would be wrong, however, to be drawn simplistically into assuming that local factors necessarily offer any more support for antiracism than is afforded by national policies. Parents can now appeal to the law to enforce racist views on the appropriateness of schools; using the proportions of white children on the roll to determine whether a traditional 'English' education will be provided.[7] Making strong, supportive links with local communities is essential for schools attempting antiracist change (Macdonald et al. 1989), but there are no easy approaches and progress is likely to be both slow and painful (see Gillborn et al. 1993: 100–7, and Chapter 6 above).

The central message of this book must, therefore, be that progress *is* possible, though never easy or complete. As Part One illustrates, the field of 'race' and antiracism is extremely complex and prone to rapid change. An awareness of this should inform our practice and analysis. The schools described in Part Two show that headteachers, teachers, students and members of local communities can come together to support and extend antiracist developments. The school case studies are not simple blueprints, but they do offer ideas about possible strategies. Most important, the school studies suggest that the struggle – though painful, slow and uncertain – is not in vain.

Notes

1 Racism and schooling

1 Interview survey carried out in June 1991 by National Opinion Polls, for *The Independent on Sunday* and the Runnymede Trust. Sample consisted of 572 African Caribbean people, 479 South Asian and 766 white. Of these 38 per cent were classified as social classes ABC1, and 62 per cent social classes C2DE (see Reid 1989: 73–4 for details of this classification).

2 There is, of course, great variety of experience and achievement between and within ethnic minority groups: not *all* minority students fail, many achieve excellent results and carve out successful careers. The pattern of experience and achievement is complex and changing, yet significant overall differences remain. Compared with their white schoolmates (of the same sex and social class), for example, African Caribbean young people are more likely to be excluded from full-time education before the age of 16 (see Chapter 2) and less likely to gain access to the most prestigious courses and institutions in higher education (see Drew et al. 1992; Taylor 1993).

3 This is not to say that all minority students experience school in the same way. There are important differences between the school experiences and achievements of different ethnic groups (see Gillborn 1990; 1992b; Mac an Ghaill 1988; 1989a).

4 During this period the use of the male generic in relation to humankind was usual and, of course, reflected deep-seated sexism (and heterosexism) in political, social and scientific discourses. On occasions throughout this book, in quotations from published material and original data, the male generic is used: it is a usage that I reject. My decision to quote original sources verbatim should not be confused with acceptance of the assumptions they embody.

5 Burt was one of the founding figures in British intelligence testing. His work was a major inspiration for authors like Arthur Jensen (1969; 1972) and Hans Eysenck (1971; 1981) who argue that genetic factors lead to differences in the

average measured intelligence of different 'races'. These intellectual debts were quickly, and conveniently, reassessed when it was revealed that Burt had probably falsified data (see Kamin 1974, 1981; Lawrence 1977). For a response to the attempted rehabilitation of Burt, see Hearnshaw (1990).

6 This understanding is adopted throughout the book, and signified by placing the term in single quotation marks. This practice is criticized by Sheila Allen (1994) who sees 'little use in it' unless used for all terms which are socially constructed and contested. I have sympathy with her position and, like Alastair Bonnett (1993: 179) do not wish to see scare-quotes around every category of identity – 'an intellectually provocative but pedantic and unpractical way of writing about human difference'. However, for the moment at least, I judge the dangers inherent in common-sense notions of 'race' to warrant inverted commas around the term.

7 The distinction between post-structuralism and postmodernism is often ill-defined, sometimes invisible. Post-structuralism is most closely associated with the work of Gilles Deleuze, Jacques Derrida and Michel Foucault – a 'heterogeneous group of French thinkers who have nevertheless participated in the common effort of subverting the notions of truth, meaning and subjectivity' (Callinicos 1990: 100). Their work, however, is also seen as a principal theme in postmodern thought, where the latter also includes first, 'cultural critiques of "modernist" art forms' and second, general theories of contemporary society that identify a movement into a post-industrial, post-capitalist and/or post-Fordist age (Green 1994: 68–72). See also Boyne and Rattansi (1990) and Sarup (1993).

8 For a classic discussion of these issues see Becker (1958).

9 I also tried to ensure that the first visit included the opportunity to wander around the school and talk with students.

10 In Chapter 5 I also draw on data collected in a third school, Forest Comprehensive.

11 Although the term 'ethnography' is increasingly applied to any form of qualitative research (cf. Hammersley 1992b: 8), I would want to retain a distinction between ethnography and the more generic notion of qualitative research.

12 Under Section 11 of the Local Government Act 1966, local authorities can apply for special funding to support the employment of additional staff necessary to respond to 'the presence within their areas of substantial numbers of people from the Commonwealth whose language or customs differ from those of the rest of the community' (Home Office 1990: 1, quoted in Bagley 1992: 1). The funding has undergone several changes, most recently with 'devastating' cuts in Home Office support; prompting the termination of successful projects and the loss of staff (see Bagley 1992; LARRIE 1992; Richardson 1993; Sofer 1994; Young 1993).

2 Discourse and policy

1 Symbolic interactionists have reacted to the development of Cultural Studies in a variety of ways. While some have attempted a synthesis of concerns and approaches (see Becker and McCall 1990) others have moved to reject

fundamental assumptions at the heart of mainstream interactionist theory (Denzin 1992).

2 Following Hall (1992a) and McCall and Becker (1990), I use 'discourse' with specific reference to talk and text. Although some writers include 'acts and their consequences' as part of the 'discursive field' (Goldberg 1993: 41), we should be careful not to lose sight of key differences between action and talk/text.

3 I use the term 'legitimate' in preference to 'benign'. Where the latter suggests a position that *may* be favourable (but at least is not antagonistic towards 'race' equality), 'legitimate' appeals directly to issues of power and suggests a more active engagement with the key issues (see note 4 below).

4 The advantage of adopting the legitimate/spurious distinction is that it places centre-stage questions about 'race' and ethnicity in the social formation. No discourse can be judged without reference to the subjects that it addresses. Decisions about whether 'race' and ethnicity are genuinely implicated in the issue will often be difficult to answer with certainty. This forces us to critically consider discourse within a wider context, as part of social relations, not as an ultimate definer of reality in its own right.

5 This is a clear example of the complex and dynamic character of 'racial' signifiers in contemporary discourse: a reminder of the importance of Goldberg's comments (quoted at the beginning of this chapter).

6 Similar arguments have surfaced in other European countries (Husbands 1994). Note also that the deracialized discourse of the New Right has begun to appropriate the term 'ethnic', returning it to one of its earliest – derogatory – meanings as a term for 'lesser breeds' (Williams 1983: 119).

7 It is interesting to remember Enoch Powell's distinction (quoted earlier) between a citizen of the UK and an 'Englishman'. Major's deployment of 'Britain' and 'the United Kingdom', in the two speeches, also clearly fulfils different discursive functions that have direct relevance to the new racism.

8 An investigation into political campaigns by local party organizations in London revealed evidence of 'pandering to racism' by members of both the Labour and Liberal Democrat parties (Liberal Democrats 1993; Runnymede Trust 1994).

9 Source: *Channel 4 News*, 17 September 1993.

10 Similarly, the Hillgate Group's support for separate Islamic schools was offered within a wider 'insistence that all children "be provided with the knowledge and understanding that are necessary for the full enjoyment and enhancement of British society". Nothing, they said, was more important than to "reconcile our minorities, to integrate them into our national culture" . . . (Hillgate Group 1987: 4)' (Whitty 1992: 299).

11 The School Curriculum and Assessment Authority (SCAA) replaced the National Curriculum Council (NCC) and the School Examination and Assessment Council (SEAC) on 1 October 1993.

12 Exclusions are more common among secondary age students. Data on England and Wales suggest that around 85 per cent of permanent exclusions are of secondary school students. Where possible, therefore, the columns in the figure refer to exclusions from secondary school. Also, males tend to outnumber females who are excluded by a ratio of between four and five to one (DFE 1993a: 4).

13 It must be remembered that these data only refer to reported cases of official exclusion. It is well known that some students and/or their parents are pressured into 'volunteering' to leave a school's roll. There is no reason to assume that such 'informal exclusions' are less common among African Caribbean young people (Advisory Centre for Education 1993; Office for Standards in Education 1993: 2).

14 This figure is not included in the official report (Nottinghamshire County Council 1991), but can be calculated on the basis of the number of secondary students excluded by ethnic group (ibid.: 134, Table F8) and the total number of secondary students in each ethnic group (ibid.: 129, Table F3).

3 Racism and research

1 By *'progress'* is meant the difference between a student's level of attainment at two different time points; say, the progress made between the second and the final year of secondary education. By *'achievement'* is meant the student's performance in final examinations, usually at the end of their school careers.

2 Although not an ethnographic study, Sally Tomlinson's research on decision-making in special education (Tomlinson 1981) also stands as a significant contribution to this area.

3 Mac an Ghaill refers to 'people of Asian and Afro-Caribbean origin as black' so as to highlight their 'common experience of white racism in Britain' (Mac an Ghaill 1988: 156).

4 The pseudonym 'City Road' is wholly fictitious.

5 For a useful discussion of social class, gender and sexuality as factors in the social construction of 'normality' and disciplinary 'problems' see Carlen et al. (1992) and Gleeson (1992).

6 In the space available here I can do no more than sketch a reply to some of Foster's criticisms of my research. For those interested in the specifics of the debate, the best solution is to compare my analysis of life in City Road (Gillborn 1990; especially Chapters 2 and 3) with the parody presented in Foster's critiques (Foster 1992b; 1993a).

7 Both Gomm and Foster conducted their PhD research under Hammersley's supervision.

8 I understand (from personal communications) that the three are now jointly writing a book about issues of equality in educational research.

9 Although the classical sociological discussion of unintended consequences is provided by Merton (1963), the concept is not necessarily bound to functionalist analyses (Giddens 1984: 12).

10 A notable exception is when the academy (or its chosen gatekeepers) judge their own position inadequate: Hammersley describes as 'suppression' the view of a journal referee who opposed the publication of 'Foster's dubious arguments' (Hammersley 1993b: 448).

11 By critical research I mean work that challenges received wisdom in the best traditions of the sociological imagination: I do not mean the specific approach outlined by Lee Harvey (1990) and applied by Troyna (1994) where 'an overt

political struggle against oppressive social structures' is an essential element in the research. Although sociological research offers the potential to contribute to such struggles, there are obvious limitations in attempting to build this overtly into every project.

12 There are many excellent books on research methods which offer a solid introduction and outline a variety of practical, theoretical and methodological issues. Among the best places to start are Burgess (1984a and b), Delamont (1992), Hammersley and Atkinson (1983), Robson (1993) and Rose and Sullivan (1992). These are general books on qualitative and/or quantitative research. For brief discussions of research issues specific to 'race' and ethnicity in education see Mac an Ghaill (1989b) and Troyna and Carrington (1989).

13 This view underlies Part Two of this book. In presenting an empirical study of antiracism in multi-ethnic schools, the role and significance of students and their communities emerges as a critical factor.

4   Theorizing identity and antiracism

1 There is a substantial literature that addresses both the specific issues raised in Rushdie's book, the range of Islamic responses and the manipulation of the affair by different political interests (in the UK and elsewhere). I do not intend to rehearse those arguments. My interest, here, is in the ways the affair throws into relief the de-centring of contemporary subjectivities.

2 One of the most active Muslim communities in the UK has been centred on Bradford, an overwhelmingly working-class community, many of whom migrated from rural areas (cf. Modood 1990a).

3 Like the term 'New Right', this conception of a 'New Left' is, of course, an ideal type (in the sociological sense of a simplification that brings together certain ideas and positions for the sake of analysis). By definition, many writers building on the considerable range of postmodernist cultural criticism would question the usefulness of a term like 'New Left' – rooted, as it is, in a modernist conception of right/left politics. Paul Gilroy has stated, for example, that 'Dealing seriously with questions of racism and nationalism makes it very hard to draw those lines' (Gilroy, in Puranik 1993). Nevertheless, it is a useful heuristic for a range of theorists who, while retaining a broad commitment to anti-oppressive politics (characteristic of the political left), have attacked antiracism – often building their critiques on a broadly postmodernist understanding of the making and breaking of subject identities. In their questioning of traditional left ideas and assumptions these writers echo the New Left of the 1960s, though their inspiration and analyses are markedly different (see Hoggart 1992: 215).

4 For critical accounts of New Right attacks on antiracism in education see Demaine (1993); Gillborn (1990: ch. 6), Troyna and Carrington (1990; ch. 1).

5 We must be careful not to stereotype local authority antiracism – as some politicians and academics have in the past. There is great variety among approaches at the local level (see Troyna and Williams 1986). Nevertheless, Gilroy's picture of 'municipal' antiracism clearly articulates with practice in certain contexts.

6 The title of the piece, 'The end of anti-racism', appears to be deliberately provocative. Certainly it does not reflect Gilroy's attempts to distinguish a particular target for his critique (municipal 'race' politics): 'I must emphasize that I am thinking *not* of anti-racism as a political objective, or a goal which emerges alongside other issues from the daily struggles of black people, from the practice of community organisations and voluntary groups, or even from the war of position which must be waged inside the institutions of the state' (Gilroy 1990: 72, emphasis added).

7 We should also remember that throughout the 1980s central Government successfully limited the autonomy of the local state – even to the point of abolishing the GLC (Lansley et al. 1989; Troyna and Carrington 1990).

8 I address these points in detail in Chapter 7.

9 See also Hewitt (1986).

10 Part Two of this book examines how teachers and students have worked on such strategies in practice.

11 Rattansi defines racism as 'discourses which group human populations into "races" on the basis of some biological signifier – for example, "stock" – with each "race" being regarded as having essential characteristics or a certain essential character (as in the phrase "the British character", or in the attributions to "races" of laziness, rebelliousness, or industriousness) and where inferiorization of some "races" may or may not be present' (Rattansi 1992: 36).

5 The politics of school change

1 Although, as a whole, the teaching profession has a fairly good track record in the stand against racism, no one should forget that some openly racist teachers still work in our schools (cf. Mac an Ghaill 1988; Mirza 1992; Wright 1986). Additionally, of course, there is the problem of unintended racism through assumptions and actions – often well-meaning – that disadvantage minority students (see Chapter 3).

6 Antiracism and the whole school

1 The reference to 'some' is significant. Students sometimes use accusations of racism as a strategy in relations with peers and/or staff (see Chapter 8 for more on this). This is not a reason, however, for dismissing any accusation without treating it seriously.

2 This is not to say that, on occasion, minority students do not make such accusations unjustly (see Chapter 8).

3 Although I have copies of all the written responses, further analysis (for example, by student age and ethnic origin) is not possible because most are anonymous.

4 The fact that many teachers were surprised by students' sensitive and detailed responses is, perhaps, indicative of stereotyped views of working-class young people as generally less caring and perceptive.

5 See Chapter 8 for a discussion of student involvement in policy-writing at Garret Morgan School.

6 'Ownership' is a buzz word in the literature on the management of change; successful change, it is argued, can only happen where people feel a sense of personal investment – ownership – in the new structures. Like 'whole-school', the concept of 'ownership' has suffered from under-theorization. From a micropolitical perspective ownership is unlikely ever to be totally shared, but this study confirms that some form of personal involvement/investment, improves the chances of real change.

7 Antiracism in the classroom

1 Here I am using the terms 'Western' and 'non-Western' to parody the (erroneous) colloquial use that equates the former with white people and the latter with black and other 'less advanced' peoples (cf. Hall 1992a; Said 1978).
2 A measure of the significance of these developments is how often rightist discourses of derision focus on attempts to introduce anti-oppressive work into science and mathematics. Consider, for example, Margaret Thatcher's party conference speech of 1987 (quoted in Chapter 2) and an article in *The Daily Mail* which described 'ethno-mathematics' and 'anti-sexist education' as 'lessons in mumbo jumbo' (Massey 1994). Interesting that the latter dismisses such work using a phrase with racist origins (see *Oxford English Dictionary*).
3 It is imperative that more focused work is seen as an *additional* and *complementary* element to antiracism elsewhere in the curriculum; it is not a substitute for work in core and foundation subjects.
4 By 'conventions' I mean both the formal content of the lesson (as prescribed by syllabuses, work programmes and the National Curriculum) and the discursive 'codes' and 'rules' that tacitly structure and define the 'proper' (i.e. officially sanctioned) content and form of lessons within a particular subject discipline (Bernstein 1990; Whitty et al. 1994).
5 The project sent questionnaires to 1 in 4 secondary schools in England and Wales (N = 1431). A response rate of 42 per cent was achieved.
6 There has been a significant increase in academic writing on citizenship. Unfortunately, much of the work on education seems almost completely to ignore matters of 'race' and ethnicity (see, for example, Edwards and Fogelman 1993).
7 It is important to keep sight of the pervasive influence of social class. Despite all this complexity, class remains strongly associated with achievement, regardless of ethnic origin and gender (Drew and Gray 1990).
8 Within Seacole parts of the programme are known variously as 'the enrichment programme' and 'race awareness'. The titles are often used interchangeably and the latter does not reflect a detailed concern with Race Awareness Training (Katz 1978) – an approach which has been widely criticized for failing to recognize the wider structural factors that support and extend racism in society (Gurnah 1984; Sivanandan 1985). For the sake of consistency, and to avoid confusion, I wanted to find an alternative title to describe the programme. I have chosen to use the phrase 'people's education' in this context to highlight both the shared transformative goals and as a reminder of the constant threat of co-option, posed by a system that is deeply implicated in the reproduction of existing social inequalities.

9 The first courses were run in the mid-1980s.

10 The plural is deliberate. There is no single 'correct' approach to antiracist teaching. As this account illustrates, different styles of interaction and discourse (between teacher and student; between student and issues) work differently according to the particular context.

11 For further detail on antiracist and antisexist counselling in secondary schools see Gillborn et al. (1993) Chapter 4.

12 The school estimates that around 75 per cent of students live in economically disadvantaged areas of the city. Around half are entitled to free school meals.

13 See Chapter 9 for more on the threat to antiracism posed by changes to Section 11.

8   Student perspectives

1 Brand-named clothing is frequently a focus for verbal and physical harassment (see Gillborn et al. 1993: ch. 3; Tattum 1993).

2 See Chapter 6 for details of this.

3 In response to this issue, some schools temporarily exclude all students guilty of fighting – whatever the provocation. While this might appear to offer a simple solution, it is not one that students support and may only do further damage to a school's attempt to develop anti-oppressive education (cf. Gillborn 1993; Gillborn et al. 1993).

4 See especially Chapter 4 and Stuart Hall (1992c) on the end of the essential black subject.

9   Rethinking racism and antiracism

1 A third school, Forest Boys', also features in Chapter 5 where I examined the range of factors that united the schools in their initial attempts to become antiracist institutions.

2 Elsewhere I have examined how these tensions were played out in Forest Comprehensive, providing a stern test of the school's emerging antiracist ethos (Gillborn 1992a). See also Chris Searle's account of student's responses to the conflict (Searle 1992).

3 The tripartite system emerged following the 1944 Education Act and embodied the idea that there were different 'types' of student; the academically gifted, those who were more technically able, and those who (in the words of the Norwood report, 1943) 'deal more easily with concrete things than ideas' (Cox 1979: 119). One of the principal arguments against this system was its inequitous treatment of students, particularly the way it reflected and reinforced social class differences (see Halsey et al. 1980).

4 This is not to dismiss the importance of academic achievement: I have argued that academic success is *especially* important for minority students (Gillborn 1990: ch. 5). The point is that in attempting to maximize levels of academic achievement, schools might sacrifice other aspects of their work and concentrate unduly on students where good examination grades seem most possible. The potential for racism (unintended and/or institutional) is obvious.

5 For example, several papers used the figure on 'percentage of half days missed' as a basis for identifying schools with exceptionally poor attendance records: *The Guardian* listed twelve schools in this way, *none* of which appeared in the list of 100 'worst schools for truancy' in *The Sun*.

6 Dearing's recommendation, that 'value added' approaches be explored, does not answer these points. Dearing's version of 'value added' seems to refer to a simple calculation of raw academic progress between two test points; ruling out any more sophisticated attempt to judge schools' 'effectiveness' after taking account of factors such as social class (Dearing 1993: 77; Dearing 1994: 80–1).

7 Notable examples in the late 1980s and early 1990s are the cases in Dewsbury, Wakefield and Cleveland. In each case white parents used legislation to move their children from multi-ethnic schools and into predominantly white schools (see Vincent 1992).

References

Advisory Centre for Education (1993) *Findings from ACE Investigations into Exclusions*. London, ACE.

Afro-Caribbean Education Resource (ACER) Project (1985) *Anti-Racism in Practice: Professor Stuart Hall Assesses the Implications of ACER Materials*. Video cassette VC SH. London, Inner London Education Authority.

Allcott, T. (1992) 'Anti-racism in education: the search for policy in practice'. In D. Gill, B. Mayor and M. Blair (eds) op. cit., pp. 169–82.

Allen, S. (1994) 'Review of D. Morgan and L. Stanley (eds) *Debates in Sociology*, Manchester. Manchester University Press', *Sociology*, 28(1): 301–4.

Anderson, B. (1989) 'Anti-racism and education – strategies for the 1990s', *Multicultural Teaching*, 7(3): 5–8.

Apple, M.W. (1992) 'Constructing the captive audience: Channel One and the political economy of the text', *International Studies in Sociology of Education*, 2(2): 107–31.

Aronowitz, S. and Giroux, H.A. (1991) *Postmodern Education: Politics, Culture and Social Criticism*. Oxford, University of Minnesota Press.

Assistant Masters and Mistresses Association (AMMA) (1987) *Multi-Cultural and Anti-Racist Education Today*. London, AMMA.

Atkinson, P., Delamont, S. and Hammersley, M. (1988) 'Qualitative research traditions: a British response to Jacob', *Review of Educational Research*, 58(2): 231–50.

Back, L. (1993) 'Race, identity and nation within an adolescent community in South London', *New Community*, 19(2): 217–33.

Bagley, C.A. (1992) *Back to the Future: Section 11 of the Local Government Act 1966: LEAs and Multicultural/Antiracist Education*. Slough, National Foundation for Educational Research.

Ball, S.J. (1981) *Beachside Comprehensive: A Case Study of Secondary Schooling*. Cambridge, Cambridge University Press.

Ball, S.J. (1987) *The Micro-Politics of the School: Towards a Theory of School Organization.* London, Methuen.

Ball, S.J. (1990a) *Politics and Policy Making in Education: Explorations in Policy Sociology.* London, Routledge.

Ball, S.J. (ed.)(1990b) *Foucault and Education: Disciplines and Knowledge.* London, Routledge.

Ball, S.J. (1993) 'What is policy? Texts, trajectories and toolboxes', *Discourse,* 13(2): 10–17.

Ball, S.J. (1994) 'Some reflections on policy theory: a brief response to Hatcher and Troyna', *Journal of Education Policy,* 9(2): 171–82.

Ball, S.J. and Shilling, C. (1994) 'At the cross-roads: education policy studies', *British Journal of Educational Studies,* 42(1): 1–5.

Banton, M. (1988) 'Race'. In E. Cashmore (ed.) op. cit., pp. 235–7.

Barker, M. (1981) *The New Racism: Conservatives and the Ideology of the Tribe.* London, Junction Books.

Barthes, R. (1972) *Mythologies.* London, Jonathan Cape.

Barton, L. and Oliver, M. (1992) 'Special needs: personal trouble or public issue?' In L. Barton and M. Arnot (eds) *Voicing Concerns: Sociological Perspectives on Contemporary Educational Reforms.* Wallingford, Triangle Press.

Bates, I. and Riseborough, G. (eds)(1993) *Youth and Inequality.* Buckingham, Open University Press.

Baudrillard, J. (1983) *Simulations.* New York, Semiotext(e).

Becker, H.S. (1958) 'Problems of inference and proof in participant observation', *American Sociological Review,* 23: 652–60. Reprinted in H.S. Becker (1970) *Sociological Work: Method and Substance.* New Brunswick, N.J., Transaction Books, pp. 25–38.

Becker, H.S. (1967) 'Whose side are we on?', *Social Problems,* 14: 239–47. Reprinted in H.S. Becker (1970) op. cit., pp. 123–34.

Becker, H.S. (1970) *Sociological Work: Method and Substance.* New Brunswick, N.J., Transaction Books.

Becker, H.S. (1980) Unpublished interview with Jef Verhoeven.

Becker, H.S. (1986) *Writing for Social Scientists: How to Start and Finish Your Thesis, Book, or Article.* Chicago, University of Chicago Press.

Becker, H.S. and McCall, M.M. (eds)(1990) *Symbolic Interaction and Cultural Studies.* Chicago, University of Chicago Press.

Bernstein, B. (1971) *Class, Codes and Control, Volume I: Theoretical Studies Towards a Sociology of Language.* London, Routledge & Kegan Paul.

Bernstein, B. (1974) *Class, Codes and Control, Volume I: Theoretical Studies Towards a Sociology of Language.* 2nd (revised) edn. London, Routledge & Kegan Paul.

Bernstein, B. (1975) *Class, Codes and Control, Volume III: Towards a Theory of Educational Transmissions.* London, Routledge & Kegan Paul.

Bernstein, B. (1977) *Class, Codes and Control, Volume III: Towards a Theory of Educational Transmissions,* 2nd edn. London, Routledge & Kegan Paul.

Bernstein, B. (1990) *The Structuring of Pedagogic Discourse: Volume IV, Class, Codes and Control.* London, Routledge.

Beynon, J. (1984) '"Sussing out" teachers: pupils as data gatherers:' In M. Hammersley and P. Woods (eds) op. cit., pp. 121–44.

Bhavnani, K.-K. (1991) *Talking Politics*. Cambridge, Cambridge University Press.

Bhavnani, K.-K. with Collins, D. (1993) 'Racism and feminism: an analysis of the Anita Hill and Clarence Thomas hearings', *New Community*, 19(3): 493–505.

Blair, M. and Woods, P. (1992) *Study Guide 1: Racism and Education: Structures and Strategies*. Open University Course ED356: 'Race', Education and Society. Milton Keynes, The Open University.

Blumer, H. (1965) 'Sociological implications of the thought of George Herbert Mead'. In B.R. Cosin et al. (eds)(1971) op. cit., pp. 11–17.

Blumer, H. (1976) 'The methodological position of Symbolic Interactionism'. In M. Hammersley and P. Woods (eds)(1976) op. cit., pp. 12–18.

Boateng, P. (1989) Unpublished paper presented to the *Speaker's Commission on Citizenship Seminar*, April.

Bolam, R., McMahon, A., Pocklington, K. and Weindling, D. (1993) *Effective Management in Schools*. London, HMSO.

Bonnett, A. (1993) 'Forever "white"? Challenges and alternatives to a "racial" monolith', *New Community*, 20(1): 173–80.

Bowe, R. and Ball, S.J. with Gold, A. (1992) *Reforming Education and Changing Schools: Case Studies in Policy Sociology*. London, Routledge.

Boyne, R. and Rattansi, A. (1990) 'The theory and politics of postmodernism: by way of an introduction'. In R. Boyne and A. Rattansi (eds) op. cit., pp. 1–45.

Boyne, R. and Rattansi, A. (eds)(1990) *Postmodernism and Society*. London, Macmillan.

Bradbury, M. (1975) *The History Man*. London, Secker & Warburg.

Brah, A. (1992a) 'Difference, diversity and differentiation'. In J. Donald and A. Rattansi (eds) op. cit., pp. 126–45.

Brah, A. (1992b) 'Women of South Asian origin in Britain: issues and concerns' in P. Braham, A. Rattansi and R. Skellington (eds) op. cit., pp. 64–78.

Brah, A. (1993) '"Race" and "culture" in the gendering of labour markets: South Asian young Muslim women and the labour market', *New Community*, 19(3): 441–58.

Braham, P., Rattansi, A. and Skellington, R. (eds)(1992) *Racism and Antiracism: Inequalities, Opportunities and Policies*. London, Sage.

Brandt, G.L. (1986) *The Realization of Anti-Racist Teaching*. Lewes, Falmer.

Brehony, K.J. (1992) '"Active citizens": the case of school governors', *International Studies in Sociology of Education*, 2(2): 199–217.

Brewer, J. (1994) 'The ethnographic critique of ethnography: sectarianism in the RUC', *Sociology* 28(1): 231–44.

Bulmer, M. (1986) 'Race and ethnicity'. In R.G. Burgess (ed.) *Key Variables in Social Investigation*. London, Routledge, pp. 54–75.

Burgess, R.G. (1983) *Experiencing Comprehensive Education: A Study of Bishop McGregor School*. London, Methuen.

Burgess, R.G. (1984a) *In the Field: An Introduction to Field Research*. London, George Allen & Unwin.

Burgess, R.G. (1984b) *The Research Process in Educational Settings: Ten Case Studies*. Lewes, Falmer.

Burgess, R.G. (1985) 'Introduction'. In R.G. Burgess (ed.) *Strategies of Educational Research: Qualitative Methods*. Lewes, Falmer, pp. 1–22.

Burgess, R.G. (1986) *Sociology, Education and Schools*. London, Batsford.

Burgess, R.G. (1988) 'A headteacher at work during the teachers' dispute'. Paper presented at the conference *Histories and Ethnographies of Teachers at Work*, St. Hilda's College, Oxford.

Burns, T. (1967) 'Sociological explanation', *British Journal of Sociology*, 18(4): 353–69.

Burstall, C. (1991) 'Arise again, Sir Cyril', *The Guardian*, 9 July, p. 21.

Callinicos, A. (1989) *Against Postmodernism: A Marxist Critique*. Cambridge, Polity.

Callinicos, A. (1990) 'Reactionary Postmodernism?' In R. Boyne and A. Rattansi (eds) op. cit., pp. 97–118.

Carlen, P., Gleeson, D. and Wardhaugh, J. (1992) *Truancy: The Politics of Compulsory Schooling*. Buckingham, Open University Press.

Carr, W. (1991) 'Education for citizenship', *British Journal of Educational Studies*, 39: 373–85.

Carr-Hill, R. and Drew, D. (1988) 'Blacks, police and crime'. In A. Bhat, R. Carr-Hill and S. Ohri / Radical Statistics Race Group (eds)(1988) *Britain's Black Population: A New Perspective*. 2nd edn. Aldershot, Gower, pp. 29–60.

Carrington, B. and Wood, E. (1983) 'Body talk', *Multiracial Education*, 11(2): 29–38.

Carter, B. and Green, M. (1993) 'Naming difference: "race thinking", politics and social research'. Paper presented at the British Sociological Association annual meeting, University of Essex, April.

Carter, B., Green, M. and Sondhi, R. (1992) 'The one difference that "makes all the difference?": schooling and the politics of identity in the UK', *European Journal of Intercultural Studies*, 3(2/3): 81–9.

Carter, B. and Williams, J. (1987) 'Attacking racism in education', in B. Troyna (ed.) op. cit., pp. 170–83.

Cashmore, E. (1987) *The Logic of Racism*. London, Allen and Unwin.

Cashmore, E. (ed.)(1988) *Dictionary of Race and Ethnic Relations*. 2nd edn. London, Routledge.

Cashmore, E. and Troyna, B. (eds)(1982) *Black Youth in Crisis*. London, George Allen & Unwin.

Centre for Multicultural Education (CME) (1993) *Sagaland: Youth Culture, Racism and Education*. London, Greenwich Central Race Equality Unit.

Clifford, J. and Marcus, G.E. (eds)(1986) *Writing Culture: The Poetics and Politics of Ethnography*. Berkeley, University of California Press.

Cohen, P. (1992) '"It's racism what dunnit": hidden narratives in theories of racism'. In J. Donald and A. Rattansi (eds) op. cit., pp. 62–103.

Commission for Racial Equality (CRE) (1992a) *Response to Choice and Diversity, A New Framework for Schools*. London, CRE.

Commission for Racial Equality (CRE) (1992b) *Set to Fail? Setting and Banding in Secondary Schools*. London (CRE).

Commission for Racial Equality (CRE) (1992c) *Secondary School Admissions: Report of a Formal Investigation into Hertfordshire County Council*. London (CRE).

Commission for Racial Equality/Runnymede Trust (1993) 'The debate so far' Conference paper 9. *Choice, Diversity, Equality: Implications of the Education Bill*. A Working Conference, 30 January.

Connolly, P. (1992) 'Playing it by the rules: the politics of research in "race" and education', *British Educational Research Journal*, 18(2): 133–48.

Cosin, B.R., Dale, I.R., Esland, G.M., Mackinnon, D. and Swift, D.F. (eds)(1971) *School and Society: A Sociological Reader* 2nd edn. London, Routledge & Kegan Paul with Open University Press.

Cross, M. (1989) 'Soapbox', *Network: Newsletter of the British Sociological As-'sociation*, 43: 20.

Cross, M. (1990) 'Editorial', *New Community*, 17(1): 1–4.

Cox, R.E. (1979) 'Education'. In David C. Marsh (ed.) *Introducing Social Policy*. London, Routledge & Kegan Paul.

Dearing, R. (1993) *The National Curriculum: An Interim Report*. London, School Examinations and Assessment Council.

Dearing, R. (1994) *The National Curriculum and its Assessment: Final Report*. London, School Curriculum and Assessment Authority.

Deem, R. (1994) 'Free marketeers or good citizens? Educational policy and lay participation in the administration of schools', *British Journal of Educational Studies*, 42(1): 23–37.

Delamont, S. (1992) *Fieldwork in Educational Settings: Methods, Pitfalls and Perspectives*. London, Falmer.

Demaine, J. (1989) 'Race, categorisation and educational achievement', *British Journal of Sociology of Education*, 10(2): 195–214.

Demaine, J. (1993) 'Racism, ideology and education: the last word on the Honeyford affair?', *British Journal of Sociology of Education*, 14(4): 409–14.

Denzin, N.K. (1992) *Symbolic Interactionism and Cultural Studies: The Politics of Interpretation*. Oxford, Blackwell.

Department for Education (DFE) (1992) *Exclusions: A Discussion Document*. London, DFE.

Department for Education (DFE) (1993a) 'A new deal for "out of school" pupils – Forth', *DFE News*. 126/93, 23 April.

Department for Education (DFE) (1993b) 'Exclusions from school', Circular No. 3 in *'Pupils with Problems': Draft Circulars*. London, DFE.

Department for Education (DFE) (1994) 'New tables latest stride in information revolution – Patten', *DFE News*, 45/94. London, DFE.

Department for Education/Welsh Office (1992) *Choice and Diversity: A New Framework for Schools*. London, HMSO.

Department of Education and Science (DES) (1989) *National Curriculum: From Policy to Practice*. London, HMSO.

Dhondy, F. (1974) 'The black explosion in British schools', February, *Race Today*, pp. 44–7.

Dickinson, P. (1982) 'Facts and figures: some myths'. In J. Tierney (ed.)(1982) op. cit., pp. 58–85.

Donald, J. and Rattansi, A. (1992) 'Introduction'. In J. Donald and A. Rattansi (eds) op. cit., pp. 1–8.

Donald, J. and Rattansi, A. (eds)(1992) *Race', Culture & Difference*. London, Sage.

Douglas, J.W.B. (1964) *The Home and the School*. London, McGibbon & Kee.

Drew, D. and Gray, J. (1990) 'The fifth year examination achievements of Black young people in England and Wales', *Educational Research*, 32(3): 107–17.

Drew, D. and Gray, J. (1991) 'The Black-White gap in examination results: a statistical critique of a decade's research', *New Community*, 17(2): 159–72.

Drew, D., Gray, J. and Sime, N. (1992) *Against the Odds: The Education and Labour Market Experiences of Black Young People*. Youth Cohort Study of England and Wales, Research and Development Report No. 68. Sheffield, Employment Department.

Driver, G. (1979) 'Classroom stress and school achievement: West Indian adolescents and their teachers'. In V. Saifullah Khan (ed.) *Minority Families in Britain: Support and Stress*. London, Macmillan, pp. 131–44.

Drouet, D. (1993) 'Adolescent female bullying and sexual harassment'. In D. Tattum (ed.) op. cit., pp. 173–88.

Dubberley, W.S. (1988) 'Humor as resistance', *International Journal of Qualitative Studies in Education*, 1(2): 109–23.

Duncan, C. (1988) *Pastoral Care: An Antiracist/Multicultural Perspective*. Oxford, Basil Blackwell.

During, S. (1993a) 'Introduction'. In S. During (ed.)(1993b) op. cit., pp. 1–25.

During, S. (ed.)(1993b) *The Cultural Studies Reader*. London, Routledge.

Dyer, R. (1988) 'White', *Screen*, 29(4). Reprinted in R. Dyer (1993) op. cit., pp. 141–63.

Dyer, R. (1993) *The Matter of Images: Essays on Representations*. London, Routledge.

Edwards, J. and Fogelman, K. (1993) *Developing Citizenship in the Curriculum*. London, David Fulton.

Eggleston, J. (1991) 'Facing the realities of a no win situation', *Times Educational Supplement*, 25 January, p. 29.

Eggleston, S.J., Dunn, D.K. and Anjali, M. (1986) *Education for Some: The Educational & Vocational Experiences of 15–18 year old Members of Minority Ethnic Groups*. Stoke-on-Trent, Trentham.

Elton, Lord (1989) *Discipline in Schools: Report of the Committee of Enquiry*. London, HMSO.

Epstein, D. (1993) *Changing Classroom Cultures: Anti-Racism, Politics and Schools*. Stoke-on-Trent, Trentham.

Eysenck, H.J. (1971) *Race, Intelligence and Education*. London, Temple Smith.

Eysenck, H.J. (1981) in H.J. Eysenck versus L. Kamin *Intelligence: The Battle for the Mind*. London, Pan.

Featherstone, M. (1988) 'In pursuit of the postmodern: an introduction', *Theory, Culture and Society*, 5(2–3): 195–215.

Foster, P. (1990a) *Policy and Practice in Multicultural and Anti-Racist Education*. London, Routledge.

Foster, P. (1990b) 'Cases not proven: an evaluation of two studies of teacher racism', *British Educational Research Journal*, 16(4): 335–49.

Foster, P. (1991) 'Case still not proven: a reply to Cecile Wright', *British Educational Research Journal*, 17(2): 165–70.

Foster, P. (1992a) 'Teacher attitudes and Afro/Caribbean educational attainment', *Oxford Review of Education*, 18(3): 269–81.

Foster, P. (1992b) 'Equal treatment and cultural difference in multi-ethnic schools: a critique of the teacher ethnocentrism theory', *International Studies in Sociology of Education*, 2(1): 89–103.

Foster, P. (1993a) '"Methodological purism" or "a defence against hype"? Critical readership in research in "race" and education', *New Community*, 19(3): 547–52.

Foster, P. (1993b) 'Some problems in establishing equality of treatment in multi-ethnic schools', *British Journal of Sociology*, 44(3): 519–35.

Foster-Carter, O. (1987) 'The Honeyford affair: political and policy implications.' In B. Troyna (ed.)(1987) op. cit., pp. 44–58.

Foucault, M. (1972) *The Archeology of Knowledge*. London, Tavistock.

Foucault, M. (1977) *The Archeology of Knowledge*. London, Tavistock.

Foucault, M. (1980) *Power/Knowledge: Selected Interviews and Other Writings 1972–1977*, trans. C. Gordon. Brighton, Harvester.

Fox, S. (1990) 'The ethnography of humour and the problem of social reality', *Sociology*, 24(3): 431–46.

Fuller, M. (1980) 'Black girls in a London comprehensive school.' In M. Hammersley and P. Woods (eds)(1984) op. cit., pp. 77–88.

Furlong, V.J. (1984) 'Black resistance in the liberal comprehensive.' In S. Delamont (ed.) *Readings on Interaction in the Classroom*. London, Methuen, pp. 212–36.

Gaine, C. (1987) *No Problem Here: A Practical Approach to Education and Race in White Schools*. London, Hutchinson.

Gannaway, H. (1976) 'Making sense of school.' Reprinted in M. Hammersley and P. Woods (eds)(1984) *Life in School: The Sociology of Pupil Culture*. Milton Keynes, Open University Press, pp. 191–203.

Gibson, M.A. (1991) 'Minorities and schooling: some implications.' In M.A. Gibson and J.U. Ogbu (eds) *Minority Status and Schooling: A Comparative Study of Immigrant and Involuntary Minorities*. New York, Garland, pp. 357–81.

Gibson, M.A. and Bhachu, P.K. (1988) 'Ethnicity and school performance: a comparative study of South Asian pupils in Britain and America', *Ethnic and Racial Studies*, 11(3): 239–62.

Giddens, A. (1984) *The Constitution of Society*. Cambridge, Polity.

Giddens, A. (1990) *The Consequences of Modernity*. Cambridge, Polity.

Gill, D. and Levidow, L. (eds)(1987) *Anti-racist Science Teaching*. London, Free Association Books.

Gill, D., Mayor, B. and Blair, M. (eds)(1992) *Racism and Education: Structures and Strategies*. London, Sage.

Gillborn, D. (1987) 'The Negotiation of Educational Opportunity: The Final Years of Compulsory Schooling in a Multi-Ethnic Inner City Comprehensive. Unpublished PhD thesis, University of Nottingham.

Gillborn, D. (1990) *'Race', Ethnicity and Education: Teaching and Learning in Multi-Ethnic Schools*. London, Unwin-Hyman/Routledge.

Gillborn, D. (1992a) 'Citizenship, "race" and the hidden curriculum', *International Studies in Sociology of Education*, 2(1): 57–73.

Gillborn, D. (1992b) 'Ethnicity and educational achievement in the United Kingdom: policy and practice in a racist society.' Paper presented at the American Anthropological Association annual meeting, San Francisco.

Gillborn, D. (1993) 'Racial violence and harassment.' In D. Tattum (ed.)(1993) op. cit., pp. 161–72.

Gillborn, D. (1994) 'The micro-politics of macro reform', *British Journal of Sociology of Education*, 15(2): 147–64.

Gillborn, D. and Drew, D. (1992) '"Race", class and school effects', *New Community*, 18(4): 551–65.

Gillborn, D., Nixon, J. and Rudduck, J. (1993) *Dimensions of Discipline: Rethinking Practice in Secondary Schools*. London, HMSO.

Gilroy, P. (1987) *There Ain't No Black in the Union Jack*. London, Hutchinson.

Gilroy, P. (1988) *Problems in Anti-Racist Strategy*. London, Runnymede Trust.

Gilroy, P. (1990) 'The end of anti-racism', *New Community*, 17(1): 71–83.

Giroux, H.A. (1991a) 'Democracy and the discourse of cultural difference: towards a politics of border pedagogy', *British Journal of Sociology of Education*, 12(4): 501–19.

Giroux, H.A. (1991b) 'Postmodernism and the discourse of educational criticism.' In S. Aronowitz and H.A. Giroux (1991) op. cit., pp. 57–86.

Glass, D. (ed.)(1954) *Social Mobility in Britain*. London, Routledge & Kegan Paul.

Gleeson, D. (1992) 'School attendance and truancy: a socio-historical account', *Sociological Review*, 40(3): 437–90.

Goffman, E. (1959) *The Presentation of Self in Everyday Life*. Harmondsworth, Penguin.

Goldberg, D.T. (1993) *Racist Culture: Philosophy and the Politics of Meaning*. Oxford, Blackwell.

Goldstein, H. (1987) *Multi-level Models in Social and Educational Research*. London, Griffin Press.

Goldthorpe, J., with Llewellyn, C. and Payne, C. (1980) *Social Mobility and Class Structure in Modern Britain*. Oxford, Clarendon Press.

Gomm, R. (1993) 'Figuring out ethnic equity', *British Educational Research Journal*, 19(2): 149–65.

Gore, J.M. (1993) *The Struggle for Pedagogies: Critical and Feminist Discourses as Regimes of Truth*. New York, Routledge.

Grace, G. (1991) 'Welfare Labourism versus the New Right: the struggle in New Zealand's education policy', *International Studies in Sociology of Education*, 1: 25–42.

Green, A. (1994) 'Postmodernism and state education', *Journal of Education Policy*, 9(1): 67–83.

Green, P.A. (1983) 'Male and female created He them', *Multicultural Teaching*, 2(1): 4–7.

Green, P.A. (1985) 'Multi-ethnic teaching and the pupils' self-concepts'. In the Swann Report, *Education for All: Final Report of the Committee of Inquiry into the Education of Children from Ethnic Minority Groups*. London, HMSO, pp. 46–56.

Grinter, R. (1985) 'Bridging the gulf: the need for anti-racist multicultural education', *Multicultural Teaching*, 3(2): 7–10.

Gundara, J., Jones, C. and Kimberley, K. (eds)(1986) *Racism, Diversity and Education*. London, Hodder & Stoughton.

Gurnah, A. (1984) 'The politics of racism awareness training', *Critical Social Policy*, 11: 6–20.

Hall, S. (1983) 'The great moving right show'. In S. Hall and M. Jacques (eds) *The Politics of Thatcherism*. London, Lawrence & Wishart.

Hall, S. (1988) 'The meaning of New Times'. In S. Hall and M. Jacques (eds)(1989) *New Times: The Changing Face of Politics in the 1990s*. London, Lawrence & Wishart with *Marxism Today*.

Hall, S. (1990) 'Encoding, decoding'. In S. During (ed.)(1993b) op. cit., pp. 90–103.

Hall, S. (1992a) 'The West and the Rest: discourse and power'. In S. Hall and B. Gieben (eds) *Formations of Modernity*. Oxford, Polity, pp. 275–320.

Hall, S. (1992b) 'The question of cultural identity'. In S. Hall, D. Held and T. McGrew (eds) (1992) op. cit., pp. 274–316.

Hall, S. (1992c) 'New ethnicities.' In J. Donald and A. Rattansi (eds)(1992) op. cit., pp. 252–9.

Hall, S., Critcher, C., Jefferson, T., Clarke, J. and Roberts, B. (1978) *Policing the Crisis*. London, Macmillan.

Hall, S. and Gieben, B. (eds)(1992) *Formations of Modernity*. Cambridge, Polity.

Hall, S., Held, D. and McGrew, T. (eds)(1992) *Modernity and its Futures*. Cambridge, Polity.

Hall, S. and Jacques, M. (eds)(1989) *New Times: The Changing Face of Politics in the 1990s*. London, Lawrence & Wishart with *Marxism Today*.

Hall, V. (1993) 'Women in educational management: a review of research in Britain.' In J. Ouston (ed.) op. cit., pp. 23–46.

Halsey, A.H., Heath, A.F. and Ridge, J.M. (1980) *Origins and Destinations: Family, Class, and Education in Modern Britain*. Oxford, Clarendon Press.

Halstead, M. (1992) 'Ethical dimensions of controversial events in multicultural education.' In M. Leicester and M. Taylor (eds)(1992) op. cit., pp. 39–56.

Hamilton, P. (1992) 'The Enlightenment and the birth of social science.' In S. Hall and B. Gieben (eds) op. cit., pp. 18–58.

Hammersley, M. (1990) *Classroom Ethnography: Empirical and Methodological Essays*. Milton Keynes, Open University Press.

Hammersley, M. (1991) *Reading Ethnographic Research*. London, Longman.

Hammersley, M. (1992a) 'A response to Barry Troyna's "Children, 'race' and racism: the limits of research and policy"', *British Journal of Educational Studies*, 40(2): 174–7.

Hammersley, M. (1992b) *What's Wrong with Ethnography?* London, Routledge.

Hammersley, M. (1992c) 'On feminist methodology', *Sociology*, 26(2): 187–206.

Hammersley, M. (1993a) 'On methodological purism: a response to Barry Troyna', *British Educational Research Journal*, 19(4): 339–41.

Hammersley, M. (1993b) 'Research and "anti-racism": the case of Peter Foster and his critics', *British Journal of Sociology*, 44(3): 429–48.

Hammersley, M. (1994) 'On feminist methodology: a response', *Sociology*, 28(1): 293–300.

Hammersley, M. and Atkinson, P. (1983) *Ethnography: Principles in Practice.* London, Tavistock.

Hammersley, M. and Gomm, R. (1993) 'A response to Gillborn and Drew on "race", class and school effects', *New Community*, 19(2): 348–53.

Hammersley, M. and Woods, P. (eds)(1976) *The Process of Schooling: A Sociological Reader.* London, Routledge & Kegan Paul with Open University Press.

Hammersley, M. and Woods, P. (1984) 'Editors' introduction.' In M. Hammersley and P. Woods (eds) *Life in School: The Sociology of Pupil Culture.* Milton Keynes, Open University Press, pp. 1–4.

Hannan, A. (1993) 'Review of "Policy and Practice in Multicultural and Anti-Racist Education" by Peter Foster', *Educational Review*, 45(1): 95–7.

Hargreaves, A. (1981) 'Contrastive rhetoric and extremist talk'. In L. Barton and S. Walker (eds) *Schools, Teachers and Teaching.* Lewes, Falmer, pp. 303–29.

Hargreaves, A. (1982) 'The rhetoric of school-centred innovation', *Journal of Curriculum Studies*, 14(3): 251–66.

Harvey, D. (1989) *The Condition of Postmodernity.* Oxford, Basil Blackwell.

Harvey, L. (1990) *Critical Social Research.* London, Allen & Unwin.

Haviland, J. (1988) *Take Care, Mr Baker!* London, Fourth Estate.

Hearnshaw, L.S. (1990) 'The Burt affair – a rejoinder', *The Psychologist*, 3(2): 61–4.

Hebdige, D. (1989) 'After the masses.' In S. Hall and M. Jacques (eds) op. cit., pp. 76–93.

Henriques, J. (1984) 'Social psychology and the politics of racism'. In J. Henriques, W. Hollway, C. Urwin, C. Venn and V. Walkerdine (1984) *Changing the Subject: Psychology, Social Regulation and Subjectivity.* London, Methuen.

Hewitt, R. (1986) *White Talk Black Talk: Inter-Racial Friendship and Communication amongst Adolescents.* Cambridge, Cambridge University Press.

Hillgate Group (1987) *The Reform of British Education.* London, Claridge Press.

Hoggart, R. (ed.)(1992) *Oxford Illustrated Encyclopedia of Peoples and Cultures.* Oxford, Oxford University Press.

Home Office (1990) *Section 11 of the Local Government Act 1966* (Circular No. 78/90). London, Home Office.

Honeyford, R. (1989) 'At last . . . the truth about black pupils', *Daily Mail*, 9 June.

Hood, R. with Cordovil, G. (1993) *Race and Sentencing.* Oxford, Clarendon Press.

Husbands, C.T. (1994) 'Crises of national identity as the "new moral panics": political agenda-setting about definitions of nationhood', *New Community*, 20(2): 191–206.

Huyssens, A. (1984) 'Mapping the post-modern', *New German Critique*, 33: 5–52.

Jameson, F. (1984) 'Postmodernism, or the cultural logic of late capitalism', *New Left Review*, 146: 53–92.

Jensen, A.R. (1969) 'How much can we boost IQ and scholastic achievement?', *Harvard Educational Review*, 39(1): 1–123.

Jensen, A.R. (1972) *Genetics and Education.* London, Methuen.

John, G. (1990) 'Taking sides: objectives and strategies in the development of anti-racist work in Britain' in *London 2000*. London, Equal Opportunities Unit. Quoted in B. Troyna and R. Hatcher (1992) op. cit., pp. 200–1.

Jones, N. (ed.)(1989) *School Management and Pupil Behaviour*. Lewes, Falmer.

Joynson, R.B. (1989) *The Burt Affair*. London, Routledge.

Kamin, L.J. (1974) *The Science and Politics of IQ*. Harmondsworth, Penguin.

Kamin, L.J. (1981). In H.J. Eysenck versus L. Kamin *Intelligence: The Battle for the Mind*. London, Pan.

Katz, J. (1978) *White Awareness: A Handbook for Anti-Racism Training*. Oklahoma, University of Oklahoma Press.

Keise, C. (1992) *Sugar and Spice? Bullying in Single-Sex Schools*. Stoke-on-Trent: Trentham.

Kellner, D. (1988) 'Postmodernism as social theory: some challenges and problems', *Theory, Culture & Society*, 5(2–3): 239–69.

Kelly, J. (1969) *Organizational Behaviour*. New York, Irwin-Dorsey.

Kirp, D.L. (1979) *Doing Good by Doing Little: Race and Schooling in Britain*. London, University of California Press.

Klein, G. (1993) *Education Towards Race Equality*. London, Cassell.

Keysel, F. (1988) 'Ethnic background and examination results', *Educational Research*, 30(2): 83–9.

Laclau, E. (1990) *New Reflections on the Revolution of Our Time*. London, Verso.

Lal, S. and Wilson, A. (1985) *'But My Cows Aren't Going to England': A Study in How Families Are Divided*. Manchester, Manchester Law Centre.

Lansley, S., Goss, S. and Wolmar, C. (1989) *Councils of Conflict*. London, Macmillan.

Lawrence, D. (1977) 'The continuing debate on heredity and environment', *Patterns of Prejudice*, 2(3): 5–9.

Leech, K. (1988/89) 'Background paper: a recent addition to the anti-anti-racist literature'. In *Race and Immigration: Runnymede Trust Bulletin*, No. 221, December 1988/January 1989, pp. 12–13.

Leicester, M. (1986) 'Multicultural curriculum or antiracist education: denying the gulf', *Multicultural Teaching*, 4(2), pp. 4–7.

Leicester, M. (1989) *Multicultural Education: From Theory to Practice*. Windsor, NFER/Nelson.

Leicester, M. and Taylor, M. (eds)(1992) *Ethics, Ethnicity and Education*. London, Kogan Page.

Le Lohe, M.J. (1989) 'Political issues', *New Community*, 16(1): 137–44.

Levin, R. (1991) 'People's education and the struggle for democracy in South Africa'. In E. Unterhalter et al. (eds) op. cit., pp. 117–30.

Lewis, R. (1988) *Anti-Racism: A Mania Exposed*. London, Quartet Books.

Lewisham Education (1991) *Pupil Exclusions from Schools, Summer Term 1990 – Spring Term 1991*. London, Lewisham Education Authority.

Liberal Democrats (1993) *Political Speech and Race Relations in a Liberal Democracy: Report of an Inquiry into the Conduct of the Tower Hamlets Liberal Democrats in Publishing Allegedly Racist Election Literature between 1990 and 1993*. London, Liberal Democrats.

Local Authorities Race Relations Information Exchange (1992) *Guide to Section*

11 *Funding: The 1992/93 Section 11 Allocation.* LARRIE Research Report No. 3. London, LARRIE.

Lyotard, J.-F. (1984) *The Postmodern Condition.* Minneapolis, University of Minnesota Press.

Mabey, C. (1986) 'Black pupils' achievements in Inner London', *Educational Research*, 28(3): 163–73.

Mac an Ghaill, M. (1988) *Young, Gifted and Black: Student–Teacher Relations in the Schooling of Black Youth.* Milton Keynes, Open University Press.

Mac an Ghaill, M. (1989a) 'Coming-of-age in 1980s England: reconceptualising Black students' schooling experience', *British Journal of Sociology of Education*, 10(3): 273–86.

Mac an Ghaill, M. (1989b) 'Beyond the white norm: the use of qualitative methods in the study of Black youths' schooling in England', *International Journal of Qualitative Studies in Education*, 2(3): 175–89.

Mac an Ghaill, M. (1994) *The Making of Men: Masculinities, Sexualities and Schooling.* Buckingham, Open University Press.

Macdonald, I., Bhavnani, R., Khan, L. and John, G. (1989) *Murder in the Playground: The Report of the Macdonald Inquiry into Racism and Racial Violence in Manchester Schools.* London, Longsight.

Macdonell, D. (1986) *Theories of Discourse.* Oxford, Basil Blackwell.

Major, J. (1993) Extract from a speech to the Conservative Group for Europe. *Conservative Party News* 188/93, 22 April.

Marcuse, H. (1964) *One Dimensional Man.* Boston, Beacon Press.

Marland, M. (1990) 'A mirror to our work', *The Guardian*, 27 November, p. 20.

Massey, I. (1991) *More than Skin Deep: Developing Anti-Racist Multicultural Education in Schools.* London, Hodder & Stoughton.

Massey, R. (1994) 'How new teachers get PC lessons in mumbo jumbo', *Daily Mail*, 21 March.

Maughan, B. and Rutter, M. (1986) 'Black pupils' progress in secondary schools: II. Examination achievements.' *British Journal of Developmental Psychology*, 4(1): 19–29.

McCall, M.M. and Becker, H.S. (1990) 'Introduction.' In H.S. Becker and M.M. McCall (eds) op. cit., pp. 1–15.

McCarthy, C. (1990) *Race and Curriculum: Social Inequality and the Theories and Politics of Difference in Contemporary Research on Schooling.* Lewes, Falmer.

McCarthy, C. and Apple, M.W. (1988) 'Race, class and gender in American educational research: towards a nonsynchronous parallelist position.' In L. Weis (ed.) *Class, Race & Gender in American Education.* Albany, State University of New York Press, pp. 9–39.

Mead, G.H. (1934) *Mind, Self, and Society.* Chicago, University of Chicago Press.

Mears, T. (1986) 'Multicultural approaches to science'. In J. Gundara, C. Jones and K. Kimberley (eds) *Racism, Diversity and Education.* London, Hodder & Stoughton.

Merton, R.K. (1963) *Social Theory and Social Structure.* Glencoe, Free Press.

Miles, R. (1993) *Racism after 'Race Relations'.* London, Routledge.

Mills, C.W. (1959) *The Sociological Imagination.* Harmondsworth, Penguin.

Mirza, H.S. (1992) *Young, Female and Black*. London, Routledge.

Mkatshwa, S. (1985) 'Keynote address: National Consultative Conference on the Crisis in Education', University of Witwatersrand, Johannesburg, 28–29 December. Quoted in H. Wolpe and E. Unterhalter (1991) op. cit., p. 10.

Modood, T. (1989) 'Religious anger and minority rights', *Political Quarterly*, July, pp. 280–4.

Modood, T. (1990a) 'British Asian Muslims and the Rushdie affair', *Political Quarterly*, April, pp. 143–60.

Modood, T. (1990b) 'Catching up with Jesse Jackson: being oppressed and being somebody', *New Community*, 17(1): 85–96.

Modood, T. (1992) *Not Easy Being British: Colour, Culture and Citizenship*. Stoke-on-Trent, Runnymede Trust and Trentham Books.

Modood, T. (1993) 'Muslims, incitement to hatred and the law.' In J. Horton (ed.) *Liberalism, Multiculturalism and Toleration*. Basingstoke, Macmillan, pp. 139–56.

Mortimore, P., Sammons, P., Stoll, L., Lewis, D. and Ecob, R. (1988) *School Matters: the Junior Years*. Wells, Open Books.

Moscovici, S. (1961) *La psychoanalyse, son image et son public*. Paris, Presses Universitaire de France.

Moscovici, S. (1984) 'The phenomenon of social representations.' In R. Farr and S. Moscovici (eds) *Social Representations*. Cambridge, Cambridge University Press, pp. 3–71.

Mullard, C. (1982) 'Multiracial education in Britain: from assimilation to cultural pluralism.' In J. Tierney (ed.) op. cit., pp. 120–33.

National Association for the Care and Resettlement of Offenders (NACRO) (1988) *Some Facts and Findings about Black People in the Criminal Justice System*. London, National Association for the Care and Resettlement of Offenders.

National Association for the Care and Resettlement of Offenders (NACRO) (1991) *Black People's Experiences of Criminal Justice*. London, National Association for the Care and Resettlement of Offenders.

National Curriculum Council (NCC) (1989) *The National Curriculum and Whole School Planning: Preliminary Guidance*. Circular No. 6. York, NCC.

National Curriculum Council (NCC) (1990a) *Curriculum Guidance 3: The Whole Curriculum*. York, NCC.

National Curriculum Council (NCC) (1990b) *Curriculum Guidance 8: Education for Citizenship*. York, NCC.

National Curriculum Council (NCC) (1991) *Report on Monitoring the Implementation of the National Curriculum Core Subjects: 1989–1990*. York, NCC.

National Union of Teachers (NUT) (1992) *Anti-Racist Curriculum Guidelines*. London, NUT.

Newsinger, J. (1992) 'True confessions: some Tory memoirs of the Thatcher years – a review article'. *Race and Class*, 33(4): 83–92.

Nixon, J. (1985) *A Teacher's Guide to Multicultural Education*. Oxford, Blackwell.

Nixon, J. (1991) *Evaluating the Whole Curriculum*. Milton Keynes, Open University Press.

Nottinghamshire County Council (1991) *Pupil Exclusions from Nottingham Secondary Schools*. Nottingham, Nottinghamshire County Council Education Department.

Nuttall, D.L., Thomas, S. and Goldstein, H. (1992) *Report on Analysis of 1990 Examination Results*. London, Association of Metropolitan Authorities.

Nuttall, D. and Varlaam, A. (1990) *Differences in Examination Performance*. RS 1277/90. London, Inner London Education Authority Research and Statistics Branch.

Office for Standards in Education (OFSTED) (1993) *Exclusions: A Response to the Department for Education Discussion Paper*. London, OFSTED.

Ouston, J. (ed.)(1993) *Women in Education Management*. Harlow, Longman.

Ozga, J. (ed.)(1992) *Women in Educational Management*. Buckingham, Open University Press.

Phizacklea, A. (ed.)(1983) *One Way Ticket: Migration and Female Labour*. London, Routledge & Kegan Paul.

Phizacklea, A. and Miles, R. (1979) 'Working-class racist beliefs in the inner-city'. In R. Miles and A. Phizacklea (eds) *Racism and Political Action in Britain*. London, Routledge & Kegan Paul.

Powney, J. and Weiner, G. (1991) *Outside the Norm: Equity and Management in Educational Institutions*. London, South Bank Polytechnic.

Pryce, K. (1979) *Endless Pressure*. London, Penguin.

Puranik, A. (1993) 'Celebrate the many shades of black', *Times Higher Education Supplement*, 29 October, p. 15.

Raab, C.D. (1994) 'Theorising the governance of education', *British Journal of Educational Studies*, 42(1): 6–22.

Ramazanoglu, C. (1992) 'On feminist methodology: male reason versus female empowerment', *Sociology*, 26(2): 207–12.

Rampton, A. (1981) *West Indian Children in Our Schools*. Cmnd 8273. London, HMSO.

Ranger, C. (1988) *Ethnic Minority School Teachers*. London, Commission for Racial Equality.

Rattansi, A. (1992) 'Changing the subject? Racism, culture and education.' In J. Donald and A. Rattansi (eds) op. cit., pp. 11–48.

Reeves, F. (1983) *British Racial Discourse: A Study of British Political Discourse about Race and Race-Related Matters*. Cambridge, Cambridge University Press.

Reid, I. (1989) *Social Class Differences in Britain: Life-Chances and Life-Styles*, 3rd edn. London, Fontana.

Rex, J. and Mason, D. (1986) *Theories of Race and Ethnic Relations*. Cambridge, Cambridge University Press.

Reynolds, D. (1989) 'Effective schools and pupil behaviour.' In N. Jones (ed.) op. cit., pp. 29–44.

Richardson, R. (1992) 'Argument and subjugation: media responses to the Muslim Parliament', *The Runnymede Bulletin*, No. 253, March, pp. 2–3.

Richardson, R. (1993) 'Funding and race equality, summer 1993', *The Runnymede Bulletin*, No. 267, July/August, p. 9.

Rieser, R. and Mason, M. (eds)(1990) *Disability Equality in the Classroom: A Human Rights Issue*. London, Inner London Education Authority.

Riseborough, G.F. (1981) 'Teacher careers and comprehensive schooling: an empirical study', *Sociology*, 15(3): 352–81.

Robson, C. (1993) *Real World Research: A Resource for Social Scientists and Practitioner-Researchers*. Oxford, Blackwell.

Rose, D. and Sullivan, O. (1992) *Introducing Data Analysis for Social Scientists*. Buckingham, Open University Press.

Rowe, G. and Whitty, G. (1993) 'Five themes remain in the shadows', *Times Educational Supplement*, 9 April, p. 8.

Rudduck, J. (1991) *Innovation and Change: Developing Involvement and Understanding*. Milton Keynes, Open University Press.

Runnymede Trust (1990) *Race and Immigration: Runnymede Trust Bulletin*, No. 236, June.

Runnymede Trust (1991) *Race and Immigration: Runnymede Trust Bulletin*, No. 250, November.

Runnymede Trust (1992) *Annual Report for 1991–92: Identities and Justice – Policies, Projects, Priorities*. London, Runnymede Trust.

Runnymede Trust (1993a) *The Runnymede Bulletin*, No. 262, February.

Runnymede Trust (1993b) *The Runnymede Bulletin*, No. 267, July/August.

Runnymede Trust (1993c) *Equality Assurance in Schools: Quality, Identity, Society: A Handbook for Action Planning and School Effectiveness*. Stoke-on-Trent, Trentham for the Runnymede Trust.

Runnymede Trust (1994) *The Runnymede Bulletin*, No. 272, February.

Rushdie, S. (1988) *The Satanic Verses*. London: Viking.

Said, E.W. (1978) *Orientalism: Western Conceptions of the Orient*. London, Penguin.

Samad, Y. (1992) 'Book burning and race relations: political mobilisation of Bradford Muslims', *New Community*, 18(4): 507–19.

Sarup, M. (1993) *An Introductory Guide to Post-Structuralism and Postmodernism*, 2nd edn. London, Harvester Wheatsheaf.

Sawicki, J. (1988) 'Feminism and the power of Foucauldian discourse.' In J. Arac (ed.) *After Foucault: Humanistic Knowledge, Postmodern Challenges*. London, Rutgers University Press, pp. 161–78.

Scarman, Lord (1981) *The Brixton Disorders, 10–12 April 1981*. Cmnd 8427. London, HMSO.

Schon, D.A. (1983) *The Reflective Practitioner*. London, Temple Smith.

School Curriculum and Assessment Authority (SCAA) (1994) *Dearing: The Final Report*. London, School Curriculum and Assessment Authority.

Searle, C. (1992) 'The gulf between: a school and a war', *Race and Class*, 33(4): 1–14.

Shakeshaft, C. (1987) *Women in Educational Administration*. Newbury Park, Sage.

Shakeshaft, C. (1993) 'Women in educational management in the United States'. In J. Ouston (ed.) op. cit., pp. 47–61.

Shan, S.-J. and Bailey, P. (1991) *Multiple Factors: Classroom Mathematics for Equality and Justice*. Stoke-on-Trent: Trentham.

Short, G. (1985) 'Teacher expectation and West Indian underachievement', *Educational Research*, 27(2): 95–101.

Siraj-Blatchford, I. (1994) *Early Years: Laying the Foundations for Racial Equality*. Stoke-on-Trent, Trentham.

Sisulu, Z. (1986) 'People's education for people's power', *Transformation* 1, Durban, University of Natal. Quoted in H. Wolpe and E. Unterhalter (1991) op. cit., p. 10.

Sivanandan, A. (1985) 'RAT and the degradation of the Black struggle', *Race and Class*, 36: 1–33.

Sivanandan, A. (1988) 'Left, Right and Burnage', *New Statesman*, 27 May. Reprinted in A. Sivanandan (1990) op. cit., pp. 145–52.

Sivanandan, A. (1990) *Communities of Resistance: Writings on Black Struggles for Socialism*. London, Verso.

Sivanandan, A. (1991) 'A Black perspective on the war', *Race and Class*, 32(4): 83–8.

Skeggs, B. (1991) 'Postmodernism: what is all the fuss about?', *British Journal of Sociology of Education*, 12(2): 255–67.

Smith, D.J. and Tomlinson, S. (1989) *The School Effect: A Study of Multi-Racial Comprehensives*. London, Policy Studies Institute.

Smithies, B. and Fiddick, P. (1969) *Enoch Powell on Immigration*. London, Sphere.

Sofer, A. (1994) 'A demoralising reversal of progress', *Times Educational Supplement*, 4 February, p. 96.

Solomos, J. (1989) *Race and Racism in Contemporary Britain*. London, Macmillan.

Solomos, J. (1991) 'Political language and racial discourse', *European Journal of Intercultural Studies*, 2(1): 21–34.

Solomos, J. and Back, L. (1994) 'Conceptualising racisms: social theory, politics and research', *Sociology*, 28(1): 143–61.

Stenhouse, L. (1982) 'Introduction'. In L. Stenhouse, G.K. Verma, R.D. Wild and J. Nixon (1982) *Teaching About Race Relations: Problems and Effects*. London, Routledge & Kegan Paul.

Stone, M. (1981) *The Education of the Black Child in Britain: The Myth of Multiracial Education*. London, Fontana.

Swann, Lord (1985) *Education for All: Final Report of the Committee of Inquiry into the Education of Children from Ethnic Minority Groups*. Cmnd 9453. London, HMSO.

Tattum, D. (ed.)(1993) *Understanding and Managing Bullying*. London, Heinemann.

Taylor, M.J. (1992) *Multicultural Antiracist Education After ERA: Concerns, Constraints and Challenges*. Slough, National Foundation for Educational Research.

Taylor, P. (1993) 'Minority ethnic groups and gender in access to higher education', *New Community*, 19(3): 425–40.

Terkel, S. (1992) *Race*. London, Sinclair-Stevenson.

Thomas, S., Nuttall, D.L., and Goldstein, H. (1993) *Report on Analysis of 1991 Examination Results*. London, Association of Metropolitan Authorities.

Thompson, K. (1992) 'Social pluralism and post-modernity.' In S. Hall, D. Held and T. McGrew (eds) op. cit., pp. 222–55.

Tierney, J. (ed.)(1982) *Race, Migration and Schooling*. London, Holt, Rinehart & Winston.

Times Educational Supplement (1992) 'Patten ushers in era of opting out', 31 July, p. 5.

Tomlinson, S. (1981) *Educational Subnormality: A Study in Decision-Making*. London, Routledge & Kegan Paul.

Tomlinson, S. (1989) 'Education and training', *New Community*, 16(1): 129–36.

Tomlinson, S. (1990) *Multicultural Education in White Schools*. London, Batsford.

Tomlinson, S. (1991) 'Education and training', *New Community*, 17(3): 433–41.

Tomlinson, S. (1992) Review of David Gillborn '"Race", Ethnicity and Education: Teaching and Learning in Multi-Ethnic Schools', *New Community*, 18(2): 343.

Torrington, D. and Weightman, J. (1989) *The Reality of School Management*. Oxford, Basil Blackwell.

Troyna, B. (1984) 'Fact or artefact? The "educational underachievement" of black pupils', *British Journal of Sociology of Education*, 5(2): 153–66.

Troyna, B. (ed.)(1987) *Racial Inequality in Education*. London, Tavistock.

Troyna, B. (1988a) 'Enoch Powell'. In E. Cashmore (ed.)(1988) *Dictionary of Race and Ethnic Relations*, 2nd edn. London, Routledge.

Troyna, B. (1988b) 'The career of an antiracist education school policy: some observations on the mismanagement of change'. In A.G. Green and S.J. Ball (eds) *Progress and Inequality in Comprehensive Education*. London, Routledge, pp. 158–78.

Troyna, B. (1988c) 'Immigration laws: UK'. In E. Cashmore (ed.) *Dictionary of Race and Ethnic Relations*, 2nd edn. London, Routledge, pp. 137–40.

Troyna, B. (1991a) 'Children, "race" and racism: the limitations of research and policy', *British Journal of Educational Studies*, 39(4): 425–36.

Troyna, B. (1991b) 'Underachievers or underrated? The experiences of pupils of South Asian origin in a secondary school', *British Educational Research Journal*, 17(4): 361–76.

Troyna, B. (1992) 'Can you see the join? A historical analysis of multicultural and antiracist education policies.' In D. Gill, B. Mayor and M. Blair (eds) *Racism and Education: Structures and Strategies*. London, Sage, pp. 63–91.

Troyna, B. (1993a) *Racism and Education: Research Perspectives*. Buckingham, Open University Press.

Troyna, B. (1993b) 'Underachiever or misunderstood? A reply to Roger Gomm', *British Educational Research Journal*, 19(2): 167–74.

Troyna, B. (1994) 'Critical social research and education policy', *British Journal of Educational Studies*, 42(1): 70–84.

Troyna, B. and Carrington, B. (1989) '"Whose side are we on?" Ethical dilemmas in research on "race" and education.' In R.G. Burgess (ed.) *The Ethics of Educational Research*. Lewes, Falmer.

Troyna, B. and Carrington, B. (1990) *Education, Racism and Reform*. London, Routledge.

Troyna, B. and Hatcher, R. (1992) *Racism in Children's Lives: A Study of Mainly White Primary Schools*. London, Routledge.

Troyna, B. and Selman, L. (1991) *Implementing Multicultural and Anti-Racist Education in Mainly White Colleges*. London, Further Education Unit.

Troyna, B. and Williams, J. (1986) *Racism, Education and the State*. Beckenham, Croom Helm.

Unterhalter, E., Wolpe, H., Botha, T., Badat, S., Dlamini, T. and Khotseng, B. (eds)(1991) *Apartheid Education and Popular Struggles*. London, Zed Books.

van den Berghe, P.L. (1988) 'Race'. In E. Cashmore (ed.) op. cit., pp. 237–9.

Verhoeven, J.C. (1989) *Methodological and Metascientific Problems in Symbolic*

Interactionism. Leuven, Departement Sociologie, Katholieke Universiteit Leuven.

Vincent, C. (1992) 'Tolerating intolerance? Parental choice and race relations – the Cleveland case', *Journal of Education Policy*, 7(5): 429–43.

Watson, L.E. (1986) 'The "loser" and the management of change', *School Organisation*, 6: 101–6.

Weindling, D. and Early, P. (1987) *Secondary Headship: The First Years.* Windsor, NFER-Nelson.

Weis, L. (ed.)(1988) *Class, Race and Gender in American Education.* Albany, State University of New York Press.

West, C. (1990) 'The new cultural politics of difference.' Reprinted in S. During (ed.)(1993b) op. cit., pp. 203–17.

Westwood, S. and Bhachu, P. (1988) *Enterprising Women: Ethnicity, Economy and Gender Relations.* London, Routledge.

Whitelaw, W. (1989) *The Whitelaw Memoirs.* London, Aurum.

Whitty, G. (1985) *Sociology and School Knowledge: Curriculum Theory, Research and Politics.* London, Methuen.

Whitty, G. (1990) 'The New Right and the National Curriculum: State control or market forces?' In M. Flude and M. Hammer (eds) *The Education Reform Act, 1988: Its Origins and Implications.* Lewes, Falmer, pp. 21–36.

Whitty, G. (1992) 'Education, economy and national culture'. In R. Bocock and K. Thompson (eds) *Social and Cultural Forms of Modernity.* Oxford, Polity, pp. 268–309.

Whitty, G., Aggleton, P. and Rowe, G. (1992) *Cross Curricular Work in Secondary Schools: Summary of Results of a Survey Carried Out in 1992: Report to Participating Schools.* London, Institute of Education, University of London.

Whitty, G., Edwards, T. and Gewirtz, S. (1993) *Specialisation and Choice in Urban Education: The City Technology Experiment.* London, Routledge.

Whitty, G., Rowe, G. and Aggleton, P. (1994) 'Subjects and themes in the secondary school curriculum', *Research Papers in Education*, 9(2): 159–81.

Williams, J. (1985) 'Redefining institutional racism', *Ethnic and Racial Studies*, 8: 323–48.

Williams, R. (1983) *Keywords: A Vocabulary of Culture and Society*, revised edn. London, Fontana.

Wolpe, A.M. (1988) *Within School Walls: The Role of Discipline, Sexuality and the Curriculum.* London, Routledge & Kegan Paul.

Wolpe, H. and Unterhalter, E. (1991) 'Reproduction, reform and transformation: the analysis of education in South Africa'. In Unterhalter, E., et al. (eds)(1991) op. cit., pp. 1–17.

Woods, P. (1983) *Sociology and the School: An Interactionist Viewpoint.* London, Routledge & Kegan Paul.

Woods, P. (1986) *Inside Schools: Ethnography in Educational Research.* London, Routledge & Kegan Paul.

Woods, P. (1990) *The Happiest Days? How Pupils Cope with School.* Lewes, Falmer.

Wright, C. (1986) 'School processes – an ethnographic study'. In J. Eggleston, D. Dunn and M. Anjali op. cit., pp. 127–79.

Wright, C. (1992a) 'Early education: multiracial primary school classrooms'. In D. Gill, B. Mayor and M. Blair (eds)(1992) op. cit., pp. 5–41.

Wright, C. (1992b) *Race Relations in the Primary School*. London, David Fulton Publishers.

Young, S. (1993) 'Language cuts set to hit the poorest' *Times Educational Supplement*, 17 December, pp. 1--2.

Name index

Subject index

status quo, 59–60
stereotypes, 25, 46, 72, 85, 86, 102,
    112, 117, 125, 131, 136–7, 139,
    183, 199
    see also racism
streaming, see selection
students, 4, 42
    antiracism, support for, 122–5,
        138, 154–60
    people's education and, 142–6
    school change and, 11, 100–3
    school policy making and, 95,
        122–5, 128, 138, 153, 160–7,
        181–2
    see also, African Caribbean, Asian,
        Greek, Italian, mixed race,
        Vietnamese, white
subject departments in schools, 11,
    95, 99, 106–7, 117, 121, 129,
    130, 131–2, 133–4, 151, 182,
    188
subjectivities, see identity
Summerfield High School, 95
surveillance, antiracism and, 113–15,
    140
Swann report (1985), 33, 34
symbolic antiracism, see antiracism,
    moral
symbolic interactionism, see
    interactionism

teachers, see change, core groups,
    expectations, INSET, racism,
    stereotypes, teacher/student
    interaction
teacher/student interaction, 46–50,
    57–8, 60–2, 114, 141, 165–6,
    183–4, 194
terrorism, 158

tests, see assessment
Thatcherism, 17, 23, 27
Times Educational Supplement, 32,
    37, 188
Tower Hamlets, London Borough of,
    29
tripartite educational system, 188, 201

underachievement, 42–3
unemployment, 3
uniform and dress codes, 103–4, 110,
    116, 158
unions, teacher, 132
United States of America, 29, 71–2,
    79, 90
United States Senate, 71–2

validity, 5, 52–5
value added, see school effectiveness
victimization, see harassment
Vietnamese students, 97, 115, 145,
    159

Wakefield, 202
Welsh Office, 21, 32–3
white ethnic identity, 11, 89, 153,
    167–8, 174–5, 182
'whiteness', see white ethnic identity
white students, 38, 39, 80, 84–6, 97,
    98, 142, 143, 144, 148, 150,
    153, 154, 155–8, 159, 161,
    162–6, 167–75
    antiracism and, 153, 154, 167–75,
    182
    see also white ethnic identity
whole-school policy, 95, 98–9,
    119–25, 161–7

youth cultures, 84–5, 158, 179, 184